Expat-ing Democracy

DEMOCRACY, HUMAN RIGHTS, INTEGRATION, RADICALISATION AND SECURITY

Edited by the / Herausgegeben von der
European Foundation of Democracy

VOL./BD. 2

PETER LANG
EDITION

Nir T. Boms

Expat-ing Democracy

Dissidents, Technology, and Democratic Discourse in the Middle East

PETER LANG
EDITION

Bibliographic Information published by the Deutsche Nationalbibliothek
The Deutsche Nationalbibliothek lists this publication in the Deutsche Nationalbibliografie; detailed bibliographic data is available in the internet at http://dnb.d-nb.de.

Library of Congress Cataloging-in-Publication Data
Names: Boms, Nir T., author
Title: Expat-ing democracy : dissidents, technology, and democratic discourse in the Middle East / Nir T. Boms
Other titles: Democracy, human rights, integration, radicalisation and security ; Bd. 2. 2192-9777
Description: Frankfurt am Main : Peter Lang Edition, 2016. | Series: Democracy, human rights, integration, radicalisation and security / edited by the European Foundation of Democracy, ISSN 2192-9777 ; Band 2 | Includes bibliographical references and index.
Identifiers: LCCN 2016015839| ISBN 9783631654699 | ISBN 9783653047127 (E-Book)
Subjects: LCSH: Democratization–Middle East. | Social media–Political aspects–Middle East. | Syrians–Foreign countries–Politics and government–21st century. | Iranians–Foreign countries–Politics and government–21st century.
Classification: LCC JK1758.A91 B66 2016 | DDC 320.956–dc23 LC record available at https://lccn.loc.gov/2016015839

ISSN 2192-9777
ISBN 978-3-631-65469-9 (Print)
E-ISBN 978-3-653-04712-7 (E-Book)
DOI 10.3726/978-3-653-04712-7

Peter Lang Edition is an Imprint of Peter Lang GmbH.

Peter Lang – Frankfurt am Main · Bern · Bruxelles · New York · Oxford · Warszawa · Wien

This publication has been peer reviewed.

www.peterlang.com

Table of Contents

List of Tables

List of Charts

Introduction: Expat-ing or Exporting Democracy

This book is the culmination of more than a decade of work and engagement with activists seeking to bring democratic discourse and democratic change to the Middle East. That work began on September 11, 2001 in Washington DC where, as a young researcher, I encountered voices of Middle East expatriate who argued about the feasibility of democratic change in their native countries, a process that appeared only too appealing in the months and years that followed. Soon after, under the leadership of President George W. Bush, the US began to pursue a more assertive democracy promotion agenda, providing additional platforms and resources for those who argued that such a change could realistically be achieved.

Technology became a clear factor in these events in light of its rapid dissemination in the region and at large. Egypt had a million cell phones in 2000, 60 million a decade later and more cell phones than people in 2015. The ASDA'A Burston-Marsteller 2015 Arab Youth Survey showed a generation of connected people, 82% of whom use the Internet daily and 77% who use a smart mobile phone. Clearly, people are communicating and somebody is listening – but to what?

As a son of the region, an Israeli who thus far has had limited opportunities for constructive engagement with my own neighbors, I have become fascinated and intrigued by these voices of change. It was not difficult to enlist in a journey aimed at creating a freer, safer and more peaceful region. However, as a student of the region, I have also developed a strong sense of skepticism while beginning to inquire more about the role and reach of these foreign democracy activists. Working in a think-tank that began to examine questions about the future of the region, I was able to engage further and begin my own personal work that included various writings as well as developing a discourse on the feasibility of political change in the region. I have had the pleasure of working with a large number of groups and individuals from the Middle East on different initiatives to promote that dialogue for change. This has been a fascinating journey filled with rare encounters as well as many surprising moments of hope that took place in unexpected places like a Syrian Refugee camp or at the grave of President Anwar Sadat of Egypt. I have since traveled throughout the region and beyond to meet the individuals who dedicate their lives to the cause of freedom and peace in the Middle East, a cause that I endorse. However, I could also not escape from asking the obvious questions: How feasible are these visions? How wide is the reach of these voices? And what is the role that expatriate play in promoting a discourse on democracy and political change in the Middle East itself?

I decided to spend more time on these questions with a focus on the latter, which ended up becoming the subject of my PhD work "Technology and Democracy in the Middle East," published in 2013, a time when the "Arab Spring" inspired at least some democratic hope. The Arab uprising that began to shake the region at the end of 2010 provided a rare case study as well as a unique opportunity to further examine these assumptions and ideas. My work and research as well as the topic of this book were born out of the need to further evaluate the role of expat groups and the significance of technology in the quest for democracy in the Middle East.

While there are a number of recent works that deal with assessing the "Arab Spring" as well as the respected role of technology in forming and influencing these revolutions, this book's intended contribution lies within a unique component, the work of expat groups toward influencing the "democracy discourse" in the region. It seeks to analyze the influence of information and communication technologies (hereafter ICT) on democratization and democracy discourse in the Middle East with a focus on the work of expatriate groups who utilize ICT to advance political reforms and democratization. I am aware, as I write these lines, that the discourse on "Democratization" and "Spring" may not appear obvious at a time where radical forces like the Islamic State (ISIS) appears to have filled some of the vacuum left by the old political guard. Nervelessness, these developments - as significant as they are -do not contradict the main thesis of this work that should be seen not as an attempt to analyze the contemporary dynamics but rather as a pointer to deeper currents that will likely be indicative of events to come. Syria and Iran are used as the two central case studies that will be introduced in more detail, although the book also includes rather detailed analyses of related events in Egypt and Tunisia. The book focuses more specifically on what is sometimes dubbed "new media," which consists mainly of satellite, Internet and cellular communications, and on its relationship to the political dynamics of the Middle East. Above all, this book addresses five major questions:

1. What is the role of ICT in relation to the discourse of political reform and democratization in the Middle East?
2. How do democratic expatriate groups utilize ICT in order to deliver and convey political messages?
3. How are these messages perceived, and what is their degree of penetration in the Middle East, specifically in Syria and Iran?
4. Can expatriate opposition efforts and the use of ICT be placed within the framework of Civil Society theory?
5. What is the overall influence and potential of democratic expatriate groups for democratization in the Middle East?

Structure and Methodology

The book is divided into five chapters. Chapter 1 deals with the role of media as well as Information and Communication Technology (ICT) in the quest for democracy in the Middle East. The chapter looks into the idea of "communicating democracy" and surveys several recent historical events for which media played a role in the pursuit of democracy. The chapter also focuses on the two main countries covered in the book, Syria and Iran, and discusses the relevant technology and communication platforms that existed in them before the eruption of protests in Iran in 2009 and protests followed by a civil war in Syria in 2011.

Chapter 2 deals with the challenge of democratization in the Middle East. Naturally, democracy is a loaded word and one that is much debated. Addressing the question of "democratization" and focusing on efforts to promote democracy in the Middle East implies that democracy *should* be promoted and that it *can* be promoted using a variety of policy, advocacy, educational, and technological tools. Both assumptions about the feasibility of democratization and about the benefit or even the right to pursue a democratization agenda are not taken for granted. The chapter spends some time examining the foundations of the "democratization" agenda, including its merits and limitations.

Chapter 3 deals with diasporas, political diasporas and political change. The phenomena of political diasporas has not received significant attention in the literature, although there are ample instances in which diasporas and political expat groups have been able to change societal and political dynamics in their host countries. This phenomenon has been witnessed in Czechoslovakia, Venezuela, Poland, El-Salvador, Spain, Argentina, South Africa, the Philippines, Turkey, Iran and Iraq to name just a few. Communication has long served opposition groups who began their political campaigns by advocating for competing ideas and political platforms. In this regard, it is important to stress that ICT is not expected to create dissent or lead the opposition effort. Rather, ICT is expected to serve the opposition and empower its ability to communicate messages, particularly to communicate with those in the opposition who are based outside of their native lands. The degree of that empowerment and service will be further examined in this chapter.

Chapter 4 offers a synopsis of the main questions that this book seeks to explore. The analysis featured in the book was built during fieldwork and was further developed as events continued to unfold in the region. This chapter also incorporates the insights gained from extensive field interviews conducted in the period preceding the upheavals in the Middle East.

Chapter 5 serves as a synopsis of this work. It delves into the present day and to the Arab uprisings that served as the ongoing case study for this work. The chapter deals with two additional case studies, Egypt and Tunisia, which enabled me to glean additional insights into the relationship between virtual differences and actual change.

Due to the contemporary character of this work, and the fact that some of the necessary data could not easily be found in a university library, it became apparent that a more comprehensive field survey would be needed in order to collect the needed data and gain access to additional resources and content that otherwise may not have been available. The Delphi Survey method was selected as a feasible solution since it was geared toward "expert-based" data collection that enables the collection of specific data, as well as gaining a broader perspective on issues relevant to the research. My personal contacts with the interviewees often resulted in access to new resources and individuals whom I found invaluable to the research process. A modified Delphi technique was selected for this study, based on a Delphi model of Linstone and Murray (1975). According to the methodology used for a general Delphi study, a pilot (or pre-Delphi[1]) process was initiated, followed by one main round of Delphi questionnaires given to a group of established experts in seven categories:

1. Scholars who were working on Iran, with a focus on Iranian media and the work of the Iranian opposition
2. Scholars who were working on Syria, with a focus on the Syrian media and the work of the Syrian opposition
3. Scholars and policy experts who were working on issues of democratization and media in the Middle East
4. Journalists and writers who were writing from and/or about the region
5. Journalists and professionals who were working or had worked in state-funded agencies (i.e. VOA, BBC Arabic/Farsi, Kol Israel).
6. Activists in the expat pro-democracy camp in Iran
7. Activists in the expat pro-democracy camp in Syria

Over 60 in-depth interviews were conducted during the Delphi and pre-Delphi process, the results of which informed my research and the writing of this book. Additional interviews were conducted following the completion of the study and during the writing phase. Appendix I provides details on the list of interviews conducted and the affiliations of the individuals involved. The interview data is detailed in Chapter 4 as well as incorporated into the text of work.

While converting the text of the dissertation into this book, with an eye to making it more accessible to a general audience, I chose to limit the amount of references in the body of the text and I converted most of them to footnotes. Those interested in the original source material should refer to the bibliography section.

A large number of people have accompanied me in the past decade as I traveled the region, collected materials and began my academic pursuits. At first these were dissidents and activists who provided energy and

1 For the purpose of this work and in light of the complexity of the questions at hand, I decided to utilize a "pre-Delphi" pilot process which was focused on constructing the Delphi process itself: (a) defining the research process, (b) identifying key questions, (c) identifying criteria for the selection of interviewees, and (d) identifying an initial list of potential interviewees.

inspiration and who escorted me on journeys of a lifetime. I thank the inspiration and direction given by Professor Gabriel ("Gabi") Ben-Dor who provided ongoing guidance and helped me work through complicated methodological problems. I would also like to thank Adam Briscoe, the bright and young scholar who assisted me with good advice and excellent editing insights while compiling this work and to Dr. Chelsi Muller for her valuable reviews and insights.

Nir Boms
April, 2016

Chapter 1: Media & Technology's Function in the Quest for Democracy

1.1 Communicating Democracy in the Middle East

The concept of democracy promotion or "democratization" has troubled researchers since the dawn of political science research and has been a subject of much debate since 1830, a time when even Great Britain—in some ways the most democratic European nation of that era—allowed barely 2% of its population to vote for one of its Houses of Parliament. As will be further discussed, "democrats" – or those who believe that liberal values and basic human freedoms should serve as a basis for political governance – hold that the values of democracy should be promoted, and that an effort should be made to influence political systems to move in this direction or at least to become more protective of human rights and individual freedoms. The founders of democracy envisioned it as a just and universal system that offers inalienable rights to all. They also saw it as a paradigm of governance that challenges the traditional authoritarian system and hence one that should be promoted.

Promoting the "democratic paradigm," as will be further discussed in Chapter 2, was historically an intellectual pursuit, a task for local democracy forces. Following WWII, this began to change and democracy promotion gradually expanded to other domains. The Cold War, solidifying a bi-polar international system, served as a convenient platform to translate the "democracy promotion" agenda to action. Democracy promotion was no longer an abstract idea but rather a "soft power" tool and a means to "influence foreign governments, foreign publics, and world public opinion through the non-forcible projection of culture, ideology and political value systems."[1]

Values and culture are instilled in a community or society when there is a steady promulgation of ideas. One of the first concrete actions following WWII was the creation of Radio Free Europe in 1949 under the motto "Free

1 See Robert Pee (2014), "The Cold War and the Origins of US Democracy Promotion," USSO, May, 2014.

Media in Unfree Societies." The radio, which gradually grew in its coverage, was aimed at offering an alternative media environment while challenging Soviet propaganda. Radio Liberty followed suit, airing in the Soviet Union. Language coverage grew and gradually expanded beyond Europe and the Iron Curtain, reaching Asia and the Middle East. The communist side reciprocated with similar steps as well.[2] Both the Western Allied governments and the Soviet Union could never have produced or maintained sufficient public support and jingoism for the long conflict without the media's contribution to the emerging "war of ideas." Following the collapse of the Soviet Union at the end of the Cold War, the topic of "democratization" received additional attention in light of new data which demonstrated links between democracy, economic prosperity, international stability, and peace as well as a positive, contemporaneous relationship between media liberalization and democratization.[3]

Following the events of Sept. 11, 2001 and the launch of the "war on terror," more attention was shifted to the Middle East, a region which still suffers from a significant "democracy deficit." In this respect, the process of democratization in the Middle East was also framed as a potential long-term policy answer to the problems of fanaticism and terrorism, two traits appearing to have prevalence in the region. Naturally, these issues came to a head again in 2010 as the region claimed its own "Arab Spring" with attempts to trigger democratically oriented revolutions in Tunisia, Egypt, Yemen, Syria and the Gulf. These attempts that seemed to be spontaneous, young, and heavily broadcast proved to be a hopeful sign of the young "Facebook generation" that became mature enough to lead a change. However, the failure of most of these attempts, the introduction of the expression "Islamic Winter" in place of "Arab Spring," and overall turmoil brought some of the basic questions back to the table: Can democracy be established and can it flourish in the Middle East? Can the moderate camps assume positions of leadership? What was the meaning of these "Facebook revolutions?" And can technology play a constructive role in helping moderate camps alter the balance of political power?

---

2 See T. Doherty (2003).

3 See Kant, 1981; Buchanan, 1984; Inglehart, 1997, 2003; Rummel, 1997, Moore, 2003 and Pasek, 2006.

The Middle East is still characterized as a region that is reluctant to welcome cultural, societal, or political changes. The Middle East has not been heavily influenced by the waves of democratization that have doubled the number of democracies in the world during the last two decades, and quadrupled them since the end of the Second World War. Alongside this process, the past two decades have witnessed the emergence of a shift in the balance of power since the end of the Cold War and the establishment of the US as the global hegemon, the one remaining superpower in the world. The end of the Cold War and the beginning of the unipolar era was not free from clashes, which were often triggered by new nationalist sentiments and/or religious awakenings. Some of these newer conflicts, such as those in former Chechnya, Yugoslavia, Sudan, and later in Pakistan, Afghanistan and Iraq aligned their key players according to old and familiar lines of ethnic, national or religious divisions. These developments also resulted in the creation of 35 new countries in the world since 1990, many of them affiliated with ethnic or religious groups that sought further independence such as Armenia, Azerbaijan, Croatia, Macedonia, Tajikistan, Turkmenistan, Serbia, Slovakia and recently, South Sudan. The Middle East saw the emergence of three de-facto (although not yet recognized by the UN) states, Palestine, Kurdistan and the Islamic State. This discourse, which was further, delineated by Samuel Huntington's seminal work *The Clash of Civilizations and the Remaking of World Order*, triggered additional research in an attempt to evaluate the possible reasons for the lack of change in the political environment of the Middle East.

The literature, which will be further reviewed in this work, has long focused on the potential contribution of media and new media to democracy and civil society. Much of the literature has described the media as a fourth branch of government[4], or a watchdog, which safeguards the democratic process. The relationship between media and social change has been framed by classic works such as *Four Theories of the Press,* which explains existing relationships specifically between media and government.[5] The four models of these relationships, Authoritarian, Libertarian, Social Responsibility Theory and Totalitarian, shed light on the different ways in which media

4 See Coronel, 2008, p. 2; Emery, 1971; Lichtenberg, 1990, p. 2.

5 Siebert, Peterson, and Schramm, 1956.

works vis-à-vis government and society. These models are differentiated according to parameters which include the purpose of a given media structure, its ownership, the control of media and the limitations placed upon it (that is, what cannot be published). Although this taxonomy was later criticized as simplistic and insufficient,[6] or as failing to pass the test of modern times[7], scholars continued to follow the lead of Siebert, Peterson and Schramm by developing more acute models in order to explain the relationship between the media, society and politics.

Katz and Lazarsfeld (1955) developed the important concept of opinion leaders and formulated the two-step flow of communication theory, which frames the relationship between media and public opinion. Their study shows that opinion leaders – also called "primary group" leaders – serve as intermediaries between messages and public opinion. Leaders of the primary groups are also the main players in the media environment, and their opinions will therefore be evaluated initially on their primary group credentials and later on the merits of their message. In other words, since opinions and value systems are formed in primary groups, their leaders (or gatekeepers) serve as the best agents for changing those opinions, irrespective of any others, which may circulate in the media or elsewhere. Other studies have further established this point. In a study by Kalichman and Hunter (1992), data was gathered in Chicago before and after the November 7, 1991 televised press conference by popular basketball player Earvin "Magic" Johnson, in which he announced his retirement from professional basketball after being diagnosed as HIV positive. The researchers found a marked change in perceptions of AIDS, with an increased concern over the disease and greater interest in AIDS-related information. They also found that all the men interviewed in the study had heard or read about Magic Johnson's HIV infection; the majority (86%) had engaged in frequent discussions about AIDS with their friends during the three days following his news conference and most reported that their interpersonal interactions with peers had reinforced their concerns about HIV and AIDS. Juxtaposed with new media technology, these ideas have since developed to show how a relatively small group of activists and citizen journalists can help form

6 See Altschull, 1994.
7 See McLeod and Blumler, 1989.

an alternative information environment, which challenges the narrative presented by state-sanctioned media.

Before Lazarfeld, Charles Mills (1951) had already warned against the manipulative functions of the media, which are likely to strengthen the power of the dominant elite that has greater access to them. For Mills, mass media can influence the creation of a "mass society," characterized by the "transformation of public into mass." The impact of the mass media is crucial in this "great transformation," because it shifts "the ratio of givers of opinion to the receivers" in favor of small groups of elites who control or have access to it.[8] Moreover, mass media outlets engage in one-way communication not allowing feedback, thus obliterating another feature of a democratic public sphere.[9] Jürgen Habermas (1989) echoed Mills's warning but offered a remedy by arguing that critical media can actually revitalize the public sphere and that it contributes to the process of democratization. He sought to do this by "setting in motion a critical process of public communication through the very organizations that *mediatize* it."[10]

The emergence of new media appears to have strengthened these convictions. Kellner (2000) argues that the rise of the Internet helps this revitalization by expanding the realm for democratic participation and debate, through the creation of new public spaces for political intervention. He also argues that the state-controlled public broadcasting system "collapsed in the era of globalization where commercially-based cable television has marginalized public broadcasting" and that the new media outlets "have multiplied information and discussion, of an admittedly varied sort, and thus provide potential for a more informed citizenry and more extensive democratic participation."[11]

Likewise, Benkler (2006) contends that Internet technologies are transforming key social infrastructures, including those supporting the "public sphere" which he defines as "a particular set of social practices that members of a society use to communicate about matters they understand to be of public concern and that potentially require collective action or

---

8 Mills, 1951, p. 298.
9 Ibid.
10 See Habermas, 1989, p. 232.
11 See Kellner (2000), p. 280 and quote from page 278.

recognition."[12] For Benkler, the new model of media created by information and communication technology (ICT) is inherently more democratic, inclusive, and interactive when compared to older methods of mass-media production and control. He proposes that Internet technologies—even under conditions of censorship—can undermine the control of oppressive regimes, so that it can function as a catalyst for democracy. This work will attempt to put some of his assertions to the test.

The Arrival of Technology to the Middle East

Information and communication technology (ICT) is a relatively new medium that has only recently become available to groups in the Middle East. In the last two decades, its rate of penetration has accelerated significantly, particularly in the areas of Internet and satellite communication. Pan-Arabic television networks like Al Jazeera and Al Arabiya have changed the map of Arabic broadcasting and challenged the previously existing monopoly on communications held by most governments in the region. The Internet, which finally made its way to the Middle East, has created another powerful source of free information and a series of new challenges to governments, which quickly sought to limit its influence.

According to the InternetWorldStats/ Nielsen ratings, Between 2001 and 2011 the increase in Internet usage throughout the Middle East grew by 1,987%.[13] In real numbers, the number of Internet users in the region grew from 3,284,000 in the year 2000 to 90,000,000 in 2012. In 2009, – at the eve of the "Arab Spring" the number of Internet users in the Middle East reached 45 million, nearly matching the average world penetration of 24.7% and at the end of 2013 it reached 103 million, or 45% penetration.[14]

Cell phone penetration demonstrated a similar growth. According to the World Bank statistics, the MENA region has grown 40-fold, since the year 2,000 where 16.5 million users were listed. InternetWorldStats notes

12 See Benkler, 2006, p. 177; p. 212–13.

13 See Shannak, Rifat O (2011), "Using Web Analytics to Measure the Effectiveness of Online Advertising Media: A Proposed Experiment" in European Journal of Economics, Finance and Administrative Sciences Vol 42, P. 91. (Accessed on January 5th, 2015).

14 See InternetWorldStat.

a 60- fold growth in cell phone usage in Egypt between 2000 and 2010, from one to 60 million users. Official 2011 numbers from Egypt's Ministry of Communications and Information Technology report a 30.05% Internet penetration rate, and a cell phone penetration rate of 91.32%.[15]

The Pew Research Center surveys on mobile technology released in February of 2014 reported that 95% of Jordanians, 88% of Egyptians and Tunisians, and 86% of Lebanese nationals claim they own a mobile phone. These numbers were overall higher than those in the US where only 90% of American adults reported owning a cell phone.

Furthermore, the market research group, eMarketer, estimates that in 2014, more than nine in 10 web users go online via mobile phones and that 94.0% of Internet users in the Middle East and Africa go online via mobile phones at least once per month[16].

In a region where approximately 60% of the population is under the age of 24, the younger generation has been galvanized by these changes and was quick to adopt them. On the other hand, the traditional players, namely governments and the Islamist establishment, have also engaged the Internet by developing their own means of messaging along with a sophisticated system of governmental censorship and control.

---

15 Ministry of Communications and Information Technology, Arab Republic of Egypt,"ICT Indicators in Brief: February 2011," <http://www.slideshare.net/ArabCrunch/egypt-ict-sector-in-brief-feb-2011>

16 Emarketer, "In Middle East and Africa, Nearly All Web Users Are Mobile," January 6th, 2014.

Table 1.1: Middle East Internet Users, Population and Facebook Statistics

MIDDLE EAST	Population (2014 Est.)	Users, in Dec-00	Internet Usage 31-Dec-13	% Population (Penetration)	Internet % users	Facebook 31-Dec-12	User Growth (2000–2007)	User Growth (2000–2010)
Bahrain	1,314,089	40,000	1,182,680	90.00%	1.10%	413,200	293.30%	1523.30%
Iran	80,840,713	250,000	45,000,000	55.70%	43.30%	n/a	7100.00%	13180%
Iraq	32,585,692	12,500	2,997,884	9.20%	2.90%	2,555,140	188.00%	2500.00%
Israel	7,821,850	1,270,000	5,537,870	70.80%	5.30%	3,792,820	191.30%	314.40%
Jordan	6,528,061	127,300	2,885,403	44.20%	2.80%	2,558,140	526.00%	1268.30%
Kuwait	2,742,711	150,000	2,069,650	75.50%	2.00%	890,780	444.50%	633.30%
Lebanon	4,136,895	300,000	2,916,511	70.50%	2.80%	1,587,060	216.70%	233.30%
Oman	3,219,775	90,000	2,139,540	66.40%	2.10%	584,900	254.70%	1274.10%
Palestine (West Bk.)	2,731,052	35,000	1,512,273	55.40%	1.50%	966,960	660.00%	917.10%
Qatar	2,123,160	30,000	1,811,055	85.30%	1.70%	671,720	866.30%	1353.3%
Saudi Arabia	27,345,986	200,000	16,544,322	60.50%	15.90%	5,852,520	2250.00%	4800.%
Syria	22,597,531	30,000	5,920,553	26.20%	5.70%	n/a	4900.00%	13016.7%
United Arab Emirates	9,206,000	735,000	8,101,280	88.00%	7.80%	3,442,940	132.40%	414.%
Yemen	26,052,966	15,000	5,210,593	20.00%	5.00%	495,440	920.20%	1360 %
Gaza Strip	1,816,379	n/a	n/a	n/a	n/a	n/a	n/a	n/a
TOTAL Middle East	**231,062,860**	**3,284,800**	**103,829,614**	**44.90%**	**100%**	**23,811,620**	**920.20%**	**1360.20%**

Source: Nielsen//NetRatings, InternetWorld Stats, September, 2007–September 2014, <http://www.Internetworldstats.com/stats5.htm>

Technology and Political Camps in the Middle East

As a means of distinction throughout this book, it is important to note the significant political camps that are operating throughout the Middle East. Traditionally, the region was comprised of two main camps: one affiliated with the governmental elite and the other with Islamist groups. I will also refer to a third camp, the liberal and often secular, "pro-democracy" opposition that consists of a variety of intellectuals, small organizations, political forums and activists (both country-based and expatriate).[17] It should be noted that these are broad generalizations since significant variation exists within the ranks of each camp and, particularly following recent events where we have witnessed significant changes in the structure of both Governments and their contenders in the region. The Islamist opposition – mainly the Muslim Brotherhood, and later more radical groups such as al-Qaida, Jabhat al-Nusra, and ISIS were able to gain political influence mainly in Tunisia and Egypt (for a brief period in 2013) as well as Syria and Iraq. With the addition of Gaza and Turkey, two additional places in which Islamist parties lead governments, we should conclude that Islamist parties can no longer be dubbed as simply "opposition" or contenders. On the other hand, the fact that the Muslim Brotherhood in Egypt and Saudi Arabia were outlawed and defined as a terrorist group in 2014 brings us back to a more traditional Middle Eastern outlook.

The "government camp" has seen its share of turmoil with overthrows of heads-of-state in Tunisia, Libya, Egypt and Yemen and different degrees of reforms and co-optation of opposition groups in Jordan, Morocco, Saudi Arabia and the Persian Gulf. Throughout the region we are now beginning to see new types of political orders while other countries such as Libya, Iraq and Syria continue to bleed without any political order in sight. The liberal camp, the camp that triggered the "Arab Spring," achieved the least amount of success as it has failed to solidify (and organize) itself to a degree sufficient enough to acquire political power. Exceptions to this case being Northern Iraq (the Kurdish area) that can be considered more aligned with

17 I use the term "pro-democracy opposition" to describe a mixture of groups who oppose the government on the one hand but who also share similar agendas regarding the issues of democratization and political reforms in the region.

the liberal/secular camp and the new coalition government in Tunisia, the liberal camp as a whole was unable to gain political victories at the end of 2014. However, as I intend to argue, a number of variables may contribute to a process of solidification and political maturity of the liberal camp. These include the liberal discourse that has been amplified and continues to challenge the emerging new political structures, the push back against the Islamist movements and the fear by countries like Egypt and Saudi Arabia of radical influences (which has led their ban the Muslim Brotherhood), and the fact that the region has not yet filled its political vacuum. These factors may help the liberal camp to solidify power and become a future political contender. As will be discussed in the following chapters, as the "Arab Spring" progressed, liberals made some attempts to acquire political power in Egypt, Tunisia, Syria and Iraq.

The region's governments, which seek to secure political continuity, usually revert to the objective of merely maintaining the status quo. They have been successful at doing so by asserting control over the means of communication. Understanding that technology would become a major player in social mobilization, they tried to limit its influence by asserting control over its usage and distribution. Most governments in the Middle East are still the official Internet providers, which enables them to maintain control over content and communication and to censor web sites run by their opposition or otherwise sensitive web sites.[18] In a similar fashion, some governments have attempted to limit the use of satellite technology by blocking and scrambling satellite and radio signals.[19] In order to further engage with the war of ideas, Middle Eastern governments have established their own satellite networks along with an Internet infrastructure.

The Islamist groups, which usually form the largest opposition camps, have also quickly realized the potential of ICT. They were quick to establish sophisticated Internet and satellite platforms such as Hizbullah's *Al Manar* television station, Hamas's *At Fatat* web site for youth, and the Muslim Brotherhood's *Ikwan*. They have also developed sophisticated Internet platforms in order to strengthen and enhance their organizational abilities. In his detailed work on the subject, Gabriel Weiman (2004) elaborates on

---

18 See Mendels, 1996; The ONI, 2005; Zarwan, 2005.
19 See AFP, August 14th, 2006.

eight different ways in which contemporary extremist, Islamist or terrorist groups have used the Internet, ranging from psychological warfare and propaganda to such practical functions as fundraising, recruitment, data mining and coordination of actions. By 1998, around half of the thirty organizations designated as "Foreign Terrorist Organizations" (hereafter FTO's) under the US Antiterrorism and Effective Death Penalty Act of 1996 maintained a web site; and by the year 2000, virtually all groups listed as FTO's had established their presence on the Internet. A scan of Internet use in 2003–2004 revealed hundreds of web sites serving terrorist groups and their supporter.[20] Veerasamy and Grobler summarize the main reasons for terrorists and radical groups using the Internet, they contend that it is inexpensive and available worldwide, it offers little or no regulation along with an anonymous multimedia environment, it has the ability to shape coverage in the traditional mass media, and it is able to serve as a global fundraising mechanism.[21]

Likewise, moderates and pro-democracy opposition groups were quick to utilize ICT to create their own satellite, radio and Internet platforms. Considering the Internet's availability, sophistication, low cost, and the possibility of creating a virtual world independent of physical distance, it was no surprise that expatriate groups would also make it their medium of choice. Unlike governments on the one hand and the Islamist establishment on the other, the scattered and far less-organized pro-democracy camp had little or no means of communication through which it could advance its ideas. Facing a harsh societal and cultural climate that would not allow overt political activity, the pro-democracy opposition was severely crippled in its ability to organize internally, mobilize and disseminate its ideas. For decades, governments and Islamist groups maintained a variety of media outlets including newspapers and television and radio programs, which were tightly controlled and pursued an agenda that left little room for the dissenting ideas of the opposition. While ICT was merely an additional communication vehicle on top of pre-existing communication platforms for governments and Islamists, ICT quickly became one of the only available means for the dissemination of ideas among pro-democracy opposition

---

20 See Weiman, 2004, p. 6.
21 See Veerasamy and Grobler, 2011 p. 2.

groups (which lacked the same media access). It also served as a powerful tool for communication and coordination between political activists within the region as well as expatriate political communities around the world.

A few preliminary words about diaspora and expat groups should be mentioned here. As Chapter 3 argues, the phenomena of political diasporas is far from new and history provides many cases where diasporas and political expat groups were able to change political environments in their host countries. Such cases occurred in Czechoslovakia, Venezuela, Poland, El-Salvador, Spain, Argentina, South Africa, and the Philippines, Iran and Iraq, to name just a few. Communication has long served opposition groups who began their political campaigns by advocating for competing ideas and political platforms in their host countries. In this regard, I contend that ICT is not expected to create dissent or lead the opposition; rather, ICT is expected to serve the opposition and empower its ability to communicate its message, particularly for those in the opposition who are based outside of their native lands. The degree of that empowerment and effectiveness will be further examined in the pages ahead.

The role of ICT as a catalyst for the dissemination of ideas and as a means of coordination within the pro-democracy camp is a recent phenomenon in the Middle Eastern context. The influence of ICT and its use by the opposition has not yet been adequately researched. This study will attempt to assess that influence on the process of democratization in the Middle East and on the democracy discourse in Syria and Iran. The book will further attempt to analyze the scope and scale of the discourse by assessing the influence of ICT on the activities and accomplishments, as well as the solidification of the pro-democracy camp inside and outside the Middle East.

1.2 Media, New Media and Democracy

> *"There are only two forces that can carry light to all the corners of the globe... the sun in the heavens and the Associated Press down here."*
>
> Mark Twain

"Knowledge is power" wrote Francis Bacon in 1597. Malcolm X later added "The media is the most powerful entity on earth." As carriers of "knowledge" the media is a significant player in the political arena, a fact that helps explain historical and contemporary attempts by governments and policy players to gain control over them. Print media (such as books and newspapers) was pivotal to the emergence of the nation-state as the principle modern unit of collective action.[22] During the American Revolution printed pamphlets with essays like Thomas Paine's "Common Sense" played a key role in establishing the independence movement.[23] During the French Revolution, print was used to pass short notes that were used for the same purpose. More than 40,000 such notes were used by all political camps.[24] In Europe, the telegraph and train were used during the revolutions of 1848, a period which has been called the "Spring of Nations," as means of communication between the different rebel groups. These revolutions were not isolated phenomena. In his book, *The Age of the Democratic Revolution, 1760–1800*, historian R.R. Palmer notes that democratic revolutionaries in Europe and the US were in contact with each other, learned from each other's experiences, and even planned their strategies and tactics in accordance with one another.[25]

Media has played an important role in contemporary revolutions as well. The *Bager Revolucija* (Bulldozer Revolution) is the name given to the wave of protests that occurred in October 2000 and which led to the fall of Yugoslav President Slobodan Milošević. The name of this revolution is derived from the actions of one Ljubisav Đokić who drove his heavy equipment vehicle into the headquarters of the Serbian state television station, the most visible symbol of the old Yugoslav system. Three years later, Rustavi-2, an independent, Western-funded television station, led the efforts to oppose Georgian President Eduard Shevardnadze, accused of attempting to "steal" the Georgian elections of 2003. In spite of various government attempts to

---

22 Anderson, B. (1983)" *Imagined Communities: Reflections on the Origins and Spread of Nationalism.*" London and Tambini and Damian (2000) "The civic networking movement: the internet as a new democratic public sphere?" In: Crouch, Colin and Tambini, Damian and Eder, Klaus, (eds.) Citizenship, markets and the state. Oxford University Press, New York, US.

23 See Walker, 2000 pp. 521–2.
Chapter 6:[25] Reichardt, Rolf (2012), " The French Revolution as a European Media Event," in *European History Online (EGO),* published by the Leibniz Institute of European History (IEG), Mainz 2012-08-27.

25 Robert, R. Palmer (1959), The Age of the Democratic Revolution. A Political History of Europe and America, 1760–1800, Princeton University Press.

sabotage the station and intimidate its employees, Rustavi-2 became one of the chief mobilizers of the crowd. Journalists such as Giorgi Sanaya, a popular anchorman for Rustavi-2 known for his investigations that exposed political corruption, led early the campaign against Shevardnadze. In 2001, Sanaya produced a documentary that exposed official corruption during the country's transition to privatized electricity. Sadly, he was murdered in July of 2001 and his murder was widely viewed as politically motivated. Nevertheless, his journalistic reports helped galvanized mass protests against Shevardnadze and led to the fateful events of 22 November 2003 when his opponents physically prevented him from opening the new session of parliament in what came to be known as the Rose Revolution.[26]

In Ukraine in 2004, some 500,000 people marched in protest against election fraud, corruption, and repression. This sparked the Orange Revolution, now regarded as one of the earliest revolutions in which the Internet and cellular phones played a significant role. Joshua Goldstein of Harvard's Berkman Center for Internet and Society authored a study that delineated the way in which a relatively small group of activists and citizen journalists helped create a distinct information environment that challenged the narrative presented by state-sanctioned media.[27] Moldova's 2009 revolution has already been coined the "Twitter Revolution[28]" due to the role played by the social networking and microblogging service "Twitter" in coordinating the protests in the Piața Marii [Maria Square] in Chişinău, Moldova's capital.[29]

The degree of freedom of the press, or freedom of the media, in a given society can also serve as a measure of the strength of its democratic system. Nevertheless, the relationship between media, society and democracy is

---

26 Idsvoog Karl, "Journalism Rises And Stumbles In The Republic of Georgia" in *eJournal US,* 16 April 2008, (http://iipdigital.usembassy.gov/st/english/publication/2008/05/20080518193617wrybakcuh0.8979303.html#axzz2dDDEDhUP accessed August 28th, 2013).

27 Goldstein, Joshua. "The Role of Digital Networked Technologies in the Ukrainian Orange Revolution," *Berkman Center Research Publication* No. 2007–14 (2007).

28 See 5 Allagui, Ilhem. "Multiple Mirrors of the Arab Digital Gap." In *Global Media Journal*, No. 14 (2009).

29 For more on this issue see Morozov, 2009, and the role that the hashtag "#pman" played in driving people to the protest. An earlier example is Greece in 2008.

more complex than first impressions might suggest. Freedom of the media is highly dependent upon other variables such as the structure and division of political power and the strength of civil society and civil tradition. Furthermore, the literature is ambivalent about the nature of these relationships. Should the relationship between media liberalization and democratization be defined as positive or negative? Can freedom of the media come before democratization? Or can can there be freedom of the media only after the establishment of a democratic system?[30] The term "media" itself is also relatively new. The concept of "public opinion" first appeared in the late eighteenth century while a concern with "the masses" is noticeable from the early nineteenth century onwards, a time when newspapers were helping to fashion national consciousness by making people aware of their fellow readers.[31] According to the Oxford English Dictionary (hereafter OED) it was only in the 1920's that people began to speak of "media," and only a generation later in the 1950's that the term "communication revolution" was coined. Today the OED defines media as "the means of mass communication, especially television, radio, and newspapers collectively." In 1962, the German sociologist Jürgen Habermas described the "public sphere" as a public zone for 'discourse' in which ideas are explored and "a public view" can be expressed.

The term "new media" emerged in the latter part of the 20th century to encompass the combination of traditional media (such as film, images, music, and the spoken and written word) with the interactive power of ICT, mobile computing devices and the Internet (see Table 1.1). In the 1990's, media scholars were debating whether new media, namely content available on demand through the Internet, would displace the "old media" such as broadcasting and traditional newspaper.[32] This highlights the process of convergence—the integration of telecommunications, data communication and mass communication in a single medium—as the most important structural characteristic of new media.

In a 1990 best seller, *Being Digital*, Nicholas Negroponte who founded the MIT Media Laboratory, predicted that the "passive old media" will

30 See Pasek, 2006, p. 2.
31 See Briggs and Burke, 2002 p. 1.
32 See Jan Van Dijk, 2006, p. 7.

gradually be transformed, and that broadcasting will replaced by "narrowcasting." Predicting the growing use of personal computers, he argued that the PC would turn into "an electronic gateway for cable, telephone or satellite," with bits being "transferred at a rate that has no bearing on how they will be used." He further argued that unlike the present, censorship would be more of a function of the receiver than the sender since "the consumer will censor by telling the receiver what bits to select."[33] Government, he further argued, will lose the ability to control media and information. Others, such as Bill Gates, the founder of Microsoft, voiced similar predictions, declaring in 1985 that the TV era is over. "Television is passive entertainment," he said. "We're betting that people want to interact, choose different paths and get feedback from the machine about what they have really learned." Echoing this view, Andrew Grove, CEO of Intel Technologies, commented, "just as the 1980's saw the demolition of the vertical structure of the computer industry, so the 1990's will see the demolition of the vertical structure of the communications industry."[34]

George Gilder, former Editor-in-Chief of *Gilder Technology Report*, went even further by arguing that the new media will not transform the old one but rather destroy it: "The computer industry is converging with the television industry in the same sense that the automobile converged with the horse, the TV with the nickelodeon, the word-processing program with the typewriter, the computer-aided design program with the drafting board, and digital desktop publishing converged with the Linotype machine and the letterpress."[35] However, the crash of the dot-com companies in the first decade of the 21st century, and the media outlets' success in adapting their operations, resulted in a partial failure of these early predictions. The digital revolution matured,

---

33 See Negroponte, p. 55.

34 For the above-mentioned quotes see reference for George Gilder. Gilder is a Harvard scholar, a prolific writer, an economist and a laureate of the White House Award for Entrepreneurial Excellence. Following a literary and business career, Gilder became an early technologist who wrote in 1989 the seminal "Life After Television," that outlined the new developments in computer and fiber optic technology and predicted certain death to traditional television and telephony. Gilder continued later to establish the Gilder Technology Report, which he edited until 2007 under Forbes.

35 Ibid.

enabling interactive, portable and affordable communication without the complete destruction of the old media structures. But the process of convergence affected both providers and consumers, forcing media companies to further adapt to an emerging new media reality. In that sense, the new media is seen as both a continuation and a transformation of the old one. It brings a new dimension of interconnectivity while using many of the old tools such as TV, radio, phones and newspapers.[36]

Table 1.2: Features and Functional Activities of ICT's

Medium		Functional Interactivity					Relative degree of functional interactivity
		Multi-directional	Participant Control	Supports exchange of roles	Possibility of Feedback	Nature of communication	
Networked electronic media	Telephone	Yes	Yes	Yes	Immediate	Synchronous or asynchronous	High
	Radio Communication	Yes	Yes	Yes	Immediate	Synchronous	High
	World Wide Web	Yes	Yes	Yes	Immediate or delayed	Synchronous	High
	Email	Yes	Yes	Yes	Immediate or delayed	Synchronous	High
Networked mass media	National TV	No	No	No	Limited, delayed	Synchronous	Low
	Local TV	Limited	Limited	Limited	Limited	Synchronous	Low/ medium
	National Radio	No	No	No	Limited, delayed	Synchronous	Low
	Local Radio	Limited	Limited	Limited	Limited	Synchronous	Low/ medium

Source: Audrey N. Selian (2002, p. 6)

As Briggs and Burke note, the discovery of the media was also related to the discovery of its potential political power. Communication, as the American political scientist Karl Deutsch puts it, is "the nerves of government," especially important in large states and above all in far-flung empires. Media outlets, and certainly open and accessible media outlets, have the power to significantly and positively influence the politics of participation and democracy.[37] O'Neil argues that in modern democracies, free and independent media, elsewhere referred to as liberal media, is seen as a critical check on the power of central government. Alternatively, as noted by Lichtenberg, when media is repressed or centrally controlled, public deliberation suffers.

36 For more on this issue see Jenkins, 2006, pp. 7–10.
37 See Entman, 1989, pp. 3–5.

These same assumptions have influenced those who seek to promote the democratic system through an active policy of promoting media in non-democratic environments. Ungar, for instance, advocates an American international media policy with liberalization at its forefront. Freedom of the press, he suggests, will "build [democracies] where they do not exist."[38]

Media is also seen as a tool for political socialization, mainly through the use of state propaganda. Leninist views of the press, which prevailed in socialist and totalitarian regimes, saw it primarily as a collective propagandist and agitator; as a partner in building socialism; and as a means of creating a collective identity. But it has taken other directions as well. In Eastern cultures, the media's role is primarily to help forge a social consensus for strong governments in pursuit of economic growth. According to the school of "development journalism," which was fashionable in the 1970's in poor countries, the role of the media is to veer away from the Western fixation on conflict and disaster and promote development goals. From this perspective, the press should avoid its critical edge and instead function as an information provider and cheerleader in support of development agendas.[39]

Media and Open Society

Since the late 17th century, Enlightenment theorists had argued that publicity and "openness" provide the best protection from the excesses of power. But can openness be created and secured? Herein media has occupied an increasing role as the 'guardian of democracy' with reference terms such as "watch dog," "the fourth estate," and "the guardian of democracy" that became associated with media, especially in relation to its role in democratic or transformative societies. [40] The idea of the media as a fourth estate, or as an institution which exists primarily as a check on those in positions of political power, was based on the premise that powerful states had to be prevented from overstepping their boundaries. The press, working independently of government with its freedoms guaranteed by the state, was supposed to help ensure that this was so. During the 1980's and 90's there was

38 See Unger, p. 368.
39 See Coronel, 2008, pp. 3–4.
40 See Briggs and Burke, 2002; Coronel, 2008 p. 2; Emery, 1971; Entman, 1989; Lichtenberg, 1990 and others.

a revival and application of these ideas, especially in relation to the so-called "transition societies," which emerged following the collapse of the Soviet Union and the European Communist bloc. The notion of free media became central to the process of transforming these former "Iron Curtain" nations, and today, as Coronel has noted, "even in countries where democracy is a fairly new experiment or even in those, like China, where democracy and a free press have yet to take root, the notion of the press as watchdogs of power is embedded in the self-definition of journalists."[41]

But how important is the media for the process of democratic transformation? A number of studies have challenged this correlation and suggest that media can serve as a liberalizing instrument only after democratic reform is already in place. Media can also not liberalize on its own as Hall and O'Neil (1998) concluded in a study on the democratization process in Hungary and Romania. In Hungary they discovered that media liberalization fostered democracy only when coupled with the emerging civil society, while Romania did not experience the same transition because it lacked strong civil institutions. While scholars continue this debate in an attempt to define the media's role in political transitions, and whether "Media can do it alone," it becomes clear that media could play a role as both a trigger and as an important vehicle for the development of more open, democratic systems.[42] While we cannot argue that free and open media is the only factor that can enable a democratic transition, it can be argued that without freedom of the media, the prospects for such transitions are much slimmer.

Pasek, who used quantitative methodology to analyze data from the Freedom House's Freedom of the Press Survey and data gathered by the

41 Sheila Coronel, Dean of Academic Affairs at Columbia Journalism School Coronel, has done excellent work on this issue in many of her writings. These references are taken from a report she authored for the World Bank in 2008. See particularly, pp. 2–3.

42 On the subject of the media's role in political transitions, Bennett (1998) argued that liberal media is necessary to preserve democracy but may not play a role in building it, and Venturelli (1998) found that throughout Europe, media reform occurred in the 1990's only in already established democracies. Ogundimu explains that "the media may be able to play a stabilizing role, but it would be wrong to assume that it alone can make the difference as far as democracy goes." Scholars like Walter Emery focused on the role of US broadcasting in the formation of a society dedicated to democracy and freedom (Emery, 1971).

World Bank between 1979 and 2003, affirmed the mutual dependency of democracy and the free press. Looking at 190 countries over the course of 23 years, he found a positive, contemporaneous relationship between media liberalization and democratization, which suggests a bi-directional interaction between the two factors. In other words, his results lead to an understanding of media as part and parcel of the democratization process. Media liberalization appears to coincide with the other elements of democratization, rather than preceding or following them. And media seems to play an important role in the process of democratization, while democracy underlies media liberalization.

A second dimension of the relation between media and open society has to do with its role in safeguarding and maintaining the democratic discourse once such a discourse has been created. The media should play the role of preserving a democratic discourse in already-established democracies, though a number of studies have shown its limitations and described successful attempts to limit its independence even in established democratic societies. This, however, is not always a simple task since media can find itself subjected to other constraints even in free societies. A number of scholars and media critics noted that media is often subjected to interests emerging from ownership and reliance on elite groups.[43] Others argue that the open media market has increased its dependence on advertising revenues, and on other financial interests, to the point that it has become an anti-democratic force in society.[44]

43 Entman (1989) asserts that the American media is subjected to a "vicious circle of interdependence" due to issues of ownership and a reliance on elite groups. To become sophisticated citizens, he argues, Americans need high-quality, independent political journalism, yet to stay in business while producing such journalism news organizations would need an audience of sophisticated citizens. As Entman shows, there is no easy way out of this dilemma, which has encouraged the decay of democratic citizenship and the media's continuing failure to live up to their own highest ideals.

44 McChesney (1997) claims that the open media market has increased its dependence on advertising revenues, and on other financial interests, to the point that it has become an anti-democratic force in society. A dependent media, in his view, offers limited content, which is shaped by narrow interests and camouflaged in the garb of a free media environment. This trend, which coincides with an overall decrease in the reach of non-profit and non-commercial media (public broadcasting

Plato's assertion that "the excess of liberty, whether in states or individuals, seems only to pass into an excess of slavery,"[45] comes as a reminder that freedom, in some conditions, cannot be a guarantor for the resilience of democracy. As Entman and McChesney tell us, even in well-established democracies the media can be manipulated by market forces to the point of acting against their goal of enabling an open democratic discourse.[46]

Media appears to serve as both the trigger of democratization processes and as an indicator of its success. As an important instrument in the service of democratic discourse, the presence of free and open media appears to be a crucial condition for the very existence of that discourse. However, a free and democratic discourse, and in fact, the democratic process itself, can only exist if there are sufficient institutional powers to sustain it. While media can assist these powers, it certainly cannot replace them or serve a democratic discourse independent of civil content.

1.3 Technology and Democratization—A Driving Force or Virtual Illusion?

ICT (information and communications technology) is an umbrella term for any communication device or application, such as radios, televisions, cellular phones, internet enabled devices, computer and network hardware and software, satellite systems and other technology-driven devices. It also refers to the various services and applications associated with them, such as videoconferencing and distance learning. In an attempt to define the ICT sector, the Organization for Economic Co-operation and Development (OECD) described ICT as "products of a candidate manufacturing industry which must be intended to fulfill the function of information processing and communication including transmission and display, or use electronic processing to detect, measure and/or record physical phenomena or to control a physical process." This definition also includes "components primarily intended for use in such products."[47] Although computer technology was pioneered during

media supported by public funds) is threatening a number of developed countries such as the US, Canada, Germany, New Zealand and Sweden among others.

45 Republic 564a.

46 See Entman (1989) and McChesney (1997).

47 See Colecchia, Zabalza, Devlin and Montagnier, 2002.

World War II, its potential became greatly apparent with two developments of the 1980's. The first was the miniaturization of hardware, which resulted in a number of important innovations in the semiconductor industry (mainly the transistor, then the integrated circuit, and finally the microchip). This process led to the mass production of small and cheap computers affordable to large numbers of users. The second event was the linking of computers into networks, and the linkage of these networks through existing, telephone-based, telecommunications technologies. ICT is considered by many scholars to be positively correlated with economic development and economic growth, an issue that will be further discussed in the forthcoming pages and noted in Table 1.3.[48] Since the connection between ICT and democratization is a central theoretical pillar of this work, the next chapter will attempt to substantiate the established links between ICT, economic growth, democracy and democratization. It suggests that the links between ICT and economic growth lead in turn to a direct correlation between ICT and democratization. It supports the assertion of Seymour Martin Lipset that, "the more well-to-do a nation, the greater the chances that it will sustain democracy.[49]

Table 1.3: Economic Growth, ICT, and Democratization

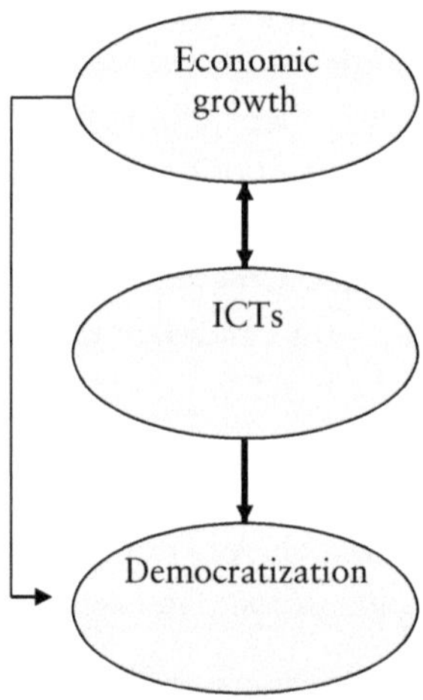

48 See Gordon R. J., 2000; Klenow and Rodriguez-Clare 1997; Ohliner and Sichel, 2001 Meijl, 1995; Raa and Wolff, 1999; OECD, 2000 and Bert 2001 and others.
49 See Lipset, 1963, p. 158.

The growth in all ICT related sectors—computers, communications and the Internet in particular—is multidimensional and in many ways, unprecedented. ICT and ICT related infrastructure became a significant global phenomenon that demonstrated unprecedented growth. Trucano (2005) reports that ICT investment in the US nearly doubled over a span of four years, from 9% of total investment expenditure in 1992 to 16.8% in 1996. This growth was related to a significant increase in the computer and data-processing services of ICT, which rose from 0.4% in 1992 to 8.1% in 1996, a twenty fold increase. ICTs are starting to be introduced in education, and interest in their use appears to be growing even in the most challenging sectors of developing countries. Data taken from the OECD shows that ICT related investment in its 34 member countries rose from less than 5% of total non-residential investment in the early 1980's to between 15% and 28% in 2001. At the end of 2013, the World Bank reported that more than 75% of the world's inhabitants now have access to a cell phone, with the number of mobile cellular subscriptions approaching 7 billion globally. This revolution is particularity evident in developing countries such as Tanzania, where mobile money agents now outnumber all other financial intermediaries by ten to one, and over half of those living on less than $2 a day in that country have access to mobile technology. The World Bank itself has been assisting that revolution and its investment in projects with ICT components have grown significantly, from about $500 million in 2006 to about $1.7 billion in 2014. The International Finance Cooperation (IFC), a member of the World Bank Group, has invested about $4.5 billion and mobilized an additional $2.7 billion of financing since 2001 in private ICT sector projects in developing countries.[50] These numbers indicate not only a trend but also a quantum leap that enabled technology to enter the 21st century as a new and viable tool in the hand of activists and dissidents from the Middle East and beyond.

The literature on ICT and non-democracies draws upon two main sources. It draws upon research on development, which investigates the role of ICT in building civil societies and implementing other development strategies. Second it draws upon research on the emerging democracies

50 Data taken from World Bank, ICT Sector Strategy.

following the collapse of the Soviet Bloc, which provided a live laboratory for democracy-building strategies. These two sources are not mutually exclusive. The so called "third wave of democratization," which will be discussed in section 2.2 of this book, has pushed aside many authoritarian regimes and begun a gradual opening-up of political systems. This process served as a catalyst for economic reforms, which brought new investors and opportunities to a large number of countries. Since the timing of the political wave coincided with the technological wave, the two were often analyzed together with particular attention to the influence of the latter on the former.[51]

According to modernization theory, low levels in factors like per-capita income, the extent of literacy and education, the degree of urbanization, and the quality as well as extent of communications media are conductive to authoritarianism, while higher levels are conducive to democracy.[52] Other theorists, such as Lipset, Moore and Rueschemeyer, have similarly argued that capitalist economic development creates growing social pressure for democratization by fostering the emergence of a middle class, bourgeoisie and working class (which seeks access to state power).[53]

To this end, the connection between technology and economic growth is well established. Robert Solow, who later won a Nobel Prize for his analysis of economic growth, had already noted in 1957 that in the United States, technological change contributed more than input accumulation to economic growth.[54] Moreover, Denison and Poullier (1968) found the same pattern in European countries such as the German Federal Republic, Italy, the Netherlands, and Norway. In 1987 Solow offered a famous paradox, which highlighted his own skepticism about the overarching positive impact

51 See Addison and Almas, 2003.

52 See Gasiorowski, 1995, p. 883.

53 See Lipset (1959) noted the influence on capitalist economy on fostering the emergence of a middle class, bourgeoisie; Moore (1966) focused on or the influence in relation to the working class and Rueschemeyer, Stephens & Stephens (1992) focused on the emerging pressure that empowered groups now have in light of their improved access to state power (Gasiorowski, 1995, p. 883).

54 See Solow, 1957, pp. 230–231. This result was also established by the early work of Abramowitz (1956) and by Denison (1962).

of ICT. Solow stated, "You can see the computer age everywhere but in the productivity statistics,"[55] meaning that growth in ICT expenditure does not necessarily reflect growth in other measures such as Gross Domestic Product (GDP) or Gross National Product (GNP). However, later studies, such as Triplett (1999) and Oliner and Sichel (2000), clarified this paradox and demonstrated the significant impact of ICT on growth and productivity. Furthermore, the detailed results of Craft (2001) suggest that ICT's contribution to growth over the last quarter of the 20th century exceeded that of steam power, and at least matched that of electricity, over comparable periods of time.[56] For developing countries, new ICT infrastructure has helped to diversify economies and decrease their dependence on natural resource endowments. This process has offset some of the geographical disadvantages of landlocked or remote countries.

Because ICT is a medium which enhances communication and enables the transfer of information in many directions, it is considered by many scholars to be a plausible catalyst for democratization and openness.[57] Most agree that ICT is to be considered a major contributor to productivity growth even though it positively affects only a few sectors of the economy.[58] Klenow and Rodriguez-Clare (1997) found that differences in technological efficiency explain the bulk of variations in income across countries worldwide. Since growth is driven by what Aghion and Howitt call "vertical innovation," technological change is enabled by firms which invest in research and development to make improved products and are thus able to outcompete older products of inferior quality. But, such a climate can only be created if an environment exists in which these companies can actually grow.[59]

Similar notions have been expressed about the relationship between ICT and democracy. ICT was found to be a key factor in accelerating democracy, since it enables users to overcome barriers of trade, access,

55 Solow Robert, New York Book Review, July 12, 1987.
56 See Crafts, 2001, p. 2.
57 See Addison, T., and A. Heshmati, 2003; Coronel, 2008, pp. 3–4; Anders, 2009.
58 Meijl, 1995; Raa and Wolff, 1999; OECD, 2000 and Bert 2001; Gordon R. J., 2000; Ohliner and Sichel, 2001.
59 See Aghion and Howitt, 1992 pp. 323, and 350–1.

communications and transportation.[60] Broadly speaking, studies suggest a linkage between economic growth and democracy, arguing that democracy will not secure itself unless a certain level of economic development has been achieved. Przeworski's (1996, 2002) seminal works on transitions to democracy focused on this very point. He and his colleagues looked at case studies of 135 countries observed between 1950 and 1990, which included forty transitions to dictatorship and fifty transitions to democracy.[61] One of their findings was that if a country passes $6,000 in per-capita income it is virtually guaranteed to succeed in its transition to democracy, while states with GDP's between $3,000 and $6,000 per capita have less than a 50–50 chance of remaining democracies. Countries with less than $3,000 are almost certain to fail in democratization. Once a democracy has been established, it is expected to last an average of about 8.5 years in a country whose per-capita income is under $1,000 per annum, 16 years if between $1,000 and $2,000, 33 years if between $2,000 and $4,000, and 100 years if between $4,000 and $6,000.[62]

Anders (2009), the director of the Swedish Development Corporation, provides a long list of the ways in which ICT has had a positive influence on societal development:

- When citizens use ICT and civil society for networking it enhances advocacy and mobilization, locally and globally.
- Blogs, Facebook and online communities create new modes of social interaction.
- The rapid and widespread use of affordable mobile telephones point to the role of mobile phones as a digital bridge and a new mass medium.
- ICT technologies assist in the documentation of human rights violations during elections, and the SMS is used for networking and mobilization.
- In government, ICT may increase accountability and transparency, acting as a counter force against corruption through more efficient administration and increased flow of information.

60 See Addison, T., and A. Heshmati, 2003; Addison, T., and A. Rahman, 2005.
61 See Przeworski, 1996, p. 39.
62 Ibid,, p. 41.

- ICT strengthens good governance by improving interactions between government and citizens.

Although most scholarship agrees with the general notion that there are positive connections between ICT, development and democratization, there are some dissenting or qualifying opinions. Both Huntington (1991) and Guillermo (1973) claim that there is a level of development beyond which the probability that a democracy will survive actually decreases. Huntington argues that both democracies and dictatorships become unstable when a country undergoes modernization, which occurs at some intermediate level of development. O'Donnell (1986) in turn, suggests that democracies may die when a country exhausts what he calls "the easy stage of import substitution." [63] He bases this assertion on his study of the breakdown of the democratic regimes in Brazil and Argentina in the mid-1960s. The political crisis was triggered by an economic crisis caused by the exhaustion of the "easy" stage of import substitution industrialization (ISI), or by acceding imports which caused a mass national debt that could not be managed. In this case, the level of economic development fostered both the exhaustion of the "easy" stage of ISI and the emergence of a politicized working class, which demanded higher wages than the government could provide. The crisis was not handled successfully and this resulted in a military regime that came to power in 1964. According to O'Donnell, certain powerful political actors believed these crises could have been resolved only by replacing these regimes with "exclusionary" bureaucratic-authoritarian regimes, because only the latter would be able to carry out the painful measures needed.[64] Responding to O'Donnell and Guillermo, Przeworski and others point to broader trends rather than the specific cases in which these trends were reversed by certain circumstances, as in the cases of Argentina and Brazil. Naturally the role of ICT is minimal in such cases, although a similar argument can be made about technology: Once ICT is embedded in a developed democracy it can, under certain circumstances, work against democratization.

---

63 See Przeworski, at el, 1991, p. 42.
64 See Gasiorowski, 1995, p. 832.

Chart 1.1: ICT Investments in Selected OECD countries

(As a percentage of non-residential gross fixed capital formation, total economy)

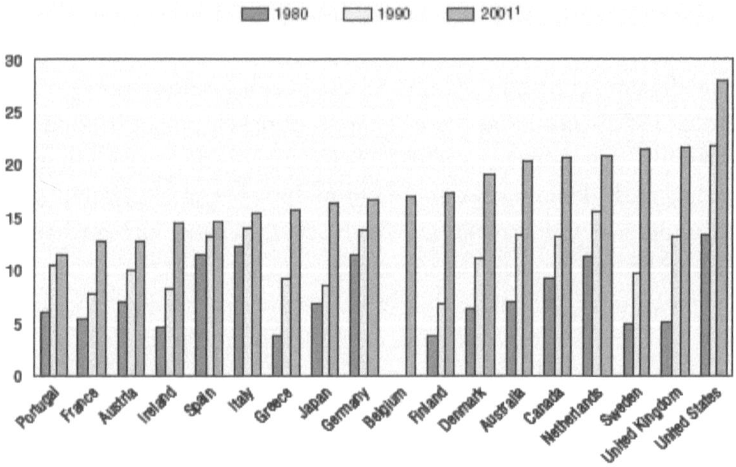

Source: OECD (2003, p. 20).

Chart 1.2: Share of ICT in the value-added, non-agricultural business sector, 2000

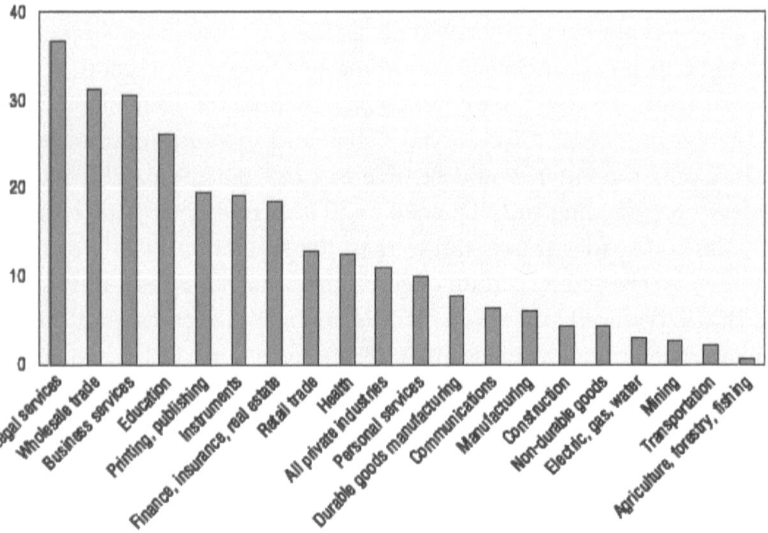

Source: Bureau of Economic Analysis, US Department of Commerce, Fixed Assets Tables, <www.bea.doc.gov>

As Chart 1.2 demonstrates, at the turn of the 21st century nearly 30% of the total stock of equipment and software in legal services, business services and wholesale trade in the United States consisted of IT and software. Education, financial services, health, retail trade and a number of manufacturing industries (such as instruments, printing and publishing) also have a relatively large share of IT capital in their total stock of equipment and software. The average for all private industries is just over 11%. The goods producing sectors (such as agriculture, mining, manufacturing and construction) are much less IT-intensive; in several of these industries less than 5% of the total equipment and software consists of IT.[65] These investments have become more efficient and affordable in light of the decreasing prices of ICT components such as computers and communication systems.

In some countries, notably the United States and Australia, there is evidence showing that industries that have invested the most in ICT (such as wholesale and retail trade) have experienced more rapid multi-factor productivity (MFP) growth, reached by the combination of labor and capital. More rapid MFP growth may also be linked to network effects arising out of the use of ICT.[66] Additional data shows that the use of ICT may help efficient firms gain market share at the expense of less productive firms, raising overall productivity. In other words, despite its "technical" nature, ICT is clearly viewed as an accelerating factor, or as a tool that can enable rapid growth.

Internet's Growth and Impact on ICT

The Internet can be used as another indicator for the rapid growth of the ICT sector. The first recorded description of social interactions enabled through a computer network was a series of memos written by J.C.R. Licklider of MIT in August 1962, discussing the "Galactic Network" concept. Licklider envisioned a globally interconnected set of computers through which data and programs could be accessed from any connected site. In essence, the concept was very similar to the Internet of today. Licklider was the first head of the computer research program at the Defense Advanced

65 See OECD, 2003, p. 22.
66 See OECD, 2003, pp. 7–8.

Research Projects Agency (DARPA), where he convinced his successors, Ivan Sutherland, Bob Taylor, and MIT researcher Lawrence G. Roberts, of the importance of this networking concept. Much of the early development of the Internet was done at MIT by researchers like Leonard Kleinrock and Thomas Merrill who connected two computers, one in Boston and the other in California, for the first time in 1965.[67] In 1969, Kleinrock described his vision for the up and coming Internet, "it would be everywhere, always accessible, always "on," and anyone would be able to plug in from any location with any computer at any time."[68] For a growing segment of people across the planet, Kleinrock's vision has already become a reality.

General public data on Internet use comes from a number of sources including ongoing research of the Central Intelligence Agency's World Factbook and Nielsen/NetRatings, which tracks the number of active Internet users for approximately 20 nations accounting for over 90% of the world's active Internet population. Additional sources include companies that focus on Internet market research. The term "active Internet user" applies to people who go online at least once in a given month. Due to its market value, data on Internet usage is available from a number of sources.[69]

Data from Netcraft, a company specializing in Internet research and tracking, shows the rapid increase in the number of Internet sites, rising from 0 to 7.8 billion in 10 years (1986–2006) and up to 52 billion in 2011 (Chart 1.3).

---

67 See Leiner & Co (2003) for a very comprehensive essay on the history of the Internet.

68 See Kleinrock, 2003, p. 5.

69 These include the Computer Industry Almanac Inc (http://www.c-i-a.com/), a company which specializes in market research reports for the PC, Internet and wireless industry and compiles Internet user data for over 50 countries. Founded in 1986, ClickZ Networks (<www.clickz.com>, a company which specializes in Internet-based marketing; Ntcraft (<www.netcraft.com>), an Internet Services Company based in Bath, England, which specializes in network security research data, and analysis for many aspects of the Internet. Netcraft has explored the Internet since 1995. Internet-related data is derived from a number of sources that attempt to trace the Internet-using populations of specific countries, mainly for commercial reasons but also for research and policy purposes.

Chart 1.3: Total Web Sites Across All Domains August 1995–May 2011

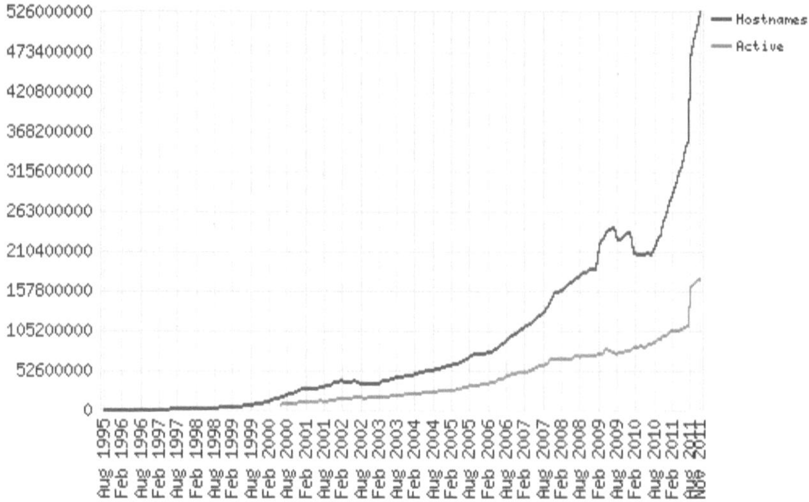

Source: Netcraft Internet Survey, <http://news.netcraft.com >

This ICT related growth presents both opportunities and threats to democracy. For established democracies, ICT offers the promise of an information-rich society in which citizens have access to a wide range of information from a variety of sources, and issues are extensively debated via interactive media. ICT is also seen as a catalyst for civil-democratic processes of citizen consultation and participation such as voting, civil participation, citizen journalism and other forms of democratic behavior.[70] For non-democracies, the main subject of this work, ICT has become a major instrument in the hands of opposition groups and regime opponents who previously had relatively little access to the means of disseminating messages. On the other hand, as already mentioned in the context of mass media, ICT can also undermine the democratic process by creating biases in the distribution of knowledge and information, thus fragmenting the discourse between increasingly differentiated policy areas and empowering non-democratic groups who are also able to utilize ICT tools.[71]

70 More on this issue see Wheeler, 1998; Escobar, 1999 and Noveck, 2000.
71 See Pratchett, p. 1218.

Nevertheless, I will argue that ICT offers more opportunities than dangers to democratic development and to the democratic system. The justification of which is shown by ICT's ability to pluralize a system of policy making, break the monopoly of old policy structures, and further enhance economic development (another important key for democratization). In a reality where the "liberal camp" has been largely unable to access media or other means of mass communication (while these means were available both to governments as well as to the Islamic camp), the prevalence and availability of ICT based communication has the potential to offer new opportunities to a camp that seeks solidification, visibility and reach.

ICT and Civil Empowerment

Early technology literature pointed to a new policy framework, which should be considered in light of the influence of ICT on the political and policy process.[72] The existing literature on policy-making has emphasized the importance of "networks," especially the effect of different types of network organizations on policy processes and outcomes. These were the "old boys networks," hierarchical in nature, more stagnated and comprised of established structures that often revolved around main centers of power such as government, military and business. These networks also had clear lines of communication and a certain degree of control over what was delivered and disseminated. This is exactly what the "new network" began to change.

Early policy scholars, such as David Truman in his work, *The Governmental Process* (1951), conceptualized a society of multiple interests that could mobilize around an almost equally limitless range of issues. Shared interests, according to this approach, will lead to the formation of groups and, later, to their politicization; but this pluralistic ideal of an interest-based policy process will need to be mediated by political structures which are far more centralized in nature. "Iron triangles" and policy networks have dominated state structures and the policy environment in a stabilized

72 For more on early technology literature see Cleveland, 1987, Grossman, 1995, Leslie, 1997.

and centralized fashion.[73] In his work on "state structures," Katzenstein (1978) argued that policy networks function as a "macro" variable, a single pattern at the broadest or deepest level of a given society which affects policy-making across all sectors. He also contended that in countries where both corporatist structures and associational systems are centralized, the two working in tandem will almost entirely dominate the policy process. In this kind of state, corporatist dynamics will be taken into consideration for most policy areas. But technology has started to change all of that, and Leslie (1997) predicted that some of these old paradigms may become obsolete as the Internet offers a prototype of a completely different model for governing policy networks.[74]

Like Leslie, Grossman (1995) argued that technology would change the access to power and the policy-making process. Focusing his work on the institutional effects of the ICT revolution, he argued that the US political system is transforming itself into an "electronic republic" with strong elements of direct democracy. Speaking about the weakening of traditional institutions, he argued that "The big losers in the present-day reshuffling and resurgence of public influence are the traditional institutions which have served as the main intermediaries between the government and its citizens: the political parties, labor unions, civil associations, even the commentators and correspondents in the mainstream press."[75] Technology is able to fragment the electorate and assist in the creation of new groups that can now design "particular appeals crafted for audiences with specific interests."[76] Through the use of ICT, activists can reach out more quickly, almost instantly, to a widely dispersed network of supporters. Computers, he further argues, can now allow for the emergence of unknown candidates or special interest groups that can reach out to citizens directly, avoiding parties or other related channels that had previously served as a screening mechanism.

---

73 "Iron triangles" is a term coined by Ralph Pulitzer in 1919, referring to the policy-making deadlock between government military and industry leaders. It is used to describe a policy formation process that is dominated by strong players and that can often create a deadlock.

74 See Leslie, 1997, p. 4.

75 See Grossman, 1996, p. 161.

76 Ibid., p. 156.

The authors draw a useful distinction between plebiscitary democracy (a direct vote in which an entire electorate is asked to either accept or reject a particular proposal) and "communitarian democracy," which they define as "participation in public space—in the meetings and assemblies, the deliberations and persuasions which distinguish the democratic process and make participation in it a transformative lesson in the common good."[77] Whereas older technologies, such as TV, promoted centralization by the virtue of having one message without a real ability of responding to it, ICT enables decentralization down to the community level. While scholars have concerns about plebiscitary politics (which are based on a direct vote), their assessments of the impact of ICT on interest group activity are positively correlated. Interest groups can use technology to break down the barriers to participation and activism by drawing upon groups that have historically been non-participatory, such as women who stay at home. Through this specialized targeting method the interest groups can mobilize support more quickly, and subsequently raise funds more efficiently.

Cleveland's work, which focuses on the consequences of the "informatization" of society, has reached similar conclusions. Cleveland argues that populations now demand participation and networking rather than command and control; that decision-making takes place more openly because of the openness of information; and that governments, try as they might, cannot hope to control information. According to Cleveland, ICT will increase the access to power since "the fusion of computers and communications will further empower the many to participate in making policy in domains to which the few, with their moth-eaten monopolies of knowledge, will have to yield more and more access."[78]

In sum, the literature agrees that ICT has the potential to weaken established institutions and networks, to improve access to power, to increase transparency and in general to weaken the ability of governments to control and manipulate information. These features, which give the citizen more participation and tools of control, have changed the policy process more gradually than was originally anticipated.

77 Ibid,, p. 23.
78 See Cleveland, 1987, p. 64.

ICT in a Non-Democratic Environment

This discussion of ICT as a pluralizing mechanism and as a vehicle to increase transparency, public awareness and public participation, is relevant to democracies and non-democracies alike; however, a non-democratic environment which stifles debate and often brutally rejects attempts to alter its hierarchical structures will pose more complex challenges to theoretical arguments about ICT's potential influence. In addition, the fact that other non-state actors (such as terrorist groups) will often excel in their use of ICT makes the claim that ICT exerts a positive influence on democracies and democratization even more problematic. Though a discussion of these other non-state actors is beyond the scope of this work, I would like to point out that this is a well-researched subject in light of its increased importance to state and security institutions worldwide. Since the Internet became a major operational and recruitment mechanism for terrorist groups, a great deal of research has been invested in tracing and studying this phenomenon, which poses new challenges to a growing number of states in the world.

Another qualifying opinion comes from scholars who are critical of the presumed influence of technology, particularly the Internet and social media, on political activism and democracy. Malcolm Gladwell and Rami Khouri have both observed that this presumption is simply overrated since despite the real scope of the phenomenon, it has not demonstrated any significant results. Writing before the Arab Spring, Khouri contends, "We must face the fact that all the new media and hundreds of thousands of young bloggers from Morocco to Iran have not triggered a single significant, lasting example of change in Arab or Iranian political culture."[79] Gladwell argues that the despite the large number of individuals involved in social networking activities with political causes, the actual associated circles of activists it generates is much smaller and is based, like other such circles before the Internet era, on more intimate ties of friends and acquaintances. He agrees that social networking can involve a significant number of individuals in political campaigns, but stresses the fact that this involvement is of "low intensity." "How did the campaign get so many people to sign up?" he asks about the case of Sameer Bhatia, a young Silicon Valley

79 See Khouri, 2010.

entrepreneur who was diagnosed with leukemia and needed a bone marrow transplant.[80] An orchestrated social-media campaign resulted in nearly twenty-five thousand new people registering on the bone marrow database, and a match was located for Bhatia. While Gladwell agrees that this example can be used as proof of the ability of social media to mobilize, he argues that the campaign was successful only because people were not asked to do much more than click a few times on a computer. He also brings examples of large Facebook groups which revolve around political issues such as Darfur; though these groups easily attract over a million members, when they are asked to contribute funds the number drops significantly, and the average donation of a "committed" member is lower than 10 cents.[81] These arguments do not necessarily negate the connection between technology, development and democratization, but rather they give "new technology" a more realistic role to play.

In sum, the majority of studies agree that ICT offers more opportunities than challenges to the democratic process. Because it contributes to the pluralization of the policy system, weakens the monopoly of old policy structures and further enhances economic development, ICT has the potential as well as the ability to help emerging democracies and strengthen existing ones.

1.4 Syria and Iran: Case Studies

Syria and Iran present very different cases of Internet penetration, considering the differences between the two societies, their level of development and the two governments' approaches to the issue of technology and the Internet. The latest Nielsen/InternetWorld Stats figures (see Table 1.1) show an impressive 34.3% penetration rate in Iran (with a population of 67 million), compared to less than half of that in Syria (16.4% with a population of 22 million). The Internet environment is likewise different in the two countries (Iran's is much more developed). Both countries have experienced a recent attempt to transform their political system in which liberal and pro-democracy forces played an important role. In Iran, that attempt – termed

---

80 See Gladwell, 2010.
81 See Gladwell, 2010, pp. 5–6.

the "Green Movement" – was crushed relatively quickly in 2009. In Syria, following Tunisia and Egypt, launched its own uprising in 2011. Battles are still being waged as I write these words. The following paragraphs will delve into both the history and censorship of the Internet in both countries and will attempt to frame the technological terrain that became available as the uprisings in each country began.

According to The OpenNet Initiative (ONI), the telecommunications market in Syria is the most regulated in the Middle East, and it is also among the least developed. In 1996, Syria was included on a short list of twenty countries that still had absolutely no e-mail or Internet connection. In the same year, Syrian Prime Minister Zuabi authorized the Syrian Telecommunications Company (EST) to enter the Internet age. The Prime Minister was encouraged to do so by Bashar Al-Assad, who served as the president of the Syrian Information Technology Association from 1995 to 1999 (before becoming President of Syria in 2000).[82] Following an initial evaluation, a larger pilot project was inaugurated to connect governmental agencies to the World Wide Web. At its inception in 1997, the pilot project had a maximum capacity of 150 subscribers, including the President's departments, the Prime Minister, local and national leaders of the Ba'ath Party, ministries, military departments, state-owned companies, universities, Arab and international organizations as well as news agencies, hospitals and chambers of commerce.[83] In addition, Kawakibi estimates that over 65,000 Syrians were "illegally" connected to the Internet via Lebanese, Jordanian and Turkish Internet providers.[84]

Although the pilot project was deemed successful, connectivity expanded very slowly under the watchful eyes of the Syrian government. Human Rights Watch found that "until 1999, Syria was one of the rare countries in the world which was connected to the global Internet network but did not allow its citizens to access it, in spite of official speeches and declarations praising this tool."[85] In early 1999, another pilot project was launched by

82 See Dholakia, et al, 2003, p. 52.
83 See Kawakibi, 2010, p. 2.
84 More on the history of Internet in Syria see Salam Kawakibi, 2010.
85 Quoted in Kawakibi, p. 2.

EST to provide email services inside the country.[86] Soon afterwards, the authorities also allowed access to international email and other services offered by the Internet, such as browsing the web and file exchange via FTP (file transfer protocol). Following the second pilot, two types of subscriptions were made available: email-only service or email plus web surfing. The authorities gradually increased the number of "entitled" subscribers and accepted subscriptions from private companies (both commercial and industrial). The progress was still slow, since it entailed bureaucratic procedures like obtaining papers that granted "legitimate" access to the Internet. Keep in mind that at this time Syria had only one Internet host, EST.[87] This practice also opened the door to a scam in which people would get hold of documents certifying their membership in an "entitled" profession without actually practicing it. It also became clear that access was being carefully filtered and monitored by the government, which soon began to take measures against those who downloaded or forwarded "banned" messages.

Another reason for the slow progress of Internet integration emerged during an interview with Syria's Minister of Communication Arm Salim in 1999, in which he explained Syria's approach to the Internet. In order for the President, Hafez al-Assad, to feel comfortable promoting a particular technology, it was required to meet the following criteria:[88]

1. It should benefit the majority of the Syrian people. Technology geared toward the elite is not favored because such people have the resources and means to get what they want without government assistance.
2. It should not disrupt the social structure or adversely affect the middle class, and should be within the means of the masses.
3. It should have a direct impact on Syria's overall social and economic development.
4. It should not jeopardize Syrian independence or security concerns.

In 2001, the Syrian Information Technology Association entered the market with subscription offers that were more flexible, while still complying with the regulations—namely the requirement for users to belong to specific

86 See SANA report, 1999.
87 See Dholakia, et al, 2003, p. 53.
88 Quoted in Goldstein et al, 1999, p. 57.

professions. Nevertheless, Internet service remained expensive and was largely unaffordable. The year 2005 saw increasing growth in the Internet sector with the arrival of two other private service providers on the market, Aya and CEC, along with the Italian satellite Internet provider Best-Italia. In 2007, mobile-phone operators Areeba (later MTN) and Syriatel also entered the Internet market.[89] These developments indicated a certain change of tone and indeed, Amr Salem, the Minister of Communications and Technology, stated in 2006 that he would like to distribute "one million affordable computers with Internet connection." Salem also proposed removing customs duties on IT hardware. Finally, the Syrian government envisaged creating several high-tech parks in Syria in order to attract foreign investment in IT.[90] At the end of this wave of reform, four private access providers (Aya, Cec-Sy, ZAD and SyriaTech) were allowed to share the market with the state-controlled STE. This resulted in a significant growth of Internet users. Reporters Without Borders (RSF) found that in 2009 there were 40 times more users than in 2004, an upsurge which has further prompted the authorities to control news posted online.[91]

Syria managed its Internet surveillance by entrusting it to two government bodies: the Syrian Telecommunications Establishment (STE) and the Syrian Information Organization (SIO), which controls bandwidth. It maintains a very tight grip over its Internet traffic and shows little tolerance for "unauthorized" Internet use. Syria is featured as an Internet rights violator, and constantly appears as an "enemy of the Web" in the ratings of Reporters Without Borders, which stated that "After China and Vietnam, the Syrian Arab Republic is one of the world's most repressive."[92] An RSF report said the government "censors opposition and independent news web sites, barring access to those which deal with Syrian policy, monitor[ing] online activity to silence dissident voices, and jailing Internet users and bloggers."[93] The government admits to censoring "pro-Israel and hyper-Islamist" web sites such as those run by the illegal Muslim Brotherhood, and those which

89 See Kawakibi, p. 3.
90 Ibid.
91 See RSF, 2009, p. 19.
92 See Reporters Without Borders, 2010.
93 See Dholakia, et al, 2003, p. 52l; RSF 2009, p. 19.

call for autonomy for Syrian Kurds. Former Minister of Technology and Communications Amr Salem has said in defense of these practices that "Syria is currently under attack ... and if somebody writes, or publishes or whatever, something that supports the attack, they will be tried."[94]

In addition to the above-mentioned sites, Syria maintains a long list of banned web sites, which include opposition sites, human rights sites, Israeli sites, and occasionally popular sites like Facebook, YouTube and Amazon. Other blocked sites include the London-based, online Arabic editions of *Al-Quds al-Arabi* and *Asharq al-Awsat*; the liberal Arabic news portal, elaph.com; the online edition of the Kuwaiti newspaper *Al Seyassah*; and the US-based web site of the *Arab Times*, and the Islam-oriented news and information portal, Islam Online. The list of banned sites changes and updates frequently. Since the government controls the main Internet gateway, surveillance and control becomes easier. To ensure centralized censorship of the web, it uses systems such as Thundercache, a sophisticated Canadian made software which allows web site surveillance at the ISP level and enables filtering by searching for keywords banned by the authorities. According to its manual, the system also allows for monitoring and controlling a user's dynamic Web-based activities, identifying and blocking the installation of spyware, slowing access to certain sites, and denying or allowing the downloading of specific applications.[95] It appears that Syria was able to upgrade its censorship system using American equipment as well. BlueCoat systems of Sunnyvale, California admitted in October of 2011 that their filtering equipment, which enables a user to block web sites or record when people visit them, is operating in Syria. The equipment was not sold to Syria but reached it following a sale to the U.A.E that was diverted to Syria.[96] These censorship systems appear to work well. Diebert is a company that tests for blocked web sites and in a 2006 comparative study of 21 countries, it found that Syria is able to effectively block many local web sites (84% of those tested, mostly in Arabic), though it had less success in blocking foreign web sites (16%). The vast majority of the political sites tested (95%) were

---

94 See Taylor, 2007.
95 This information is taken from the manual of the software. See Platinum, 2010.
96 See Soone and Stecklow, 2011.

found to be blocked.[97] Syria was able to block major parts of the Internet a few times during the 2011 wave of protests.[98]

Aside from their technical capabilities, the Syrian authorities have several legislative tools at their disposal: The penal code, the state of emergency law which was put into effect in 1962, and the repressive 2001 Press Code (which was amended in 2005 to cover online publications), enables the regime to accuse activists, bloggers and other Internet users of illegal use of the Internet or of endangering state security. It can also use articles 286 and 287 of the penal code, which criminalize spreading news abroad; and decree number 6 of 1965, which criminalizes "publishing news aimed at shaking the people's confidence in the revolution."[99] These legal mechanisms have been used often, and in 2007, Reporters Without Borders described Syria as the biggest prison for cyber-dissidents in the Middle East because of the number of arrests and the frequency of which online activists are mistreated.[100] Here are some examples of such practices:

Habib Saleh was tried in December 2008 for publishing articles calling for democracy in Syria on the liberal online magazine, Elaph.com (which is censored in Syria), and was given a three-year prison sentence in March 2009. Saleh was convicted of "weakening national sentiment" under article 285 of the criminal code. Blogger Tariq Biasi received a three-year sentence for "weakening national sentiment" due to some comments he published on his blog about the Syrian security services. Osama Kario was jailed for a joke he put on his blog in 2007, which mocked the "three no's of Khartoum." Omar Ali Abdallah was sentenced to five years in prison in 2006 for contributing to an Internet forum that was deemed seditious by the authorities. Lawyer and web site editor Abdallah Souleiman Ali was detained 12 days for "persisting in publishing legal and political articles criticizing the role of the government" on his web site, Al Nazaha. Tal al-Mallohi, a 19-year-old female high school student who encouraged the Syrian government to do more for the Palestinians, was put in jail in September 2010 on charges of spying. A number of other bloggers such as Ahed al

97 See Chadwick Andrew and Philip 2008, p. 330.
98 See Flock, 2011.
99 See ONI, 2009b.
100 See RSF, 1997.

Hendi, Kareem Arabji, Habib Saleh, Firas Saad, Mohammad Badi, Dak al Bab and Homam Hassan Haddad were harassed, arrested or jailed by the authorities because of what they wrote or posted on other web sites. They were prosecuted under article 287 of the Syrian criminal code ("damaging state prestige"), or under similar articles such as damaging "state integrity" and weakening "national feeling."[101] In 2009, the Committee to Protect Journalists ranked Syria third in a list of the ten worst countries in which to be a blogger given the number of arrests, level of harassment, and tight restrictions that online writers in Syria have faced.

Another form of censorship is regulations that aim to ensure that the government has oversight over bloggers and web site administrators. On 25 July 2007, former Minister of Telecommunications Amr Salem announced a decision by the Prime Minister that all web site administrators would be required to "publish the names of article authors and those posting comments clearly and in detail."[102] Failure to comply with this would expose administrators to penalties and an inability to access their sites. In March 2008, security officers verbally ordered owners of Internet cafes to register all visitor data and to keep daily records of each client's full name, mother's name, ID or passport number, the number of the computer station used and the log in and log out times. Cafe owners were forced to hand in these records to the security authorities.

This was the reality at the beginning of the uprising and as demonstrations began in Syria in March 2011. A noteworthy event took place on January 17th of that year, just 2 days after Ali was deposed in Tunisia: Syrian police in Damascus captured and beat a young man for unknown reasons. A large crowed assembled next to the police station shouting "thieves, thieves" evoking a common practice in which corrupt policemen demand money to release an innocent man. Footage of the incident was uploaded to the Internet where hundreds of people can be seen next to the police headquarters, protesting while taking videos and pictures with their cellular phones.[103] The episode scared the regime enough to send the Minister of Interior, Mohammad Sammour (also showed in the video), to assure the

---

101 More on this issue see Taylor, 2007, RSF, 2009, p. 19; Worth, 2010.

102 See OpenArabNet, Syria report, 2010.

103 See https://www.youtube.com/watch?v=5L5H-8BZ6UU

crowds that justice would prevail. Pictures and videos of demonstrations and battle scenes seen later on have fueled the Syrian Revolution since its inception. People like Basil al Sayid, a young citizen-journalist who chronicled the Syrian siege of Homs for months until he documented his own death by the regime in December of 2011, became a symbol of the quest for freedom in Syria. In this sense it is important to notice that the means of ICT technology were dispatched long before weapons came to the scene. Since then, the Internet has continued to serve as an active arena of the uprising for all parties joining the fight.

Internet in Iran

The history of the Internet in Iran began in January 1993, when Dr. Larijani, Director of the Institute for Studies in Theoretical Physics and Mathematics (IPM), sent Iran's first electronic mail message, a greeting to administrators at the University of Vienna. Unlike in Syria, the growth of the Internet in Iran has been fast and transparent. In 1995, *Newsweek* commented "If the computer geeks are right, Iran is facing the biggest revolution since the Ayatollah Khomeini.... outside Israel, Iran has the most comprehensive site for information browsing in the Middle East."[104]

The Middle East Economic Digest (MEED), quoting statistics prepared by Pyramid Research, suggests that Internet users in Iran have rapidly increased from 250,000 in 2000 to 450,000 in 2001, a 30%increase every six months.[105] InternetWorldStats estimates that as of June 2011 there were 36,500,000 Internet users in Iran, representing a 46.9% penetration with the highest growth rate in the Middle East. ONI calculated an average Internet growth of 48% from 2000–2008.[106]

Internet development in Iran was supported by the government as an alternative means of scientific and technological advancement during the troubled economic period following the Iran-Iraq War in the late 1980s. The Iranian government encouraged the use of the Internet by allowing commercial and educational sectors to access it without interference. Iran's

104 See Bogart, 1995, p. 36.
105 See Rahimi, 2003, p. 114
106 InternetWorldStats, 2011 ONI, 2009b, p. 2.

first computer network was established within the university system where Iran's first national academic network (IRANET.IPM) was created. The Data Communication Company of Iran (DCI), an arm of the state Telecommunications Company, took it upon itself to set up the first Internet switchboards in Iran, which quickly became available in most Iranian cities by 1995. But the prices of these services were still expensive: leased lines with a speed of 9600 bps were 40,000 rials ($9.50 US dollars) per month. Dial-up lines on the other hand were cheaper, 5,000 rials ($1.19) per month plus a 500,000-rial ($199) deposit, plus the usual connection time and volume charges.[107] These prices began to drop toward the end of the twentieth century to the equivalent of $40 per month for an individual account (with an additional $16 per 200 kilobytes of traffic). This was still expensive considering that salaries in Iran at the time averaged the equivalent of about $180 a month. A satellite GulfSat link was offered for about $625 per month on top of a $30,000 set-up fee.[108]

In those early days, the Iranian government maintained a relatively open Internet environment while exercising some control over the main Internet "pipeline." Iran's Public Switched Telephone Network (PSTN) provided the connections based on modems and connected end users to Internet Service Providers (ISPs), while DCI provided the backbone for high-speed and high-capacity data communications between various points throughout the country.[109]

IRANET, which became available in 1993, offered full Internet access, e-mail services, electronic publishing and web site design. It helped many Iranian organizations to establish an online presence and conduct business in a relatively flexible market-driven environment. Given the academic sector and the help of ISPs like IRANET, commercial industries in Iran developed an active Internet presence.

In the early 1990s, tensions began to emerge between the bureaucratic agencies, such as the High Council of Information (HCI), the DCI (a branch of the Telecommunication Company in Iran), and the emerging private technology sectors. The two sides differed primarily over how to improve

---

107 See Javid, 1995.
108 See Johari, 2002, p. 81.
109 Ibid, p. 82.

the quality and availability of network access under the pressure of accelerated demand. As a result, new ISPs were allowed to enter the market and the state information agencies became increasingly weaker. Making their first appearance in 1994, Iranian ISPs created dynamic institutional bases for the development of the Internet in Iran.[110] Over 100 private ISPs have joined the market since 1994.[111]

These developments led to the establishment of a sophisticated net that exceeded the current Internet programs of some European nations. By 2001, Tehran alone boasted 1,500 Internet cafes, making it one of the leading countries in the Middle East in terms of the number of Internet cafes per major metropolitan area.[112] *The Guardian* reported in February 2002 that ParsOnline, one of the biggest Internet service providers in Iran, was offering "Asymmetric Digital Subscriber Line (ADSL) connections at 2 Mbps [megabits per second], four times faster than that available to home users [in London], and for people out of ADSL attachment zones, there are wireless links available, running at 5 Mbps, something unheard of in the UK."[113] Computers became widely available and even the government began its digital age with Supreme Leader Khatami's web site, which was launched ahead of the 1997 election and was able to show the election results in a live web cast. Encouraged by the government, most clerics, even those in the notoriously conservative holy city of Mashad, developed web pages. They were among the last to join all of Iran's government ministries, government-run media networks, grand ayatollahs, mosques and other governmental agencies in maintaining active web sites.[114]

This significant growth should be attributed to demographics as well. The post-revolution baby boom in Iran led to a significant rise in both the number of universities (especially private ones) and the number of students enrolled at those universities (especially female students). As at other universities around the world, all of these students received access to the Internet through their educational institutions. At the same time, the literacy rate

110 See Rahimi, 2003, pp. 115–116.
111 See Abbas, 2002, p. 81.
112 See Rahimi, 2003, p. 116.
113 See Babak, 2003, p. 3.
114 See Hammersley, 2002.

also dramatically increased since 1979, rising from 59% to 77.1% in 2003. Iranian schools and universities began producing large groups of educated youth who were mostly unemployed and in search of new ways to express themselves.[115]

The Internet has quickly become an important medium of communication and expression, and this development is reflected in Iranian society. A growing network of web sites and blogs has made Farsi one of the languages most widely used by bloggers. Much of this growth happened after September 2001 due to the work of Hossein Derakhshan, a young Iranian journalist who created a simple how-to blog guide in Farsi. In 2004, there were an estimated 60,000–75,000 blogs in Iran, with Farsi being the fourth most-popular language for online journals. This is a significant figure compared to neighboring countries such as Iraq, where there were no more than 50 known bloggers in the same year.[116] The effect of these Internet technologies extends beyond the major urban areas as well. Students who return from urban universities to their towns and villages strive to remain connected and in the process, introduce their rural families and friends to the capabilities of the Internet. It is this phenomenon in particular which has made the Internet revolution reach farther, wider, and deeper than would otherwise be expected in a developing country like Iran.[117]

The importance of the Internet in Iran became the focus of a great deal of media attention following the infamous elections of 2009. Sites such as YouTube and Twitter enabled protesters to document the aggressive and brutal actions with which the Iranian government attempted to quell the protests. Despite the regime's censorship efforts, which aimed at stopping the flow of images and stories, information was able to escape in large quantities. The Green Movement, the emerging opposition movement, quickly adopted the concept of "one person, one reporter." This movement made a concerted effort to publish images and videos from Iran.[118] This caused the government to significantly increase its oversight of Internet activity, and it soon occupied a leading spot on the list of notorious Internet oppressors.

115 See Rahimi, 2003, p. 116.
116 See Alavi, 2004; Kelly & Etling, 2008 p. 2.
117 See Rahimi, 2003, p. 117.
118 See Shahab and Mousoli 2010, p. 6.

Internet Censorship in Iran

As mentioned before, the Iranian government was well aware of the power and utility of the Internet, and initially chose to allow its development and growth without significant constraints. However, this technological endorsement did not prevent the Iranian government from enforcing an increasingly stringent censorship regime. As early as 2003, the government began a systematic campaign of implementing more Internet restrictions. The Open Net Initiative called the current censorship policy implemented by the Iranian regime "one of the most extensive filtering systems in the world."[119] Its conduct in matters of censorship also earned Iran the title, leading "enemy of the Internet," according to the Internet report of Reporters Without Borders.[120] This system of censorship has grown to be more sophisticated, and Iran now employs domestically produced technology for identifying and blocking objectionable web sites, thus reducing its reliance on Western filtering technologies.[121]

Illegal suppression of the press in Iran began long before the Internet. The Iranian government maintains a number of mechanisms which help enforce this policy. The Supreme National Security Council, which is charged with defending the country from external enemies, is the primary enforcement arm of censorship policies. The council produces writing guidelines and sends instructions to newspaper editors that order them to write within certain limits. The Iranian judiciaries along with the Intelligence Ministry are working to enforce and punish journalists and bloggers who do not comply. Other security agencies could also be mobilized to exert pressure on journalists and newspapers. Arash Sigarchi, an Iranian journalist and former editor of *Gilan-e Emrooz* offers a number of illustrations of these mechanisms, which have become more active during the tenure of President Mahmoud Ahmadinejad. "The Ministry of Information and Security—Iran's intelligence ministry—began to summon all newspaper journalists to ask them to cooperate with the system. Their message was clear, those who cooperate can work; those who do not will go to prison. Those who

119 See ONI, 2009a, p. 1.
120 See RSF, 2010a, p. 1.
121 See ONI, 2009a, p. 1.

cooperated with the regime received economic privileges. Some of my former colleagues chose to accept the regime's offers and today hold positions of power."[122]

Speech restrictions extend over a broad range of topics, including religion, immorality, social harmony and politics. The government has been shutting down reformist papers for years while maintaining a strong censorship regime over radio and TV stations. The Internet, a communications outlet that enjoyed relative freedom, quickly became the only available source of independent news and information and as such caught the attention of the Iranian government.[123] The legal and institutional basis for the technical filtering system began with a series of decrees passed down by the Supreme Council of the Cultural Revolution (SCRC) in December 2001. An inter-agency committee, the Committee in Charge of Determining Unauthorized Sites (CCDUS), was set up in 2002 to set criteria for identifying web sites should be blocked. Its regulations required ISPs to employ filtering systems and be subject to censorship. Regulatory agencies in Iran charged with policing the Internet began to expand in 2004, when the chief of the Iranian Judiciary, Ayatollah Mahmoud Shahroudi, announced new "cyber laws" defining punishments for "anyone who disseminates information aimed at disturbing the public mind through computer systems."[124]

Although Iran's 2005 Development Plan called for enhanced broadband penetration, and despite the fact that it was developing related infrastructure including a cyber-optics network, in October 2006 the Ministry of Communications and Information Technology (MICT) issued an order designed to limit household access to broadband Internet, forbidding ISPs from providing Internet connectivity to households and public Internet access points at speeds greater than 128 kilobytes per second. This policy, which restricts the ability of Internet users to download multimedia content and use VOIP applications, was intended to hinder access to online, alternative media sources that may have competed with the tightly controlled radio and television outlets in Iran. In 2009, Open Net Initiative (ONI) reported that "Iran is the only country in the world to have instituted an explicit cap

122 See Arash, 2008, p. 49.
123 See Arash, 2008, p. 52; Granick, 2005 P.11; ONI, 2010, p. 1.
124 See Granick, 2005 P. 11; ONI, 2010, p. 1.

on Internet access speed for households."[125] This has affirmed complaints by owners of Internet cafes that heavy filtering "slowed down the Internet in Iran, reducing its speed by almost 50%."[126] Simultaneously, the Iranian government continues with some degree of success to jam the satellite signals of stations like VOA, BBC Persian and other opposition stations.

Internet restrictions appear to vary from one geographic location to another, but are tightened in times of unrest and tension. An example of this kind of tightened censorship occurred during the aftermath of the June 2009 election, when the Iranian government worked to "shield the outside world's view of the unrest, banning coverage of the demonstrations, arresting journalists, threatening bloggers and trying to block web sites like Facebook and Twitter, which [became] vital outlets for information about the rising confrontation."[127] During the same period Diebert noted the localization of the Iranian filtering system. Many of the blocked web sites had a higher percentage (80%) of inaccessibility in Farsi than in English (45%). The Berkman Center study on blogs found that Iranian censorship efforts focused on secular and reformist blogs, although religious and conservative blogs were also found to be blocked, but to a lesser extent.[128] While the exact number of blocked sites is unknown, Roberts, Palfrey and Zuckerman estimate it to be in the "tens of thousands."[129]

Another censorship technique is the creation the "Halal Internet," or what Iranian Deputy Minister for Economic Affairs Ali Agha Mohammad calls "an Internet that conforms to Islamic principles."[130] This highly regulated and monitored network is aimed at further solidifying the Iranian censorship efforts that have been somewhat weakened by the lack of control over the central Internet gateway. Once fully operational, it will enable a more centralized control beyond the ISP level. As a related first step, the Iranian Government were able to report on a functioning automatic "smart filtering" system able to disqualify specific messages that

125 See ONI, 2009a p. 2 and also, Shahab and Mousoli, 2010, p. 6.
126 See Najibullah, 2007.
127 See Fathi, 2009, A1.
128 See Kelly & Etling. 2008, p. 38.
129 See Roberts, Palfrey & Zuckerman, 2009, p. 3.
130 See Freedom House, 2013.

include predefined, prohibited content. At the end of 2015, Telegram users (Telegram is the most popular text messaging system in Iran with over 20 million users) have testified that attempts to send text messages including certain words or phrases have failed, and that they immediately received a message saying that the message could not be sent due to local restrictions in their country[131] Pavel Durov, and the Iranian authorities. On 20 October 2015, Telegram's CEO, Pavel Durov tweeted that access to Telegram was blocked in Iran, after the company refused to comply with the requirements of the Ministry of Communications to supply the Iranian authorities with surveillance tools for spying on citizens.[132]

As in the case of Syria, intimidation tactics were and continue to be widely used. Iranian bloggers and Internet activists are often arrested, jailed, and even killed as a result of their work. Like the regime of censorship, these activities began to intensify toward 2004.

Arash notes that in 2001, when he began to write, the Iranian government was not very aware of the Internet, so he could "get away with straight reporting." This situation began to change in 2004 when he was first arrested and eventually, in 2005, sentenced to ten years imprisonment for "cooperating with the US government, insulting the Iranian leadership, and conducting propaganda against the Islamic Republic."[133] There are countless similar examples. In 2005, blogger Mojtaba Saminejad barely escaped the death penalty for "insulting the prophets." He was found guilty of "insulting the Supreme Leader," and sentenced to two years imprisonment.[134] In December 2007, Iranian police raided more than 430 Internet cafes and other shops in Tehran during the first days of the latest campaign against "inappropriate and un-Islamic conduct." Twenty five Internet cafes were closed in that raid and 170 cafe owners were fined for "using immoral computer games and storing obscene photos," as well as for the presence of women without "proper hijab" on their premises.[135] Omidreza Mirsayafi, 29, who was convicted of "insulting Imam Khomeini and the Supreme

131 See Zimmt, Raz, 2016.
132 Ibid, P. 4.
133 See Arash, 2008, p. 51.
134 See Hamdy 2006, Sigarchi, 2008. p. 49–50.
135 See Najibullah, 2007.

Leader Khamenei" and posting "seditious" materials on his blog died in prison following lack of medical care in March 2009. His private blog focused mainly on traditional Persian music but included some political criticisms.[1] Jila Bani Yaghoob, a 2010 recipient of the Reporters Without Borders' Freedom of Expression prize, was arrested along with her husband and 20 other journalists in June 2009. Her blog, "We are journalists," brought news and political commentary from Iran and she produced more than 4,000 reports on issues such as the schooling of women, prostitution, AIDS victims, suicide among young people and the wars in Iraq, Afghanistan and Lebanon. She had undergone a number of previous arrests because of her work. Yaghoob joined over forty Internet journalists, bloggers and Internet activists behind bars in 2010.[2]

Shortly after sentencing two Iranians to death for running Internet pornography sites, the Iranian government announced the opening of an Internet police unit to help ensure proper Internet use and counter the growing popularity of web-based social networks and web based political activity.[3] The new Internet police were created to help centralize the work that was previously done by a number of other agencies and to as assist with other censorship efforts like the development of government controlled VPN networks. VPN (Virtual Private Networks) are used to bypass Internet censorship by allowing a connection via a proxy server that enables a gateway to a non-censored connection.

Recently discovered third party organizations are providing the Iranian public with such VPNs. The identities of these providers are unknown but it appears that the Iranian government controls some of them. These VPNs can easily enable the authorities to discover the identities of users and of individuals in their social networks.

Unlike the Syrian government, the Iranian government was better prepared to tackle "internet protests." The Iranian authorities were able to not only to control VPN's but also circumvention tools such as TOR, a highly sophisticated and popular online anonymity tool used by many Iranians to

1 See Cameron and Mousoli, 2010. p. 7; Parsa, 2009.
2 See RSF, 2010b, p. 4.
3 See AFP, 2011.

bypass Internet censorship. Despite its sophistication, the Iranian authorities succeeded in circumventing it as late as August 2014.[4]

Following the succession of Ahmadinejad by Hassan Rouhani in August of 2013, a lively discourse developed in Iran regarding the implications of Rouhani's promise of greater openness and rehabilitation of the country's international standing. This promise should have had an impact on the level of filtering and government censorship on the Internet including the continued ban on popular social media web sites such as Facebook and Twitter. A year later, Iran's Minister of Information and Communications Technology (ICT), Mahmoud Vaezi, attempted to clarify these policies to reporters in a press conference that took place on 21 August 2014. The Rouhani government, "never promised to open things that were filtered in the past," he said. He added that, "The Government is trying to eliminate those things that the people of this country are opposed to, and within our nation, which is a Islamic nation, families pay special attention to ethical matters and they are not happy with accessibility of these non-permitted websites."[5]

The rapid development of ICT created significant opportunities to break the once held government monopoly on information and communication. New tools, channels and platforms became available forcing governments to re-think their own media strategies while offering civilian groups new opportunities to disseminate messages and amplify their voices. While the overall impact of these developments point to the weakening of centralized government and indicates a move toward greater openness, economic growth and even democratization, the emerging civilian forces may not guarantee an immediate "democratic transition." As we have clearly seen in the Middle East, non-democratic forces that also utilize ICT among other tools, may gain the upper hand by offering a more unified and cohesive alternative due to financial and other support that may become available to some of the radical groups. Technological platforms, as will be later discussed, cannot replace physical structures, nor can they guarantee unity of rank or message (a fact that points to an advantage on the side of the more unified and hierarchical Islamist opposition). Nevertheless, these

4 See Alimerdani, 2014a.
5 See Alimerdani, 2014b.

developments must be looked at with the appropriate historical perspective and with an understanding of the given departure points. While the Islamist camp has been an established, organized political force and contender for many years, the liberal camp is much less cohesive and politically organized, but it is still young and emerging. The liberal camp's failure to acquire political positions should not overshadow other significant developments that will be further discussed in the coming pages. With the help of ICT, the liberals have been able to disseminate new ideas about the future of the region and provide a more solid political alternative, at least on the level of discourse.

While this process is still in motion as the region continues to count its dead and injured – I believe that we can already see a change in the basic balance of power and the related discourse about the possibility of change. In the words of Syrian author Sadik Jalal al-Azm:

> "Consider where each of the two sides started. Before the uprising, the regime's security agencies saw themselves as invincible, a granite block; anything that bumped into them would crumble to dust. Indeed many jailed dissidents reported upon release that during interrogation and torture officers would warn them: Why do you bother to criticize, oppose, and protest, when you know we are invincible? With a will of steel that crushes anything and anyone that stands in its way? … The revolution has destroyed this omnipotent image both within the regime and outside of it."[6]

As we will discuss further, it takes more than a virtual network to establish a functioning democracy. However, the developments are significant enough to indicate changes that may be on the horizon.

6 See Al-Azm, 2014, p. 7.

Chapter 2: The Challenge of Democratization and the Middle East

2.1 Universal Rights and Democracy Promotion: Is Democracy a Philosophy for All?

Raising the question of democratization is to accept the conceptual underpinnings and legitimacy of democracy. When it comes to democratization in the Middle East, this acceptance is associated with a certain political understanding or, at least, a philosophical believe that justifies an attempt to change an existing political structure, which has dominated the region for decades. Although this is not the primary focus of my work, it is important to understand the philosophical bases and the motivations shared by those who advance the set of ideas and values associated with the word "democracy." Investigating the factors that drive "democratization" will shed some light not only on the important role of those who work for this cause on behalf of governments or international organizations, but also on the expatriate groups who often spread these ideas.

Democracy, I will argue, has gradually grown to be a "world value," and has grown from an old idea inspired by a few, to a way of life sought after by many.[1]

From the inception of democratic thinking, its founders saw it as a new paradigm of governance, which focused on individual rights, mainly those of civil equality, justice, and equal opportunity. Such an approach challenged the way states functioned, mainly as authoritarian and highly centralized organs that were not open to decision sharing or to limited executive power.

Although democracy as a system is still relatively new, especially in its more liberal form, the discourse on rights is an ancient one. This discourse can be traced as far back as the 18th century B.C. when the Code of Hammurabi guaranteed some rights even to slaves, who were allowed to own possessions (including other slaves), do business, and eventually purchase

1 See Sen, 1999.

their freedom, which was final and binding.[2] This concept of society hastily developed and was deemed successful, to the point that today much of it is accepted by a universal consensus.

Aristotle, one of the earlier proponents of democracy, differentiated between types of political systems when he stated that, "an oligarchy is said to be that in which the few and the wealthy rule, and a democracy that in which the many and the poor are the rulers."[3] In the 5th century B.C., Thucydides, a Greek historian, stated that democracy must "afford equal justice to all," and stressed the importance of personal freedom, "...far from exercising a jealous surveillance over each other, we do not feel called upon to be angry with our neighbor for doing what he likes, or even to indulge in those injurious looks which cannot fail to be offensive, although they inflict no positive penalty."[4] These ideas contributed to the concept of "natural law," a philosophical construct that focuses on the laws of morality and reason. This construct is based on the assumption that the law cannot be divorced from moral principles. Hence, natural law relates "to the most fundamental values of everyday living. It is pertinent to the choice of the best future legal and political order, and the kind of civilization which will be most conducive to man's happiness."[5]

The philosophical linkage between morality and law attempted to clarify the legal foundation for individual rights and for the idea of justice. Sir William Blackston (1723–1780), was an English jurist who authored a historical treatise on the English common law. He went further by arguing that a norm, which does not conform to natural law, cannot be legally valid. According to Blackstone, the laws of nature were dictated by G-d himself and hence cannot be trumped by legal standards that conflict with them. Furthermore, all valid laws derive their authority from natural law, which in turn must be superior to any other laws and universally binding. Political systems and governments are then given the responsibility to implement these natural laws.[6] In accordance with these views, John Locke stated

---

2 See Richardson, 2000, pp. 16–18.
3 See Rackham, 1932, III, p. 8.
4 See Crawley, 1951, p. 104.
5 See Brown, 1960, p. V.
6 See Blackstone, 1979, pp. 38–41.

in *Two Treatises* that under the "social contract" it is the government's responsibility to protect "natural rights," which include "the right to life, liberty, and the ownership of property."[7] Locke posits that the government is responsible for securing the freedom and liberty of men, and stated, "freedom of men under government is, to have a standing rule to live by, common to every one of that society, and made by the legislative power erected in it; a liberty to follow my own will in all things, where the rule prescribes not; and not to be subject to the inconstant, uncertain, unknown, arbitrary will of another man."[8]

Rousseau expanded on this idea in *The Social Contract*, in which he defines government as the organ responsible not only for securing freedom but for maintaining it. He defines government as "an intermediate body set up between the subjects and the sovereign, to secure their mutual correspondence, charged with the execution of the laws and the maintenance of liberty, both civil and political."[9] The French historian, Alexis de Tocqueville, who visited the United States in the 1830's and wrote the modern classic *Democracy in America*, spent a significant time on questions of equality and freedom. Starting from an assumption of equality—all men are created equal—he went on to argue that men are also entitled to freedom, since that is the only vehicle that will allow the implementation of such equality. Commenting on the ideal characteristics of a democracy, he wrote:

> Let us suppose that all the people take a part in the government, and that each one of them has an equal right to take a part in it. As no one is different from his fellows, none can exercise a tyrannical power; men will be perfectly free because they are all entirely equal; and they will all be perfectly equal because they are entirely free. To this ideal state democratic nations tend. This is the only complete form that equality can assume upon earth; but there are a thousand others which, without being equally perfect, are not less cherished by those nations.[10]

For de Tocqueville, democracy was a social state, which was based on the premise that all people are equal from birth, and that men need to share the task of organizing a society. That society, according to Tocqueville,

---

7 See Locke, 1680, p. 114.
8 Ibid.
9 See Rousseau, 1792, III, p. 1.
10 See Tocqueville, 1840.

must possess the elements of equality, a task that cannot be accomplished without the existence of freedom.[11]

Thomas Jefferson drew further on these ideas when he developed what would become known as "constitutional liberalism."[12] Constitutional liberalism argues that human beings have certain natural (or inalienable) rights, and that governments must limit their own powers in order to secure these rights for citizens. The American Declaration of Independence, whose composition he supervised, states as "self-evident" the truths that "all men are created equal" and entitled to "life, liberty and the pursuit of happiness." The universal nature of these principles, and the fact that they were quickly incorporated into the American Constitution and later on into other founding declarations, encouraged the promotion of freedom and democracy not only within the emerging borders of the United States but also outside them.

Nobel laureate Amartya Kumar Sen argues that the notions of universal rights and democracy as a universal commitment are a product of the twentieth century. He explains that while the Barons who rebelled against the King of England and composed the Magna Carta saw the need as an entirely local one, the American fighters for independence and the revolutionaries in France contributed greatly to an understanding of the need for democracy as a global system. If in the nineteenth century, theorists discussed whether one country or another was "fit for democracy," In the twentieth century the discussion shifted with the recognition that the question itself was framed incorrectly. A country does not have to be deemed fit for democracy but should rather adjust to democracy. Sen further argues that democracy can be considered a world value since the notion of a system that guarantees rights will quickly become a dominant belief in the contemporary world, especially by the poor who understood that "democracy is not a luxury that can await the arrival of general prosperity."[13]

The 20th century brought the discourse of universal rights further into the international arena, via the new international organizations that were created following World War I. The League of Nations, an international organization founded by the Allied front, was created to "promote

11 See Zuns and Kahan, 2002, p. 6; Fishman, 2005, p. 17.
12 See Zakaria, 1997, p. 31.
13 See Sen, 1999, pp. 4–6.

international cooperation and to achieve peace and security."[14] Although ultimately unsuccessful, its covenant obliged League members to promote the "well-being and development" of peoples in the territories over which they had jurisdiction, as well as "fair and humane conditions of labor for men, women and children."[15] These principles were later incorporated into the mandate of the UN, signed in San Francisco on June 26, 1945. That mandate expresses the determination of the peoples of the United Nations to "reaffirm faith in fundamental human rights, in the dignity and worth of the human person, in the equal rights of men and women and of nations large and small."[16]

These ideas were translated into political action in a number of ways. President Ronald Reagan introduced sanctions against apartheid South Africa in 1986, and the Bush administration cut assistance to Uzbekistan in 2004 because of its human rights abuses. Similar resolutions associated with human rights were issued in connection with Rwanda and Sudan. More recently, human rights have triggered NATO involvement in Libya. The EU has adopted democratic criteria for membership that forces new (and existing) members to adopt a series of democratic reforms, along with an open market economy and a clean track record with regards to human rights standards.[17]

These developments, which paralleled what Huntington has termed the "third wave of democratization," and the growing number of democracies in the world, have contributed to the acceptance of democracy as "an ideal system of government" and one that "has near-universal appeal among people of every ethnic group, every religion, and every region of the world."[18] This claim can be substantiated by a number of surveys. Several major empirical research programs are monitoring public support for democratic institutions on a global scale, including the New Democracies Barometer,

---

14 See, History of the UN, http://www.un.org/en/aboutun/history

15 Ibid.

16 See UN mandate, preamble.

17 See McFaul, 2004, pp. 160–161.

18 The "third wave" is term coined by Samuel P. Huntington in his 1991 book *The Third Wave: Democratization in the Late Twentieth Century*. It refers to the growth of democracies in the world toward the end of the 20th century. It will be further discussed in section 2.2; See McFaul, 2004, p. 148.

the New Russia Barometer, the Latino Barometer, the Afro Barometer, the European Values Survey, and the World Values Survey (WVS).

The findings of the WVS (a Sweden based NGO which carried out representative national surveys in 97 societies from 1981 to 2007, containing almost 90% of the world's population) were this:

> The desire for freedom and democracy is a universal human aspiration, but it is not top priority when people grow up feeling that survival is uncertain. When basic physiological and safety needs are fulfilled, growing emphasis on self-expression values makes the emergence of democracy increasingly likely.[19]

The findings of the WVS observed an inter-generational shift toward post-materialistic values, along with a growing global tendency for self-expression, which is more prevalent among younger age groups around the world.[20] It also found a correlation between mass self-expression values and democratic institutions. Based on these trends, and on the prediction that inter-generational population replacement is likely to make these values of self-expression more widespread, it predicted that countries with authoritarian regimes were likely to become more liberalized in the next 15 to 20 years.[21] Ronald Inglehart, the president of the WVS, posits "countries which show a lower level of democracy than their citizens' values would predict, are likely to become genuine democracies." The WVS also found that economic development brings rising levels of tolerance, trust, political activism, and a greater emphasis on freedom of speech (the components of self-expression), which in turn leads to growing mass demands for liberalization in authoritarian societies and to rising levels of direct mass participation in societies that are already democratic.[22] Interestingly, in none of the countries surveyed does support for dictatorship exceed support for democracy.[23]

The "world value" argument also draws from the fact that diverse populations, countries, and groups subject to societal transitions to democracy have related to this system in a similar fashion. For example, Muslim attitudes toward democracy appear positive irrespective of the character

---

19 See Inglehart, 2007, p. 8.
20 See Inglehart 1977, 1997, and 2003; Inglehart and Abramson 1999.
21 See Inglehart, 2007, p. 8.
22 See Inglehart, 2003, p. 52.
23 See Macfaul, 2004, p. 150.

of governments in the Muslim and Arab world. Tessler analyses a subset of the WVS data in which 2,343 Egyptians were interviewed in 2000. The survey shows that most Egyptians favor democratic governance regardless of religiosity, gender or age. The Zogby polls, conducted in 2002 in Morocco, Egypt, Saudi Arabia, United Arab Emirates, Jordan, and Lebanon, show that while almost no respondents had a favorable attitude toward US policy, very substantial majorities have a positive view of a democratic educational system and a democratic form of government. In other words, while support for specific American policies remains very low, support for a freer society, education and freedom remains high.[24]

Chart 2.1: Attitudes about US Education, US Freedom and Democracy, and US Policy toward the Arabs, Among Egyptians Interviewed in 2002 (in percentages).

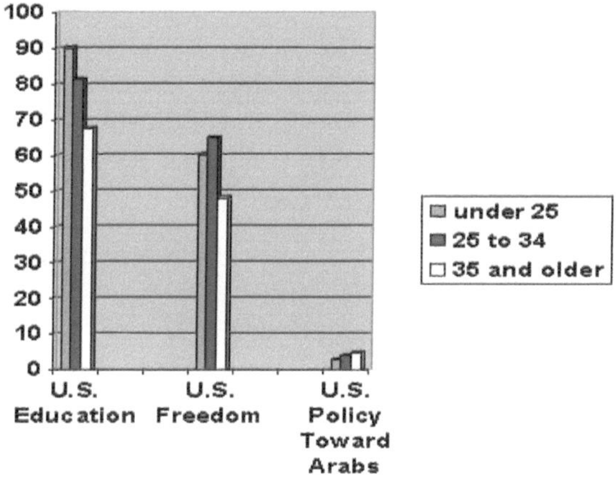

Source: Tessler (2003, p. 179)

These findings are consistent with other survey findings from the Muslim world. In 2006–2007, a research project, the Arab Barometer, conducted face-to-face interviews with large and representative national samples of ordinary citizens in seven Arab societies, Algeria, Jordan, Kuwait, Lebanon, Morocco, Palestine, and Yemen. A total of 8,555 men and women were interviewed. Respondents were asked whether they agreed or disagreed with

24 See Tessler, 2003 pp. 177–8, and Chart 2.1.

the following statement: "Democracy may have its problems, but is better than any other form of government." As shown in Chart 2.2, overwhelming majorities agreed: 74% in Jordan, 79% in Palestine, 92% in Morocco, 82% in Lebanon, 63% in Yemen, 69% in Algeria, and 85% in Kuwait. Other questions about democracy produced similar response patterns. But at the same time, similar majorities expressed their dissatisfaction with the American policy of democracy promotion. In responding to the statement: "US democracy promotion policies are good," there was a range of disagreement from 64 percent in Jordan to 73% in Algeria. Analyzing the findings, Tessler and Amaney concluded that despite the anti-Americanism resulting from Arab complaints about US foreign policy, Arab popular support for democracy has not been undermined.[25]

Chart 2.2: Support for Democracy in Seven Arab countries, the Arab Barometer Project

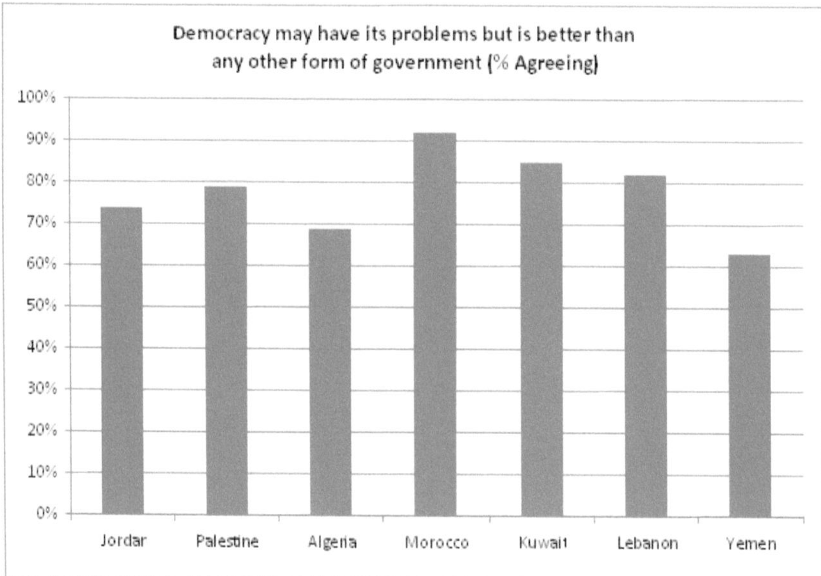

Source: (Amaney and Tessler, 2008)

25 See Amaney and Tessler, 2008, pp. 2–3.

Macfaul further argues that international resentment of US power and policies may in fact have liberated the democratic norm from its close association with the United States, particularly during the Cold War. He concludes that being both pro-democracy and anti-America is no longer a contradiction in terms, and that this notion helps to secure democracy as a leading world governance system.[26]

As a philosophy, as a value and later as a political norm, democracy appears to have established its global position. Democratic norms and discourse appear to dominate international affairs without serious challenge from competing ideologies. In more than one way, democracy has become the prevalent means of discourse and the accepted term of reference, if not the political norm. Although democracy is still far from available to the majority of the world, democratic discourse has gained a lot of momentum and democratic values appear to have gained consensus worldwide. True, this picture cannot guarantee the continuation of the third wave or the collapse of remaining dictatorships in the world, however this data helps to explain the growing role of democratic values, including self-expression and human rights in the international system. It also points to a gap between the documented aspirations and the realities of many people living in the Middle East and elsewhere who seek a "freer" environment than what is being forced on them by existing political and governmental structures.

According to the thinkers mentioned above, the principles of freedom must serve as the basis for any desired form of government, and must therefore be incorporated into the infrastructure of governmental, legislative and judicial processes. Democratic convictions, and particularly the notion of universality, helped support those who sought to encourage assertive policies of democracy promotion that eventually became pillars of American and European foreign policy.

2.2 The "Democracy Wave"

The "democracy wave," which has doubled the number of democracies in the world in a relatively short period of time (1974–1990), and quadrupled it since the end of World War II, has not impacted the Middle East. In 1950,

26 See Macfaul, 2005, p. 152.

only 22 of the 80 sovereign political systems in the world (or 28%) were regarded as democratic.[27] When the third wave of global democratization began in 1974 there were 39 democracies in the world but the percentage of democracies in the world was about the same (27%). Yet by December of 2004, following the collapse of the Soviet Bloc and a significant increase in the number of recognized states, Freedom House tallied 120 democracies. This was the highest number and the greatest percentage (63%) in the history of the world, which at that time constituted 190 countries. In the Middle East, however, aside from Israel and Turkey, no other country is classified as "democratic."[28]

The third wave of democratization began in the Iberian Peninsula in the mid 1970's with the collapse of the Salazar dictatorship in Portugal and the death of Franco in Spain.[29] It then spread to Latin America and parts of Asia in the 1980's. That wave accelerated dramatically from 1989 onwards, with the fall of the Berlin wall, the breakup of the Soviet Union, the unexpected surge of democratization in Sub-Saharan Africa, and further democratization in Asia. By the end of 1991, half the states in the world were electoral democracies (a term which will be further discussed in the next chapter), and by the mid-1990's that proportion had risen to three-fifths, where it has remained for several years. According to a UNDP development report, in the 1980's and 1990's some 81 countries took significant steps towards democracy, bringing the number of electoral democracies to 140.[30]

This dramatic expansion indicates that democracy has been gaining universal legitimacy, and may go hand in hand with Fukuyama's assertion that liberal democracy is the "end point of mankind's ideological evolution" and the "final form of human government."[31] Indeed, in its 1999 *Country Reports on Human Rights Practices,* the US State Department went so far as to identify democracy and human rights as a third "universal language" (along with money and the Internet). The State Department report also envisioned the emerging transnational network of human rights actors (both

---

27 See Diamond, 2000; Freedom House survey, 2004.
28 See ibid, Freedom House, 2005, Chart 2.1.
29 See Carothers, 1999, p. 1; Huntington, 1991, p. 2.
30 See UNDP, 2002, p. 1.
31 See Fukuyama, 1988, pp. i–ii.

public and private) becoming an "international civil society ... that will support democracy worldwide and promote the standards embodied in the Universal Declaration of Human Rights."[32]

Chart 2.3: Growth of Freedom around the World

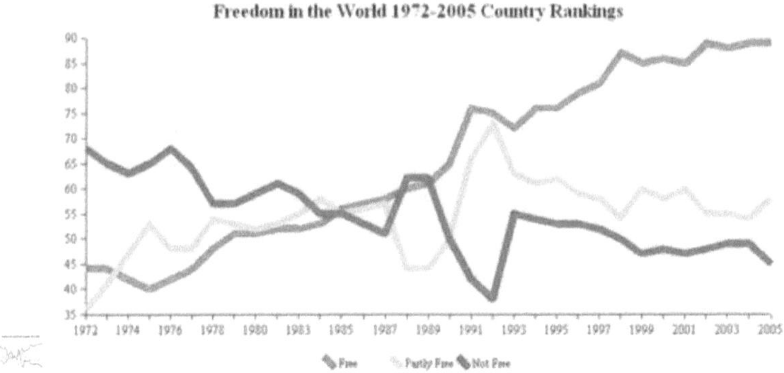

Source: "Freedom in the World" by Freedom House 1972–2005

The democracy wave did not emerge in a vacuum. Huntington identifies five changes in the world, which paved the way for the latest wave of democratic transitions:[33]

1. The deepening problems of legitimacy that authoritarian governments have faced in their inability to cope with military defeat and economic failure.
2. The burgeoning economies of many countries, which has raised living standards, levels of education, urbanization, and by default the level of civil expectations and the ability to express them.
3. Changes in religious institutions which have made them more likely to oppose governmental authoritarianism than to defend the status quo.
4. The push to promote human rights and democracy by external factors such as non-governmental organizations and the European Community.
5. Communications technology that has helped to expose the democratization processes in other countries and triggered a snowball effect.

32 See Diamond, 2000, p. 3.
33 See Huntington, 1991, pp. 5–16.

As Huntington and Diamond further point out, the third wave of democratization appears to be one of historic proportions. This has particularly held true by comparison with the "second wave" of democratization, which began after World War II but lasted less than 20 years. Following the war and the victory of the Allied forces, a number of new democracies emerged, triggering the "second wave" of democratization. However, a "second reverse wave," in which new democracies broke down in more than 20 developing countries, was quick to follow. Within a few short years, military rulers and civilian autocrats brutalized human rights, the rule of law, and reversed newly established democratic systems in countries like Argentina, Portugal, Lebanon, Czechoslovakia, Spain, Hungary and Uruguay.[34]

That, however, has not been the case for the third wave. As dictatorships around the world have fallen in societies as diverse as Chile, Bolivia, Bulgaria, Mongolia and Malawi, the forces of the free world, led by the US and Europe, have responded with measures of support to help stabilize new democratic governments. They have primarily done so by increasing levels of economic and political assistance.[35]A quarter century after the inception of the third wave of democratization, there is no significant sign that the world has entered a "third reverse wave." Not only are there more democracies than ever before but, as Table 2.1 clearly indicates, there have also been very few prominent democratic reversals. The exception to this case parallels the period known as the Arab Spring. A 2011 Freedom House report showing that the number of countries designated as "free" fell from 89 to 87, and the number of electoral democracies dropped to 115, far lower than the 2005 reported tally at 123. The 2014 report, although noting an overall democratic decline, showed a number of electoral democracies at 122, four more than in 2012.[36]

34 See Diamond, 2000, p. 3 and Table 1.1.
35 See Diamond, 2000, p. 3.
36 See Freedom House, 2011 and 2014.

Table 2.1: The Growth of Electoral Democracies, 1974–2002

YEAR	Number of Democracies	Number of Countries	Democracies as a Percentage of all Countries	Annual Rate of Increase in Democracies
1974	41	150	27.3%	n. a.
1987	71	164	43.3%	n. a.
1990	76	165	46.1%	n. a.
1991	91	183	49.7%	19.7%
1992	99	186	53.2%	8.1%
1993	108	190	56.8%	8.3%
1994	114	191	59.7%	5.3%
1995	117	191	61.3%	2.6%
1996	118	191	61.8%	0.9%
1997	117	191	61.3%	-0.9%
1998	117	191	61.3%	0
1999	120	192	62.5%	2.6%
2000	120	192	62.5%	0
2001	120	192	62.5%	0
2002	121	193	62.7%	0

Sources: Diamond, 2003. Data from Freedom House, *Freedom in the World: The Annual Survey of Political Rights and Civil Liberties, 1990–91, 1991–92,* etc. (New York: Freedom House, 1991 and years following); and *Journal of Democracy* 14, No. 1, January 2003.

More recent events including the emergence of the so-called Islamic State, Russia's annexation of Crimea and support for separatism in other parts of Ukraine highlight a worrying trend toward the resurgence of authoritarian power with willingness to employ military and other means to create and support repressive, non-democratic political structures. The new assertiveness of authoritarian governments can be seen in the conflicts in Syria and Iraq, elsewhere in the region, and beyond. However, the overall trend still reflects positive democratic developments along with challenges that have much to do with the ever-changing Middle East.

2.3 Democracy, Elections and Liberalism

The third wave and the spread of the democratic system should be further qualified not only in quantitative terms, but also in terms of their qualitative growth. Democracies do vary one from another in a number of ways, including the levels of freedom, participation, and individual rights. In order to qualify and identify trends of the third wave which was described before, the term "democracy" must first be adequately defined.

Joseph Schumpeter defines democracy as an "institutional arrangement for arriving at political decisions in which individuals acquire the power to decide by means of a competitive struggle for the people's vote."[37] In a similar fashion, Huntington defines a political system as democratic to the extent that "its most powerful collective of decision-makers are selected through fair, honest and periodic elections in which candidates clearly compete for votes and in which virtually all the adult population is eligible to vote."[38]

Robert Dahl adopts a different approach to the definition of democracy, based upon a continuum of compliance.[39] He provides a classification for democratic systems that is characterized by inclusiveness—the extent to which people under a given regime's jurisdiction have the right to participate—and by liberalization—the extent to which participants in the regime have the right to contest the conditions of rule. According to Dahl, the ideal democracy is a political system that will maintain the following characteristics:

1. Freedom to form and join organizations.
2. Freedom of expression.
3. The right to vote.
4. Eligibility for public office.
5. Competition by political leaders for support.
6. Alternative sources of information.
7. Free and fair elections.
8. Institutions for making government policies dependent on electoral results and other expressions of preference.

---

37 See Schumpeter, 1947, p. 269.
38 See Huntington, 1991, p. 7.
39 See Dahl, 1975, pp. 118–119.

Dahl recognizes that each of these conditions can be measured on a continuum of compliance, and that different regimes will vary in the degree to which these eight institutional conditions will be implemented.[40]

Dahl further identifies three types of political systems that are neither dictatorships nor democracies. The closest to the ideal of democracy are "polyarchies," which are "regimes that have been substantially popularized and liberalized, that is, highly inclusive and extensively open to public contestation."[41] Polyarchies include elements of competition (or contestation) and participation.[42] They also have elected officials, free and fair elections, inclusive suffrage, the right to run for office, as well as the freedom of expression, freedom of the press, and freedom of association. However, polyarchies fall short of the standard of pure democracy which is perceived as theoretical and unlikely to be implemented in full. The two other political structures that fall between dictatorships and polyarchies are "competitive oligarchies" and "inclusive hegemonies."[43] Inclusive hegemonies are political systems in which there is inclusive suffrage, but institutions and procedures through which citizens can express effective preferences about alternative policies at the national level are lacking. Competitive oligarchies, on the other hand, allow for a greater degree of participation that is limited to a relatively small group of citizen elites.[44]

Chart 2.4: Robert Dahl's Classification of Regimes

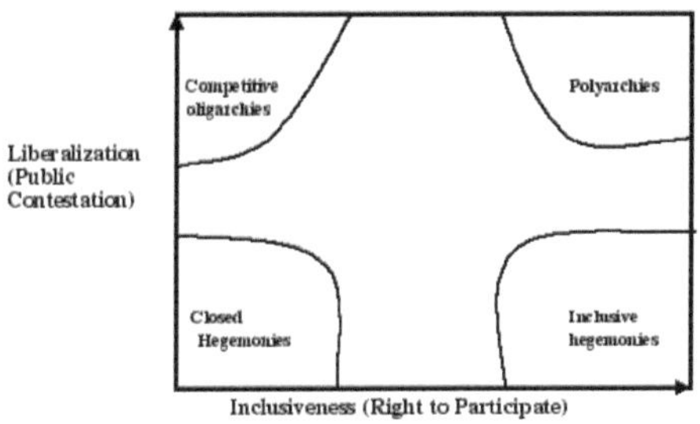

Source: Tilly (1998)

---

40 See ibid, p. 119.
41 See Dahl, 1971, p. 8.
42 See Dahl, 1989, p. 252.
43 See ibid, p. 253.
44 Se Dahl, 1971, pp. 5–7.

An additional important distinction between "electoral democracies" and "liberal democracies" is required in order to adhere to stricter indicators of freedom. Electoral democracies are characterized by a range of competing political parties that are able to gather and utilize resources in open political campaigns through a free and fair election process. Electoral democracies also require diffusion of power among different branches of government, and a regular cycle of elections in an environment, which allows for a change of the political elite among competing groups. But unlike liberal democracies, electoral democracies may still suffer serious deficits in areas such as inter-ethnic relations, discrimination against minorities and social groups, and a weak rule of law.[45] Zakaria asserts that of the 120 "democratic" countries, 50% do better on political liberties than on civil liberties. In other words, half of the "democratizing" countries in the world today are illiberal democracies.[46] According to Zakaria, "illiberal democracies" are beginning to form a new political trend. In 1990, only 22% of democratizing countries could have been so categorized, but by the end of the decade that figure had risen to 35%.[47]

The term "liberal democracy" mentioned before in the context of Fukuyama's work requires some further clarification as well. Zakaria defines liberal democracy as a "political system marked not only by free and fair elections, but also by the rule of law, a separation of powers, and the protection of basic liberties of speech, assembly, religion, and property."[48]

According to Freedom House, liberal democracies are defined as countries that have the following characteristics:

- The freedom of belief, expression, organization, and demonstration
- Protection from political repression and unjustified imprisonment
- A rule of law under which all citizens are treated equally and due process is secure
- Political independence and neutrality of the judiciary and of other institutions, including "horizontal accountability" which checks the abuse of power.

45 See Freedom House, 2000, Zakaria, 1997.
46 See Zakaria, 1997, p. 24.
47 See ibid, p. 25.
48 See Zakaria, 1997, p. 23.

- An open and pluralistic civil society
- Civilian control over the military

It should also be noted that the various dimensions of democratic character constitute a continuum, as it is hard to determine exact quantities of freedom, pluralism, lawfulness, accountability, and institutional strength, which constitute a liberal democracy.

In a study of 22 countries in Latin America where elections have been held, Larry Diamond determined that 10 of the 22 countries studied "have levels of human rights abuse that are incompatible with the consolidation of [liberal] democracy."[49] Similar developments have been observed in Africa. For six months in 1990 much of Francophone Africa had lifted its ban on multi-party politics and engaged in an electoral process. Yet, since 1991 elections have been held in most of the 45 sub-Saharan nations (with 18 different elections held in the year 1996 alone), and they were followed by violations of human and political rights. Michael Chege, a Kenyan scholar at Harvard University, surveyed the wave of democratization in Africa and concluded that the continent had "overemphasized multiparty elections...and correspondingly neglected the basic tenets of government."[50] In Central Asia, even elections held in reasonably free states such as Kyrgyzstan and Kazakhstan have resulted in strong executives, weak legislatures and judiciaries, and few civil and economic liberties. In the Islamic world, from the Gaza Strip to Egypt, Iran and Pakistan, democratization has led to an increased role for theocratic politics, eroding long-standing traditions of secularism and tolerance.[51]

These and other examples help us draw another important distinction between liberal and electoral democracies, which leads to important observations about the "democracy wave" and the state of democratization efforts. Jillian Schwedler argues that the majority of countries that began their transitions during the third wave now seem to be moving less toward democracy, and instead toward new forms of non-democratic rule. Other scholars, including major proponents of Democratic Transition (or transitology), admit that successful transitions have proven to be more the exception

49 See Diamond, 1996, p. 73.
50 See Zakaria, 1997, p. 37.
51 See ibid, p. 38.

than the rule.[52] At the same time, scholars of Middle East politics have been frustrated that transitologists tend to systematically ignore cases in the Middle East, some of which have been no less promising in their early stages than those in other parts of the world.[53] Middle Eastern regimes that increasingly adopted the rhetoric of democracy and initiated limited political openings in the 1980's and early 1990's were quickly dubbed as being "en route" to democracy, though they still failed to produce the necessary pre-conditions for it.[54] Hence, the discussion on transition to democracy quickly morphed into a discussion about the reasons for the failed transitions.

This complex picture may point toward either a theoretical problem associated with democratization theory or toward the transitional model itself, which appears far from complete and requires further adjustments in order to be able to apply it to different social or cultural environments As Carothers argues, "by describing countries in the gray zone as types of democracies, analysts are in effect trying to apply the transition paradigm to the very countries whose political evolution is calling that paradigm into question."[55] Either way, it is important to conclude that although the third wave of democracy is indeed statistically impressive, its real influence is still very much in question. The cases reviewed here further stress the difficult challenge of democratic transition, a process that requires a societal transformation that goes beyond the simple act of setting up an election booth.

2.4 Promoting Democracy in the Middle East during the 20th Century

Promoting democracy became one of the most critical issues in 20th century foreign policy, especially after World War II and in the context of the Cold War between the United States and the Soviet Union. In particular, promoting democracy has been a central pillar of American foreign policy for nearly a century.[56] Carothers argues that "American foreign policy of

---

52 See O'Donnell and Schmitter 1986, p. 3; Diamond 1999; Carothers 2002; and Schwedler, 2006, p. 4.
53 See Schwedler, 2002, p. 5.
54 See ibid, p. 6.
55 See Schmitter, 2002 p. 10.
56 See Smith, 2005 p. 4.

the past 100 years cannot be understood without serious attention to the democracy ideal," and "the history of democracy around the globe during the same period is incomplete without sustained attention to the role of the United States on the world stage."[57]

American presidents, Democrats and Republicans alike, have championed the values of freedom and democracy and have cultivated an image of the US as the leader of the free world. This notion became more acute following WWII and the beginning of the Cold War. President Eisenhower's Middle East doctrine focused on preventing Soviet influence and by extension, providing an alternative to Communism. In an address to Congress in 1957 in which he outlined a plan of action to prevent the expansion of Soviet influence in the Middle East, he stated: "the reason for Russia's interest in the Middle East is solely that of power politics. Considering her announced purpose of 'communizing' the world, it is easy to understand her hope of dominating the Middle East." In the same speech President Eisenhower declared, "Our desire is a world environment of freedom, not servitude."[58]

In his inaugural address, President Jimmy Carter articulated this idea as follows:

> We know that the best way to enhance freedom in other lands is to demonstrate here that our democratic system is worthy of emulation... The passion for freedom is on the rise. Tapping this new spirit, there can be no nobler nor more ambitious task for America to undertake on this day of a new beginning than to help shape a just and peaceful world that is truly humane.[59]

Speaking in the British Parliament in 1982, President Reagan stressed,

> While we must be cautious about forcing the pace of change, we must not hesitate to declare our ultimate objectives and to take concrete actions to move toward them. We must be staunch in our conviction that freedom is not the sole prerogative of a lucky few, but the inalienable and universal right of all human beings.[60]

A number of efforts including media programs, psychological warfare and NGO-related work have echoed these sentiments, but for the purpose of

57 See Carothers, 1999, p. 5.
58 See Eisenhower, 1957.
59 See Carter, 1977.
60 See Reagan, 1982.

this work it will suffice to mention that once the opportunity arose following the collapse of the Soviet Union, there was an even greater increase in action. Beginning in 1989, Congress and the Bush Administration proposed an increased assistance package to the countries of Central and Eastern Europe. In November of that year, the Support for East European Democracy *(*SEED*)* Act appropriated $900 million dollars for democracy assistance programs for three years. By 1992, these sums had further increased, following the dissolution of the Soviet Union in December 1991 and the passage of the Freedom Support Act in October 1992, which allocated an additional $400 million to a range of activities including democratic reform and economic privatization. From 1991–1998, the SEED allocations to Eastern and Central Europe amounted to $3.85 billion, mostly aimed at strengthening democracy as well as supporting civil society and non-governmental organizations.[61] But the US was not acting alone: by 1993 the Group of 7 leading industrialized countries (G7) pledged $43.4 billon to economic development, liberalization and democratization programs.[62]

In Europe, the 1949 Statute of the Council of Europe, which was signed by the majority of European states, was the first regional document in Europe to make a commitment to democracy. The statute affirmed a European commitment "to the spiritual and moral values which are the common heritage of their peoples and the true source of individual freedom, political liberty and the rule of law- principles which form the basis of all genuine democracy."[63]

The Cold War, however, would soon divide Europe into US-aligned Western Europe and Soviet-aligned eastern and central Europe, which did not consider democratization a policy objective. The fall of the Berlin Wall sparked a major commitment by Western European states to integrate former Communist states into their political and economic sphere. The Charter of Paris for a New Europe, signed in 1990 by the members of the Conference on Security and Cooperation in Europe (the CSCE, which in 1995 became the Organization for Security and Cooperation in Europe, or OSCE), declared democracy the "sole legitimate system of government"

61 See Ulrich, 1999, pp. 46–7.

62 See ibid, p. 48.

63 See Statute of the Council of Europe, 1949.

and made it a requirement for membership in the organization.[64] The 1991 Document of the Moscow Meeting of the Conference on the Human Dimension of the Conference on Security and Cooperation in Europe (CSCE) strengthened the Charter of Paris by referring directly to the need to deal with downfalls of democracy. The participating states expressed their "collective determination to further safeguard human rights and fundamental freedoms and to consolidate democratic advances in their territories."[65] They also agreed to increase the CSCE's effectiveness in addressing human rights concerns at "this time of profound change in Europe."[66]

Following the Cold War era, Europe saw democracy as a promising tool for the promotion of regional stability as well as a unifying basis for a common European foreign policy.[67] The Copenhagen Criteria (which determine which states are to be accepted into the EU) fall into three categories, the first of which is the presence and health of institutions that guarantee democracy, human rights, and the rule of law.[68] In that sense democratization, was not just a political trend but also a policy objective of the US and Europe, which perceived themselves as the leaders and guardians of the free world.[69] Consequently, Europe launched its own democratization initiative at its Conference of Ministers of Foreign Affairs, held in Barcelona in November 1995. The initiative, later known as the "Barcelona Initiative" or the "Barcelona Process," had three major objectives:

1. The definition of a common area of peace and stability through the reinforcement of political and security dialogue.
2. The construction of a zone of shared prosperity through an economic and financial partnership, and the gradual establishment of a free trade zone.

64 See Peck, 1998, pp. 104–105.
65 See the document of the Moscow Meeting of the Conference on Human Dimensions of the CSCE, 10th Sep–4th http://www.osce.org/odihr/elections/14310?download=true.
66 See ibid.
67 See Schraeder, 202, p. 132.
68 See ibid, p. 136.
69 See Carothers, 1999, p. 6.

3. The rapprochement between peoples through a social, cultural and human partnership aimed at encouraging understanding among cultures and exchanges among civil societies.[70]

European Foreign Ministers expressed their conviction that the "peace, stability and security of the Mediterranean region are a common asset which they pledge to promote and strengthen by all means at their disposal."[71] To this end, they agreed to "conduct a strengthened political dialogue at regular intervals, based on observance of essential principles of international law, and reaffirm a number of common objectives in matters of internal and external stability." They also agreed to "develop the rule of law and democracy in their political systems."[72]

At this point, it appeared that Europe and the United States were better coordinated, or as the Assistant Secretary of State for European and Eurasian Affairs, Daniel Fried, said they were "essentially united" in the task of advancing freedom around the world. He also said, "I believe ... Europe and the United States are essentially united in this great task. Together, we are putting the political, economic and security assets of the transatlantic community to work outside Europe in support of freedom-seekers around the world."[73]

2.5 Promoting Democracy Before and After September 11th

September 11th was a seminal moment in American history and a moment which significantly influenced the foreign policy of the United States by defining international terrorism as its preeminent national security challenge.[74] In his second inaugural address delivered in January 2005, President Bush stated, "it is the policy of the United States to seek and support the growth of democratic movements and institutions in every nation and culture, with the ultimate goal of ending tyranny in our world."[75]

70 See Barcelona Declaration, 1995.
71 Ibid.
72 Ibid.
73 See Fried, 2006.
74 See Haass, 2001.
75 See Bush, 2005.

The President also began to develop his "forward strategy of freedom," which had a specific focus on the Middle East. In his 2003 address to the National Endowment on Democracy (NED), the President stressed,

> Stability cannot be purchased at the expense of liberty. As long as the Middle East remains a place where freedom does not flourish, it will remain a place of stagnation, resentment, and violence ready for export. And with the spread of weapons that can bring catastrophic harm to our country and to our friends, it would be reckless to accept the status quo. Therefore, the United States has adopted a new policy, a forward strategy of freedom in the Middle East."[76]

Offering a new interpretation which was about to reshape an important pillar of American foreign policy, he added that "the survival of liberty in our land increasingly depends on the success of liberty in other lands," and noted that "the best hope for peace in our world is the expansion of freedom in the entire world."[77] The US was insistent that the push for democratization was not a new, but rather an old idea that was consistent with American foreign policy: in a policy address to the Baltimore Council on Foreign Relations, the assistant secretary for European and Eurasian affairs stated, "Support for freedom is not just a tactic or tool in America's national security strategy—it is THE core concept of our national grand strategy and, I believe, has been so for a century."[78]

Although the "War on Terrorism" has greatly raised the profile of democratization as a matter of policy, it has hardly clarified the issue. Following the events of September 11th, the United States appears to have faced two contradictory imperatives. On the one hand, the fight against al-Qaeda encouraged Washington to put aside its democracy rhetoric and seek closer ties with autocracies throughout the Middle East and Asia, but on the other hand US officials and policy experts have increasingly come to believe that it is precisely the lack of democracy in many of these countries that helps breed Islamic extremism.[79]

The US was willing to stand behind its verbal commitments to this new stated agenda, and acted to significantly increase the budget for

76 See Bush, 2003.
77 See Dobriansky, 2005.
78 See Fried, 2005.
79 See Carothers, 2003, p. 35.

democratization programs. The budget for these programs is allocated through a number of federally-funded programs, via departments such as the Department of State, the Department of Defense, and institutions such as NED and the US Institute of Peace, or via partnerships with American and non-American NGO's. In all of these organizations, we can trace a significant increase in the amount of resources available since 2002. In 2001 the annual allocation to these programs came to a sum of over $27 million whereas the 2004 allocations reached over $185 million.[80] The budget of the US Middle East Partnership Initiative (MEPI), which was specifically designed to promote democracy in the Middle East, climbed from $35 million in 2002 to $75 million in 2005 (Chart 2.5). The aim of the initiative, as formulated by Richard Hass who was the director of policy planning for the Department of State, was to "put an end to the United States' exceptional forgiving attitude displayed toward the lack of democracy, which found expression in accepting the theory of democratic exception of the Arab and the Muslim World."[81]

Chart 2.5: Middle East Partnership Initiative, budget 2002–2005 (in millions of dollars)

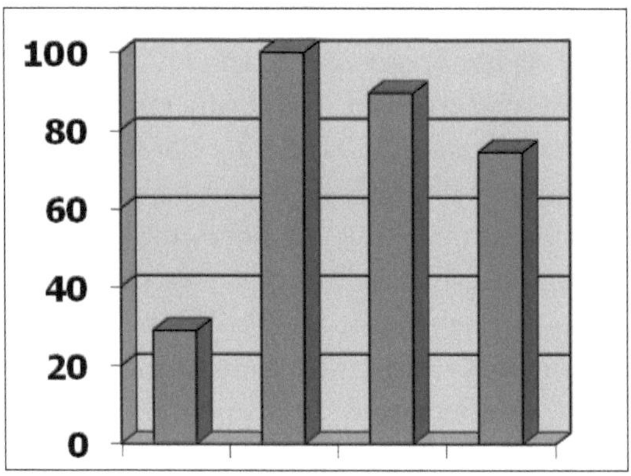

Source: GAO report to Congressional Requesters, United States Government Accountability Office (August 2005, p. 9).

80 See Yerkes and Wittes, pp. 10–11.

81 The reference to "exceptionalism" refers to accepting the notion that the nature of the Arab and Muslim regimes is not conducive to democracy. Quoted in Govrin, p. 146.

Moreover, the Millennium Challenge Account, which enables the President to provide development assistance to countries meeting eligibility criteria in the areas of democratic governance, investments in human development, and the promotion of economic freedoms has grown significantly since it was founded in 2003 with a budget of $1 billion, reaching $5 billion in 2006 (Chart 2.6).

Chart 2.6: Millennium Challenge Account Funding, 2004–2006

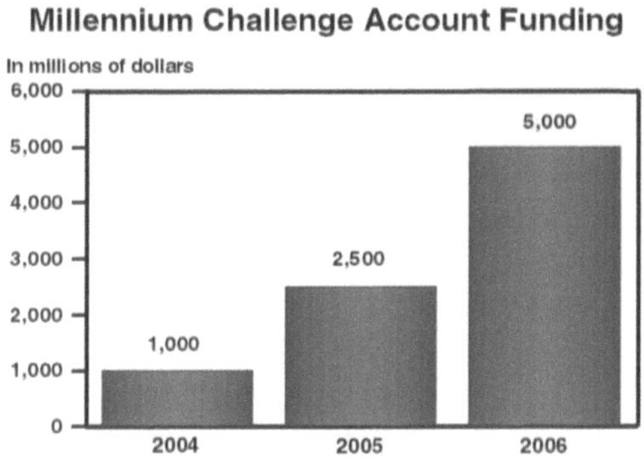

Source: The White House, Office of Management and Budget, Department of State and International Assistance Programs (April, 2006)

American-European coordination on democratization policies became more important in the post-September 11 period. The US attempted to show that the task of advancing freedom is one of concern for the Europeans as well. Knowing that an international consensus for far-reaching democratization policies is essential to their success, Daniel Fried, the Assistant Secretary for European and Eurasian Affairs at the Department of State, stated, "Europe and the United States are essentially united in this great task. Together, we are putting the political, economic and security assets of the transatlantic community to work outside Europe in support of freedom-seekers around the world."[82]

Based on the Barcelona Declaration, the EU created the MEDA (Mesures D'Accompagnement) program, which further served as the principal financial instrument for the implementation of the Euro-Mediterranean Partnership. The program offered technical and financial support measures to

82 See Fried, 2006.

accompany the reform of the economic and social structures of its Mediterranean participants including, Algeria, Egypt, Jordan, Lebanon, Morocco, Syria, Tunisia, and the Palestinian Authority. It also sought to encourage "participation of civil society and populations in the planning and implementation of development measures;" the "strengthening of democracy, human rights and the rule of law;" the fostering of "exchanges between civil society in the Community and the Mediterranean partners within the framework of decentralized cooperation through the networking of civil society actors "amongst other objectives."[83] The program further established the MED Committee to allow EU member states to advise the European Commission on implementing the MEDA Program.[84] As Chart 2.7 indicates, the budget of the MEDA program expanded significantly and reached over €11 billion Euro in the year 2006.

Chart 2.7: MEDA Program Budget (in Million Euro)

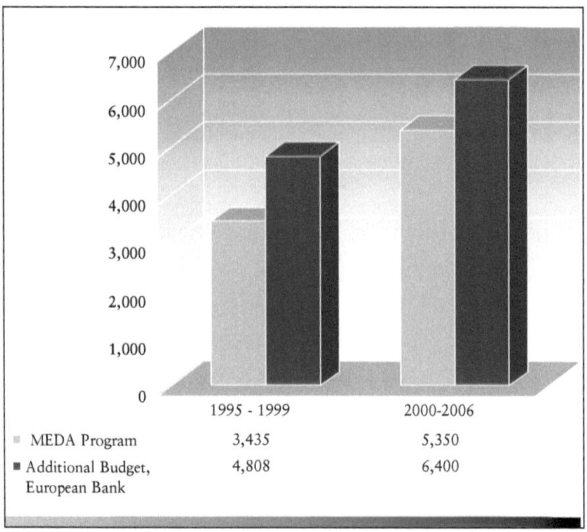

Source: Euro-Mediterranean Partnership, <http://europa.eu.int/comm/external_relations/euromed/meda.htm>

83 See Council Regulation (EC) No 1488/96 of 23 July 1996 on financial and technical measures to accompany (MEDA) the reform of economic and social structures in the framework of the Euro-Mediterranean partnership.

84 Ibid.

An additional push for democracy-promotion programs came with the help of the 2002 Human Development Report of the United Nations Development Program (UNDP). The report argued that "Democracy has proven to be the system of governance most capable of mediating and preventing conflict and of securing and sustaining well-being;" and that "for politics and political institutions to promote human development and safeguard the freedom and dignity of all people, democracy must widen and deepen."[85] This, and other subsequent reports, gave additional recognition to the merits of democratization.

In 2004, US President George W. Bush also established the "Forum on Reform in the Middle East" (a.k.a. the Abu Dhabi Forum), aimed at promoting political, social and economic reforms in the Middle East and North Africa. Backed not only by the Group of 8 leading industrial nations (G8), but also by the heads of the BEMENA (Broader Middle East and North Africa) countries, the forum was convened first in Morocco, followed by Bahrain the year after, Jordan in 2006, Yemen in 2007 and Abu Dhabi in 2008. In its concluding statement in Morocco, the forum called for "an informal, flexible, open and inclusive dialogue, devoted to strengthening democracy and the participation of civil society, to developing skills training, and to encouraging the growth of modern economies that generate wealth and that are well-integrated into the global economy."[86] It also agreed on a number of concrete programs, such as a Democracy Assistance Dialogue to promote consolidation of democratic institutions in the region, programs on education and the elimination of illiteracy, and the establishment of centers of entrepreneurial excellence.[87] The 2007 forum further established the "Foundation for the Future" with the aim of assisting Arab civil society. The forum made most of its initial grants, which amounted to $25 million annually, to relatively "safe" civil society projects.[88]

Naturally, these American-led policies were subject to criticism by the Middle Eastern partners themselves, by scholars and analysts, and by public

---

85 See UNDP, 2002, p. 1.

86 US Department of State, Fact Sheet, Office of the Spokesman, Department of State, Washington, DC December 11, 2004.

87 See Shelby, 2004.

88 See Allen, 2008.

opinion at large. First, the democratization effort was perceived as part of a wider set of US interests and concerns motivated largely by interests that often did not coincide with the interests of the region. Second, attempts at implementation (including, in the eyes of many, the invasion of Iraq and Afghanistan) appeared to be nothing more than aggressive interventions backed by methods of coercion, which contradicted the very nature of a "democratization process." In addition, a lack of clarity and focus seemed to characterize many of these efforts that were carried out by agencies and initiatives, often appearing to be at odds with one another. Third, it appeared that the majority of these democracy-promotion policies did not take the domestic reaction into account, and were often perceived as simply ineffective.[89] Some critics were even harsher: Carothers claimed that the Bush democratization doctrine actually damaged democracy-promotion efforts, arguing that democracy building during the war in Iraq, and the many American abuses of the rule of law in the war on terrorism, discredited these efforts both at home and abroad. He also argued that a "glaring gap" exists between President Bush's rhetoric of freedom, and policies aimed at securing economic and security favors from autocratic allies around the world.[90] Upon taking office in 2009, President Obama inherited a democracy promotion policy that was highly stained due to the experiences in Afghanistan and Iraq. During the Bush years, America's reputation as a global symbol of human rights and democracy declined during a time period in which democracy struggled around the world.[91] Unlike his predecessor, President Obama did not refer to democracy or to the Middle East in his first inaugural address. However, he did send a message to dictators throughout the world, stating, "to those who cling to power through corruption and deceit and the silencing of dissent, know that you are on the wrong side of history, but that we will extend a hand if you are willing to unclench your fist."[92] Addressing the Middle East in his Cairo speech of June 4, 2009, he still refrained from the word "democracy" but spoke about "governments that

89 See Dalacoura, Katerina 2005.
90 See Carothers, 2007 pp. 35–6.
91 See Carothers, 2012, p. 1.
92 See Obama, 2009.

reflect the will of the people" and the "freedom to live as you choose."[93] In September 2009, President Obama argued in the UN General Assembly that "democracy cannot be imposed on any nation from the outside," but also that "America will always stand with those who stand up for their dignity and their rights—for the student who seeks to learn; the voter who demands to be heard; the innocent who longs to be free; and the oppressed who yearns to be equal."[94]

At the end of 2010, when the Arab Spring was beginning to take shape, there was a clear change to this rhetoric. The first National Security Strategy (issued in May 2010) incorporated some references to the idea of supporting democracy promotion, stating, "America's commitment to democracy, human rights and the rule of law are essential sources of our strength and influence in the world."[95] The word "democracy" interestingly appeared more than 24 times in this document. By the time of his May 2011 address to the Middle East, an address which took place in Cairo as the Arab Spring raged, President Obama reverted to some familiar rhetoric when he made reference to the "policy of the United States to promote reform across the region, and to support transitions to democracy," and to the policy of "support[ing] political and economic reform in the Middle East and North Africa which can meet the legitimate aspirations of ordinary people throughout the region."[96] In the same speech, he justified US military involvement against President Muammar Qaddafi, claiming that the "prospect of imminent massacre" gave the US a mandate for action, and warned Syria's President Assad that he could "lead [the] transition, or get out of the way."[97] This interventionist agenda, which might have been a response to events on the ground, can certainly be seen as a departure from the President's earlier statements and actions, although the budget for democracy promotion programs diminished in the early part of Obama's tenure. The 2011 speech promised increased intervention and assistance in political reform, human rights and political and economic development.

---

93 See Obama, 2009 (a).
94 See Obama, 2009 (b).
95 See Carothers, 2012, p. 1.
96 See Obama, 2011.
97 See ibid.

In this context, he offered $1 billion of debt relief to Egypt.[98] In May of 2011, speaking to the State Department and relating to the Arab Spring, President Obama gave a passionate speech about the US commitment to democracy in which he said:

> Because of its own history and democratic values, the United States must stand with the people of the Middle East and with others who peacefully demand their universal rights and seek greater opportunities...We have the chance to show that America values the dignity of the street vendor in Tunisia more than the raw power of the dictator.[99]

Despite differences in approaches and priorities, as well as other influences such as those of the Cold War, it appears that the democratization agenda was of concern to both Americans and Europeans alike. Americans and Europeans appear to share the notion that the principles of freedom, human rights and democracy are important pillars of foreign policy and that, on a whole, they should be promoted. The events of September 11th and subsequent events related to the war on terrorism, generated fresh support for these policies and resulted in an enhancement of "democracy programs" in both the US and Europe. The issue of democratization is of concern to both American and European leaders, who have developed a variety of programs in order to promote it. Although further analysis of these programs is beyond the scope of this review, it will suffice to say that this issue has remained relevant for over seven decades, and that both Europe and the US are perceived as parties who seek to promote democracy around the world.

2.6 Democracy, Islam and Civil Society in the Middle East – Reconciling a Paradox

Can democracy prevail in the Middle East? Is Islam compatible with it? Can a strong and liberal minded civil society be created in a region that appears to be even more immersed in religious dogma and encumbered with radical Islamist movements? Can the failure of democracy in the Middle East be reversed? Each of these questions deserves a book of its own, and indeed many such books have already been written albeit without concluding this

98 See ibid.
99 See Obama, 2012.

ever-evolving debate. Since much of this book focuses on the attempt to introduce democracy into the Middle East, it is important to address at least some of these topics in the introduction and lead up to my discussion of conversations with expat leaders and democratization efforts at large.

Khalid al-Dakhil, a columnist for Al Hayyat and a professor at King Saud University in Saudi Arabia, has noted the basic difficulties the Arab society has with the concept of freedom, saying:

> The opposition to liberalism in the Arab Society is almost total: the states reject it because it destroys the foundations upon which it was established, and the people reject it because it does not fit their cultural heritage, and the elite is incapable of treating it as a binding ideology."[100]

Lebanese author Jihad al-Khazen joins Dakhil by saying, "freedom is a planet alien to our part of the Arab world, whenever implanted it dies."[101] These types of statements, however, stand in sharp contrast to the millions who marched to November 7th Square in Tunisia or to Tahrir (freedom) Square in Cairo demanding the freedom that ignited the Arab Spring. Understanding that paradox requires some background related to the structure, culture and traditions of the Arab and the Muslim world, traditions that are challenged from within and that serve as another important dimension of the regional turmoil.

It is important to begin with a note about language. Terms such as "liberalism" (in Arabic *liberaliya*), "freedom" or "liberty" (*hurriya*), "secularism" (*almaniyya* or *al-zamaniyya*), "pluralism" (*ta'addudiyya*), "citizenship" (*al-muwatana*), or "civil society" (*al-mujtama al-madani*) do not always carry the same meaning when translated into Arabic or Farsi. Many of these and related terms are new to the Arabic language and even more so within the context of democracy discourse. Nevertheless, as noted earlier, these terms were used to galvanize millions who called for freedom and democracy, construct songs of freedom, and to establish movements and parties of change.

In order to understand these dynamics, we must first further define some of the key terms that will be subsequently used and lay out some of the basic characteristics of the Middle Eastern societies.

---

100 Quoted in Govrin, 2014, p. 4.

101 See ibid, p. 6.

Civil society has been defined as "un-coerced collective action around shared interests, purposes and values, which is distinct and uncontrolled by the institutional forms of the state; family and market;" or as a "society organized outside the state."[102] The literature on civil society is vast in scope and the term can easily transcend beyond borders. There are analyses of broader civil society systems and even of terms such as "global civil society"[103], "world civil culture"[104], and "internationalization of civil society."[105] According to Keane, global civil society refers to a dynamic non-governmental network of "inter-connected social and economic institutions that straddle throughout earth and that have complex effects that are felt in its four corners." [106] While Keane admits that global civil society is still an evolving concept, it is important to note that the very attempt to coin such a large umbrella term is worthy of attention due to the interconnectivity between civil groups which also relates to the role of diaspora and expat groups.[107] With this global perspective, it is important to point out that civil society usually appears as very "liberal" and "Western" by the virtue of its definition (and as opposed to non-Western understanding of the terms that will be discussed shortly). The notion of "global civic society" is usually associated to the idea of support by of a larger democratic network as mentioned by Barr: "If civil society is one key to democracy, then global strong democracy needs and depends on a methodological internationalization of civil society.[108]"

While democracy is designed to create "societies organized outside the state," dictatorships are designed to do the exact opposite—control the

---

102 See CCS, 2004 and Bamyeh, 2006.

103 See Keane, 2003, p. 1.

104 See Keane, 2003 P 5, noting the work of Elise Boulding (1990), "Building a Global Civic Culture: Education for an Interdependent World".

105 The term appear in a variety of contexts including international aid operations, the E.U.; Human Rights and democratization. See, for example: Barber, Benjamin. "Jihad vs. McWorld: How Globalism and Tribalism are Reshaping the World". Random House, 1995, P 287.

106 See Keane, p. 8.

107 Ibid p. 18.

108 See Barr Hugh in "Democrcay at a Crossroa, International Perspectives on Critical Global Citizenship Education" 2005, Lanham, MD: Lexington Books, P. 64.

societal dynamics and shut any opposition activity that may challenge the state system. Hence, in contrast with Keane and his peers, scholars from the Middle East have offered a very different understanding of civil society and its global dimensions. Turkish scholar Serif Mardin claims that "civil society is a Western dream, a historical aspiration that does not translate to Islamist terms."[109] He argues that social justice has become a substitute for the concept of freedom in the Islamic world, and that the notion of Muslim "civil society" cannot be separated from the nature of Islamic society.[110] While the Middle East dictatorships have excelled in limiting the influence of civil society at large, the doctrine of Islam – which is codified into the majority of state charters in the region—must be examined as intrinsically related to the structure of the Muslim state and its (civil) society.

This brings us back to the debate about the compatibility of democracy with Muslim culture. The discussion of the term "democracy" in Arab Islamic literature can be traced back to Rifa`a at-Tahtawi (1801–73), a graduate of Al-Azhar University in Cairo who was sent to Paris as an emissary of Egypt's Sultan, Muhammad Ali, and returned to Egypt as an advocate of modern political thought. His 1834 book, *Takhlis Al-Ibriz Ila Talkhis Bariz* (Refining [the] Gold While Defining Paris), summarized his observations of the manners and customs of 19th century France, and praised the concept of democracy as he saw it there.[111] Other Islamic scholars felt the same way. In 1867, Khairuddin At-Tunisi (1810–99), leader of the 19th-century reform movement in Tunisia, published *Aqwam al-Masalik fi Taqwim al-Mamalik* (The Straight Path to Reforming Governments), which tackled the question of political reform in the Arab and Muslim world. While appealing to the politicians and scholars of his time to seek all possible means of improving the status and civility of their communities, he warned the general Muslim public against shunning the experiences of other nations on account of the misconception that all the writings, inventions, experiences and attitudes of non-Muslims should be rejected or disregarded.[112]

---

109 See Serif, 1995, p. 278.
110 See Sajoo, 2004, pp. 1–2; Saltzman, 2008, p. 23.
111 See Hourani, 1982, pp. 70–71.
112 See Ad-Dajani, 1984, pp. 115.

Al-Tunisi understood that a bridge must be built between science and faith, between the culture of Islam and the new ideas of liberty. Hence he implemented his plan by establishing the As-Sadiqiyah School for teaching modern arts and sciences within an Islamic framework. He asserted:

> … kindling the Umma's potential liberty through the adoption of sound administrative procedures, and enabling it to have a say in political affairs, would put it on a faster track toward civilization, would limit the rule of despotism, and would stop the influx of European civilization that is sweeping everything along in its path.[113]

Tahtawi and Tunisi were not the rule, but rather the exception. Elie Kedourie argued that Islamic beliefs, norms, attitudes, and experience have shaped a distinctive and non-modern Muslim view of politics. Muslim civilization, he argues, is unique and Muslims generally seek to distinguish themselves from the outside world. Their civilization constrains Muslims from learning about and appreciating the social and political progress achieved by others.[114] Bernard Lewis further argued that democracy, which is generally regarded as a secular concept, cannot exist alongside Islam, a religious doctrine that regulates all aspects of Muslim life. Islam in this respect accepts no separation between the law of religion and the law of the state. He argued that political participation outside a religious context is not likely to occur in Islam, and that secularism, which is a crucial element of a modern society, cannot be expected to emerge from within an Islamic society.[115] Even in the case that secularism is imported from the West, in most cases these attempts will result in clashes rather than integration and cooperation.[116] This 'clash' dynamic is partially explained by the tribal structure of Middle Eastern societies, which predates Islam and still dominates much of the societal dynamic.

Saltzman's seminal work *Culture and Conflict in the Middle East* stresses the importance of this dimension to our understanding of the region. He notes, "tribes operate differently from states, which are centralized, have political hierarchies, and have specialized institutions—such as courts, police,

---

113 See At-Tunisi, 1972, p. 185.
114 See Kedourie, 1994, p. 1.
115 See Lewis, 2002, p. 100.
116 See ibid, p. 114.

tax collectors, and an army—to maintain social control and defense."[117] Tribes, he argues, address their affairs differently than states. Security, for example, is handled through affiliation to an extended family, while a clan or a tribe can shift the balance of power in a given state due to tribal loyalties.[118] Saltzman also discusses the "tribal dynamics" which have deeply influenced Arab culture and, by extension, Islam.[119] Tribe-state dynamics are further decrypted by Mohammed Bamyeh, who argues that the history of Islam confirms that basic social structures of obligation and reciprocity tend to become less reliable once they reach the level of state politics.[120]

Referring to the compatibility of Islam and civil society, Richard Bulliet argues that Islam has fulfilled the same historical function as "the people" of the West, namely as a source of limitation on state power.[121] Whereas the evolution of political theory in the West, he argues, gradually led to the concept of "the people" as a countervailing force against tyranny, in the Islamic world that countervailing force was thought to be Islam, the submission of all—ruler and ruled alike—to God and His law.[122]

In a more restricted sense, John Kelsay identifies a mechanism in the activity of the *ulama* (an authoritative body of Muslim scholars) which he calls "limiting despotism." Their self-designated role as "heirs" to the prophet somewhat counterbalances the idea of the "caliph."[123] The terms of reference used in the Muslim world to describe social and political dynamics are different as well.

By understanding the strength of traditional cultural and religious dimensions within Muslim societies, it becomes clear that the development of civil society must take place within such frameworks, not outside of them. Bamyeh identifies structures such as shared lineages, tribes, millet, families, "urban notables" (*ayan*), merchants, the "colonial bourgeoisie," and "learned networks" (*ulama*) as Muslim societal distinctions that adopt the notion of civil discourse. These structures, he argues, help provide a

117 See Saltzman, 2008, p. 23.
118 See Saltzman, 2008, p. 24.
119 See ibid, p. 4.
120 See Bamyeh, 2006, p. 41.
121 See Bulliet, 1998, 1999.
122 See ibid, p. 190.
123 See Kelsay, 2003.

distinct social worldview, rules of membership, and patterns of relations to the outside groups as well as to the state in a way that will allow a better understanding of Muslim civil discourse.[124] Furthermore, a number of Muslim scholars have argued that Islam contains its own parallels to "democracy" and democratic values, and that a bridge between the two can be built by using a number of existing Islamic ideas. This framework includes terms such as *shurah* (consultation), *ikhtiyar* (choice), *wasatia* (moderation), *bay'ah* (oath of allegiance), and *ijma* (consensus of the Muslim community). The Quran advocates the principle of consultation, affirming that affairs should be conducted through consultation or mutual consent (*Am ruhum shura-bai nuhum*). These terms should be used as a substitute for, or at least in parallel with, Western concepts when attempting to reach a Muslim audience.[125] This view appears to be held by a number of Muslim leaders who advocate for a certain interpretation of Islam and democracy; explaining the Iranian interpretation, Khameini (the Supreme Leader of Iran) said prior to the June 2001 elections:

> Existing democracies do not necessarily follow one formula or aspect. It is possible that a democracy may lead to a liberal system. It is possible that democracy may lead to a socialist system. Or it may be a democracy with the inclusion of religious norms in the government. We have accepted the third option.[126]

A different approach is taken by some recent studies such as those of Sohail Hashmi, Abdulaziz Sachedina, and Ahmad Moussalli, who seek to articulate a theoretical conception of Muslim civil society on the basis of classical Islamic traditions rather than European theories.[127] This approach stresses three distinct historical principles, which serve as a guide to understating Islamic societies:[128]

1. The principle of partial control considers the legitimacy of the Islamic state, which was historically regarded (by constituents and rulers alike) as only one among several sources of legitimate authority. Its control was often

124 See Bamyeh, 2006, p. 41.
125 See Dajani, 2009, p. 16; Esposito and Voll, 2001, p. 3; Moussalli, 2001, pp. 16–18, p. 4.
126 See Esposito and Voll, 2001, p. 4.
127 See Bamyeh, 2006, p. 41.
128 See Bamyeh, 2003.

territorially limited to major cities, while beyond the cities—and sometimes within them—this control had to be shared with other networks of religious authorities, tribal notables, merchant guilds, Sufi orders, and vast networks of extended families. Afghanistan can be considered a modern case in which this tribal model continues to be viable.

2. The principle of free movement does away with the meaning of "borders," which would seem to contradict the notion of a global *Umma* whose domain is defined by ideological rather than political expansion. The principle of free movement and the reach of Islamic rule allowed ibn Battuta, one of the most famous travelers in Islamic history, to be trained as a judge in Morocco and yet without any further training to find employment as far away as India. In other words, a global civil society was maintained through various networks, which connected the great urban centers of the Islamic world.

3. Heteroglossia – The term "heteroglossia" was coined in the 1930's by the Russian literary scholar Mikhail Bakhtin, who considered how one literary work (usually a realist novel) could accommodate a multiplicity of voices, representing different social standpoints. It describes a condition in which a single narrative imposes order, but not unity, on the variety of voices within it. "Heteroglossia" differs from "diversity" in the sense that the community of Muslim believers does not regard itself as diverse (however diverse it may actually be). In other words, a unity imagined where diversity is a disunity proclaimed. The former allows specific voices to express themselves as though they were the voices of all, and the latter as though they were addressing people who are largely alike. While diversity is recognizable at the borderlines of communities, heteroglossia is an unrecognized, and thus unconscious characteristic of the community itself. In the Islamic context, its properties are the ones that allow the existence of a variety of social, tribal, and political orders and practices, or in other words, some diversity that is characterized as unity.

In the Islamic world, these principles have in the past supplied the conditions for the networks, institutions, habits, and practices which Europe would eventually come to define as "civil society."[129] They may also help

---

129 See Bamyeh, 2005, p. 41.

us understand some of the difficulties associated with attempts to create a "Western-style" civil society in Muslim lands, as seen in the cases of Yemen and Lebanon.

In 1990, North and South Yemen surprised the world by announcing that the two countries would unify into the new Republic of Yemen, a republic that would bring democracy to the Arabian Peninsula. Rapid democratization seemed unlikely in this mostly rural country with poor economic development and low levels of literacy; but some progress was made, which has been partially attributed to the incorporation of tribal elements into the democratic process.[130] In the port of Hodeida, the commerce-based, "modern" rationality of a city government emerged out of the "traditional" base of the Yemeni tribal system. The outcome of these developments was an arrangement in which the tribal system continued to function as a voluntary network, while tribal solidarity became interchangeable with other types of group solidarity. Another related example is the extension of the tribal ethic of mutual assistance into Yemeni diaspora networks, which stretch from Singapore to suburban America. These networks tend to revolve around extended kinship, and they owe their resilience to the absence of obvious alternatives, including the limited reach of the state system.[131]

Lebanon and the Balkans offer another perspective on the dangers associated with tribal dynamics. The millet system, which predated Lebanon, included features analogous with modern nationalism, in particular the notion that certain rights could be guaranteed or claimed only through specific forms of group association. As these countries morphed into modern nation-states, the consequences of this transformation were usually highly unpleasant, as in the cases of the Balkan conflict and the Lebanese civil wars.[132]

It was within the framework of these ideas that Islamic scholarship on the issues of civil society and democracy began to develop at the dawn of the modern Arab renaissance. In the 18th century however, the roots of this discourse can be traced to much earlier times with the works of al-Farabi (d. 950 CE) and Ikhwan al-Safa (late 10th century) who debated ideas about

130 See Carapico, 1998; Schwedler, 2002 pp. 48–49.
131 See Bamyeh, 2005, p. 41; Carapico, 1998.
132 See Bamyeh, 2005, p. 41.

the "good society" in the tradition of Plato and Aristotle.[133] During the 19th century, Muslim and Arab ideas about democracy were clearly influenced by Western thinking, and were often the product of Muslim scholars who had spent time in the West. Although they had had the opportunity to travel outside the borders of the Islamic empire, the discourse that they initiated was within a traditional context (though it was often framed by modern Islamic interpretation). Both of these groups of scholars—the earlier and the later—became increasingly aware of alternative models of governance, and their thinking reflected not only a new theological outlook, but also a new political approach that encountered many critics who refused to adopt their line of thinking.

While it is possible to point to a Muslim interpretation that supports the values of democracy, it is important to note the mentioned gap between these ideas and the political reality—a gap that was greatly exposed to the international community during the short season known as the "Arab Spring." According to Freedom House's Index of Political Rights and Civil Liberty, Muslim states have generally failed to establish democratic conduct. Mali (est. 1960) was the only Muslim country that saw the workings of a full democracy for more than five years. According to the Freedom House study, there are twelve semi-democratic Muslim states defined as partly free, and the rest (45 states) are defined as authoritarian. Moreover, 8 of the world's 15 most repressive regimes in the last decade are found in Muslim states.[134]

The last two decades have seen a great deal of writing on the issue of Islam and democracy, which is far beyond the scale and scope of this chapter, but it will suffice to say that despite the established connection between Islam and authoritative political structures, alternative Muslim frameworks do exist. The exposure to traditions of democracy and civil society may help explain the more democratic conduct of some of the Muslim opposition groups based outside their native lands. However, as the following chapter will emphasize, the most vocal opposition to democratic ideas has come from certain Islamic (or Islamist) ideologies that have continued in their

---

133 See Sajoo, 2004, pp. ix–x.
134 See Freedom House, 2001, 2004, 2005.

struggle not only against non-Muslim influences, but also against internal Muslim forces that seek political reform and democracy.

In reconciling these different views, it is important to note that any discussion of democracy and civil society in the Middle East must take into consideration culture, language, and social structures that are central to analyzing any dynamic of change. Islam is very much at the core of this dynamic and so is the influence of Islamic and Islamists groups who oppose democracy from the very beginning. Due to the small size of the secular camp and the vast influence of traditional, cultural and religious forces, it is important to focus on the creation of bridges between the Islamic framework and the democratic one.

2.7 New Threats to the Democratic Revolution

Alongside the "democracy wave," the last two decades have also seen the rise of a new global balance of power created by the end of the Cold War. The disintegration of the Soviet Union, the establishment of the United States as the sole superpower in the world and most recently, the Arab awakening. However, a series of new local and regional conflicts have also characterized the post-Cold War period, during which over 40 new countries (mostly democracies) have been established. Ethnic and religious tensions accompanied many of these conflicts, or to adopt the Huntingtonian terminology, they displayed some of the characteristics of "civilizational conflict."[135] The Middle East has served as a focal point for some of these conflicts, which expressed a tension between the leading influential "Western" powers on the one hand, and local Arab governments as well as the flag of Islam on the other. The events of September 11th caused the West to focus additional attention on the phenomenon of terrorism, which was quickly associated with "democratization" policies. Influenced by these events, President George W. Bush argued that Islamic authoritarianism breeds terror and political extremism that can only be moderated by a rapid democratization of the Muslim and Arab world.[136] This objective was clearly reflected in US policy in Iraq, and as Lawrence Kaplan wrote in

135 See Hungtington, 1993.
136 See Encarnacion, 2003, p. 1.

the days before the American invasion, "Never mind disarmament: Bush's true objective is to replace Iraq's tyrant with a regime which might have pleased the founding fathers and which would serve as a model for the democratization of the Middle East."[1]

As I have already suggested, the 21st century finds the third wave of democratization still at its peak and amplified by a growing network of political structures and alliances such as the EU, NATO, the G7 and others who support the broader objectives of democratization. But while this democratic alliance has gained strength, it has also begun to face new enemies who consider the freedoms which democracy has to offer to be a threat to their traditional way of life and existing political structures.

Sa'id Hawwa (1935–89), the leading ideologue of the Muslim Brotherhood in Syria and a close disciple of Sayyid Qutb (the founder of the Muslim Brotherhood in Egypt),articulated this position when he wrote:

> Democracy is a Greek term which signifies sovereignty of the people, the people being the source of legitimacy. In other words, it is the people that legislate and rule. In Islam the people do not govern themselves by laws they make on their own, as in democracy. Rather, the people are governed by a regime and a set of laws imposed by God.[2]

Osama bin Laden, the founder of Al-Qaeda and perhaps the most extreme contemporary representative of this ideology, attempted to frame the democratization effort as a blatant attempt at Western intervention that threatens the entire Arab and Muslim civilization. Though pockets of illiberal creeds, racist norms and anti-democratic ideologies exist throughout the world, it appears that only "Osama bin Ladenism" and its variants constitute a serious transnational ideological alternative to liberal democracy today. Bin Laden (d. 2011) can be described as a successful propagator of the set of illiberal, anti-modern, anti-democratic, and quasi-religious ideas commonly referred to as Islamic fundamentalism.[3] In his view, democratization efforts are nothing but another colonial attempt at conquest, and a declaration of war against the entire Muslim nation. In his statement from

---

1 See Kaplan, 2003, p. 21.
2 See Azzam, 1997, p. 8.
3 See Macfaul, 2004, p. 160.

October of 2001, which followed the launch of the American military intervention in Afghanistan, he said:

> I say these events have split the whole world into two camps: the camp of belief and the camp of disbelief. So every Muslim shall support his religion ... And to America, I say to it and to its people this: I swear by God the Great, America will never dream nor those who live in America will never taste security and safety unless we feel security and safety in our land and in Palestine.[4]

In his speech of December 26, 2001, he added:

> It became very clear that the West in general and America, head of the infidels in particular, bear hate and grudge against Islam and Muslims that cannot be described... Our terrorism is a good accepted terrorism because it's against America, it's for the purpose of defeating oppression so America would stop supporting Israel, who is killing our children.

Echoing the same line, Abu Baker Al Bagdadi, the self-appointed Caliph of the Islamic State noted:

> Our last message is to the Americans: Know O protector of the crusade that this war by proxy in Syria won't help you like it didn't in Iraq. Soon we will be in a direct confrontation and the sons of Islam have prepared for such a day. So watch for we are with you, watching.[5]

Similarly, former Iranian President Mahmoud Ahmadinejad, a symbol of another Islamic revolution, often stresses what he sees as a confrontation between the world of Islam and the "world of arrogance," or the West. Drawing upon the legacy of Khomeini, the founder of the Iranian revolution, Ahmadinejad speaks in terms of an "Islamic struggle" and an "Islamic front" which needs to be united against the threat posed to it by the arrogant powers of Israel and the United States. In his speech of October 26, 2005 he said:

> We are in the process of an historical war between the world of arrogance and the Islamic world, and this war has been going on for hundreds of years. In this historical war, the situation at the fronts has changed many times. During some periods, the Muslims were the victors and were very active, and looked forward, and the world of arrogance was in retreat. Unfortunately, in the past 300 years, the Islamic world has been in retreat vis-à-vis the world of arrogance... During the period of the last 100 years, the [walls of the] world of Islam were destroyed

4 See Bin Laden, 2001.
5 See Baghdadi, 2014.

> and the world of arrogance turned the regime occupying Jerusalem into a bridge for its dominance over the Islamic world...In his battle against the world of arrogance, our dear Imam [Khomeini] set the regime occupying Qods [Jerusalem] as the target of his fight...Oh dear people, look at this global arena. By whom are we confronted? We have to understand the depth of the disgrace of the enemy, until our holy hatred expands continuously and strikes like a wave.[6]

These voices, joined by Islamists, nationalists and people affiliated with the ruling elites of the Middle East, have helped launch a new war of attrition, which is taking place in Iraq, Afghanistan, Syria, and elsewhere ever since September 11, 2001. While democratization efforts attempt to pave their way, a coalition of militants, Islamic activists, and pro-regime supporters are doing their best to stifle any possible progress. These statements, and the ongoing military and terrorist activities which follow them, help to frame an important dynamic in the Middle East and an unavoidable conflict between two camps—the Western powers (along with some liberal individuals and institutions in the region) versus Islamist groups backed by religious establishments and para-military structures. The Islamist camp has demonstrated both the will and the ability to use any possible means in order to prevent the advance of foreign influence and the threatening freedom it may bring with it. Both camps have become increasingly more occupied with a new war of ideas, which has also become an internal part of the new reality in the Middle East. This bloody struggle, unfortunately, is far from over.

---

6 See Ahmadinejad, 2005.

Chapter 3: Diasporas, Political Diasporas and Expatriate Groups

3.1 The Growing Political Role of Diaspora and Expatriate Opposition Groups

The term "diaspora" is based on the Greek term "speiro," meaning "to sow" and the preposition "dia," meaning "over." The Greeks understood the term to mean migration and colonization. The Septuagint (the earliest extant Greek translation of the Old Testament from the original Hebrew which was produced near the middle of the 3rd century BCE) translated Deuteronomy 28:25 as follows: "Thou shalt be a diaspora in all kingdoms of the earth."[1]

Today, the term "diaspora" refers not only to such classic groups as Jews, Greeks, Armenians or Italians but also to a much wider category of people. This reflects global phenomena such as politically motivated uprooting, the voluntary migration of populations, global communications and transport. The term has acquired a broad semantic domain and now encompasses a number of groups such as political refugees, alien residents, guest workers, immigrants, expellees, overseas communities and ethnic and racial minorities.[2] Chander defined "diaspora" as "that part of a people, dispersed in one or more countries other than its homeland, that maintains a feeling of transnational community among a people and its homeland." [3] Robin Cohen proposed a typology of diasporas each of which has been caused by a different set of circumstances. These are, victim diasporas, labor and imperial diasporas, trade diasporas, cultural diasporas and global-deterritorialized diasporas. Cohen noted that these types of diasporas may overlap and may change character over time.[4]

Migration in a general sense is a process that both depends on social networks and is also known to create social networks.[5] Sociological,

1 See Shuval, 2000, p. 41.
2 See Ibid.
3 See Chandler, 2001, p. 1020.
4 See Vertovec, Steven and Cohen, Robin, 1999.
5 See Portes and Guarnizo, 1990; Portes, 1995.

anthropological and political science researchers have helped shed some additional light on the dynamics of diaspora and expatriate communities, including relations with their kin countries. Despite historical patterns, the data indicates that ethnic groups are not disappearing and that they appear to assimilate more slowly than anticipated.[6] Chaliand and Rageau, who traced migration of twelve diaspora groups (Jews, Armenians, Romani and Sinti (Gypsies), Native Africans, Chinese, East Indians, Irish, Greeks, Lebanese, Palestinians, Vietnamese, and Koreans), found that many of these new communities have developed mechanisms for maintaining their unique identity.[7] However, as recognized by Schiller, Basch and Szanton-Blanc, "the majority seem to maintain several identities which link them simultaneously to more than one nation."[8]

But do diasporas matter? This question is a source of debate among scholars and various academic schools of thought. Diaspora groups were not considered "significant political players" by a number of theorists, and received relatively little attention from political scientists to date. Realists, who see unitary states as the primary actors in the international arena, do not value the role that ethnic groups can play in constraining the range of a state's strategic choices. Generally, they link integrated (or homogeneous) ethnicities with a stronger state and fragmented ethnicities with a weaker or vulnerable state.[9] Likewise Waltz and others in the neo-realist school of international relations hold that foreign policy is merely an extension of domestic politics and hence relations between states can neither be understood through the rhetoric of state governments nor the competition among groups that shape it.[10] According to this approach, international relations should be viewed as the actions of other states vis a vis the anticipated actions or reactions of other states. In this framework, expatriates can make a difference only if they are able to influence the perception of anticipated state actions.

6 See Sheffer, 1997, p. 1.
7 See Chaliand and Rageau, 1995.
8 See Basch and Szanton-Blanc, 1992, p. 11.
9 See Davis and Moore, 1998.
10 See Waltz, 1979, 1996.

Constructivists on the other hand give more weight to non-state actors such as international organizations, ethnic and religious groups, and transnational groups. This approach sees states as composed of many competing actors with foreign policies that are the result of the interplay between domestic forces and perceptions of international concerns that are developed in part by expatriate and ethnic groups. Davis and Moore, Kolsto, Stack and Waltz (in his later writings) look at the contribution of external actors to the policy process and recognize the role of transnational ties between ethnic groups as a factor influencing both domestic and foreign policy. They see these "ethnopolities" as a factor in the policy and strategic decision-making process of a given state. There are a number of ways for diasporas to become involved in an attempt to influence events in the homeland. Individuals from the diaspora may continue business activities, retain family ties and remain personally involved in various "homeland matters." Individuals may also pursue social and political involvement by supporting NGO's or political platforms. Finally, they might act to funnel resources from the host country to the homeland in terms of financial support, arms, and even troops (volunteer or hired combat support services).[11]

Theory aside, there are a large number of documented cases of political diasporas that have helped to bring about significant political change in their home countries.[12] These include:

- The struggle for Czech independence by Thomas Massaric who was able to initiate the action of the allies and later lead his country
- The role of the exiled Socialist (SPD) and Communist (KPD) Parties of Germany under the Weimar Republic and particularly that of SPD that later assumed control of the occupied zones
- The contribution of the Jewish Diaspora in creating Zionism and the formation of the State of Israel
- The role of the *Acción Democrática*, an exiled Venezuelan party that was established in 1941 in Colombia and later contributed to the restoration of democracy in 1958

11 See Hockenos, 2003.

12 Some of these examples are taken from Shain (2004) who has studied the phenomena of political diasporas.

- The underground resistance army in Poland led by General Sikorski, the head of the Polish government-in-exile that assisted the Allied Powers in the battle against Nazi Germany
- The case of FMLN in El Salvador that successfully fought the US-backed Salvadoran military government
- The campaign of the exiled Catalan President, Joseph Tarrandellas, that led to a historic reconciliation agreement and unity government with Spanish Primier Suárez
- The return of Peron to Argentina following 18 years of campaigning from exile
- The role of the exiled African National Congress in ending apartheid in South Africa
- The anti-Marcos campaign of Filipinos abroad that is considered one of the most successful diasporic efforts to unseat a non-democratic regime
- The Iranian revolution that was led from France by Ayatollah Khomeini
- The case in which exiled leader Ahmed Chalabi played a major role in convincing the Americans to initiate a military intervention in Iraq
- The case of Cuba and the role of expatriate in applying political pressure (and the prior attempt to co-opt some diaspora elements in an attempt to trigger a coup against Fidel Castro)
- The case of the Sudanese opposition and Uganda that serves as a base for the Sudan Liberation Army, one of the key factions fighting Sudanese President Omar Al Bashir.
- The case of Muhammed Fethullah Gülen, the founder of the Gülen movement that is considered the most serious opposition group to the AKP despite being managed from Pennsylvania, United States.
- The more recent phenomena of foreign fighters who have joined the battles in Syria and Iraq (although the motivation for many of the recruits was more religious than classic ex-pat activism).

This rather long (but not exclusive) list makes it important to stress the significance of diasporas and their ability to trigger political change in countries around the world. Although, at times, the expat factor is more symbolic in nature (such as the case of the exiled Polish government in London that was brought back by Lech Walesa in 1990, or the return of King Zahir Shah to Afghanistan after 29 years in exile), there are other instances in which diasporas have been able to send troops, weapons and funds (as was the case in 1948 in Israel/Palestine; in Sudan and El Salvador and recently in Syria and Iraq) and there have been times when diaspora groups have been able to organize politically.

Naturally, these are not simple cases of "expat victories." Each case presents unique circumstances, and often a juxtaposition of particular political circumstances, timing, and ripeness of a given exiled group. It is also clear that the work of expatriate never takes place in a vacuum. Expat groups operate, react, and interact with the political surroundings and power structures that are in place (powers that often attempt and succeed at using these expat groups as a means to their own ends). Although the work of expatriate must be put in appropriate context, this historical review stresses that the expat phenomena is apparent in political life and that it deserves further attention in the context of this book's central question on the respective role of ICT as a vehicle used by expat groups to achieve their political objectives.

3.2 Growing Diasporas and the Phenomenon of Globalization

Diaspora and migration numbers have steadily increased since the 1990's as a result of a number of factors, including a series of political problems in Africa, Afghanistan, Bosnia, Romania, Lebanon, former Yugoslavia, Somalia, Sri Lanka, Iran, Iraq, Pakistan and Syria. The number of international migrants in the world has doubled in the last quarter of the 20th century to the point where almost 10% of the people residing in developed regions of the world are now international migrants.[13]

The variety of diaspora groups is also increasing as new groups in Europe, the Western Hemisphere and the Middle East form new ethnic and national communities around the world.[14] According to the Global Commission on International Migration (GCIM), in 2006 there were about 200 million people who lived outside their home countries while defining themselves as expatriates, asylum seekers, or willing migrants.[15] This number reflects

13 See Lukas, 2005 p. 4.
14 See Chaliand and Rageau, 1995; Sowell, 1995.
15 See Martin, 2006, p. 6.

a significant growth since 1989 when the estimated number of refugees in the world stood at 60 million.[16] According to Vertovec and Cohen, a third of the migrant population, can be counted as refugees or people who were forcibly displaced from their homes.[17] The UN refugee agency reported on World Refugee Day in 2015 that number of people forced from their homes by conflicts worldwide rose to a record 59.5 million.[18]

In parallel with the increases in migrant numbers, other changes have helped to further solidify the "diaspora identity" of these newly established communities. Before the 1960's, immigrant groups were generally expected to shed their ethnic identities and assimilate into the new social and cultural environment of their host country. Groups that were thought to be unable to assimilate were denied admission, such as the Chinese in Canada and non-whites in Australia.[19] However, in the beginning of the 1970's it became evident that assimilationist models did not work effectively. As a result, policies have changed in some societies, such that immigrants are permitted and even encouraged to maintain various aspects of their ethnic tradition. The resurgence of diasporas has affected modernization theories whose predecessors argued for faster assimilation and the disappearance of ethnic diasporas.[20] These trends are also associated with the phenomenon of globalization expressed in worldwide financial, economic, technological, and ecological interdependence in which goods, capital, knowledge, crime, culture, drugs, fashion and other materials flow across territorial boundaries.[21] Globalization, emphasizing technical, economic and cultural transformations which have undermined the significance of boundaries between nation-states, has gradually created a "flatter world" which was originally predicted to weaken nations, as well as religious and ethnic based identities.[22]

---

16 See United Nations, 1989.
17 See Vertovec and Cohen, 1999.
18 See interview with Antonio Guterres, head of UNHCR "Number displaced worldwide hits record high – UN report," BBC, June 18th, 2015.
19 See Shuval, 2000, p. 44.
20 See Kearny, 1995; Kymlicka, 1996; Shuval, 2000.
21 See Shuval, 2000, p. 26.
22 See Shaw, 2000 p. 15.

The character of globalization and the ramifications of these meta-trends on national and political identities have generated interest among scholars and philosophers. In recent years, globalization has come into focus, generating considerable interest and controversy in the social sciences, humanities, policy circles, and among the informed public at large.[23] With the term "global," scholars often refer to areas of social life beyond the national level.[24] Music and culture, for example, can now easily travel the world and cross physical borders and cultural divides by means of satellite and the Internet. The term "global trends" can have a new meaning in a more "globalized world."

On the one hand, it has become clear that globalization with its open borders, mobile job markets, accessible travel and increased accessibility to modern means of communication has made the world a little smaller and has opened up new bridges to cross cultural divides. On the other hand, some reverse trends were also associated with the "globalization" phenomena. Global trends, which came mostly from the Western world, were subject to resentment from domestic conservative forces that saw these trends both as a threat to national and religious traditions, or as a foreign (or Western) attempt to gain influence within their own sphere of influence. Tomlinson argues that globalization has been the most significant force in creating and proliferating cultural identity.[25] Portes suggests that the competitive realities of the world economy may undermine the cohesiveness of a given diaspora community and hence create communities that sit astride political borders that are "neither here nor there" but in both places simultaneously.[26] Smith argues that although globalization enabled the crossing of national and cultural boundaries and offered some unifying tendencies of modernity, the international system has appeared to become

23 See, for example, Appadurai 1996; Bauman 1998; Baylis and Smith 1997; Bhagwati 2002; Castles and Davidson 2000; Giddens 2000; Hardt and Negri 2000, Inda and Rosaldo 2001; Jameson and Miyoshi 1999; King 1997; Lechner and Boli 1999; O'Meara, Mehlinger, and Krain 2000; Sassen 1998; Shuval, 2000; Singer 2002 and Tomlinson 1999.

24 See Shaw, 2000 p. 16.

25 See Tomlinson, 1991, p. 23.

26 See Portas, 1997, p. 3.

less stable during the same time period.[27] He suggests that the intensification of contacts in a global world could lead to increased competition between resilient national cultures and end with a global "cultural war."

The global culture of the 21st century is sustained by advanced communication technologies, which provide an accelerated dispersal of information and images across boundaries and cultures. Open borders, mobile job markets, international division of labor, and increased access to modern means of transportation also enable connect immigrants with their countries of origin. At the same time, counter forces such as nationalism, ethnicity, religious fundamentalism, racism, sexism, and other forms of exclusion have adopted these new technologies as well.[28] As a result, in today's world, immigrants are less contained inside the physical and cultural boundaries of their host countries. Travel to and from their homelands and communication with their family and friends who remain there has become relatively easy. Social networks in this age are promoting and supporting immigration. These phenomena carry important implications for the maintenance of relations between immigrants and their homelands, for the persistence of traditional cultural patterns, on-going separatism, and merging into the mainstream of the host society.[29]

In sum, the new globalized world has helped enhance the diaspora phenomenon both in terms of numbers as well as in terms of character and influence. The available means of communication has helped to slow the pace of diasporic assimilation and, in parallel, to strengthen diasporic identity among the growing number of immigrants who have chosen to join diaspora communities in the last two decades. Diasporas can now maintain contacts not only with their home countries, but also with other similar diaspora communities. This trend allows for further strengthening the character of a given diaspora community, its identity, and its influence both at home and abroad.

27 See Smith, 1992.
28 See Huntington, 1994, 1997; Portes, 1989.
29 See Shuval and Leshem, 1998; Shuval 1998.

3.3 Political and Economic Roles of Transnational Diasporas

Transnational (or ethno-national) diasporas arise out of voluntary or imposed migration from an ethno-national state or homeland to one or more host countries.[30] Members of diaspora groups permanently reside in host countries, a fact which distinguishes them from transient migrants, refugees and guest workers.[31] They also maintain their ethno-national identities, which are closely connected to either myths or facts related to their homelands.[32] Transnational diasporas are a particular subset of migrants that are characterized by networks which link the migrants in the host country to their brethren in the homeland. Not all migrants actively join diaspora groups; some seek to assimilate (if allowed) into the culture of their host country or avoid drawing attention to their foreign allegiances for political reasons. Others migrate in small numbers, and therefore lack the critical mass to form an organizational core.[33] The assimilationist migrants, the unidentified and inactive members of a given diaspora, are of less concern to this study. They usually fall under the general heading of "diaspora" but do not belong to those ethno-national or transnational diaspora groups which symbolize strong identities and relations with their brethren at home. Smith defines ethno-national diasporas as groups that remain minorities in their host countries and face possible expulsion, alienation, and social, political, and economic hardships.[34] Sheffer suggests a working definition for ethno-national diasporas as "ethnic minority groups of migrant origins residing and acting in host countries but maintaining strong sentimental and material links with their countries of origin- their homelands."[35] It is important to note that diasporas and political diasporas in particular do not form right away, but rather the critical formative stage occurs only after the new migrants have overcome the initial shock of leaving their homeland. Only then can they cope with the overwhelming problems involved

30 See Sheffer, 1997, p. 3.
31 See Smith, 1981.
32 See Cavalli-Sforza, 1996, Kelass, 1991; Sheffer, 1997; Smith, 1992.
33 See Lyons, 2004, p. 5.
34 See Smith, 1981.
35 See Sheffer 1997, p. 3.

with settling in their new host country. Only once they have become more established can they turn to communal and political activities.[36]

Ethno-national diasporas seek to create a new communal solidarity, or maintain the one they already have. This solidarity is the foundation of their cultural, social, political, and economic activity. One of the most important characteristics of life in these communities is that they preserve regular contact with their homelands, whether or not their homelands are independent or sovereign states (as in the case of the Kurds or the Palestinians). They create elaborate networks that permit and even encourage exchanges of money, political support, and cultural influence with their homelands and with segments of their diaspora that exist elsewhere. This dynamic creates the potential for friction with both homelands and host countries, which is related to divided, dual or ambiguous state loyalty(ies).[37] The process by which such diasporas are created is usually referred to as "transnationalism." It may also be described as a mechanism by which immigrants forge and sustain multi-stranded social relations, which link together their societies of origin and settlement.[38]

However, despite widespread perceptions to the contrary, immigrants come to the wealthier nations not simply because they want to, but rather because it is necessary due to acute labor scarcities in the economies of those home nations. In some cases, absolute scarcities have pushed immigration in a certain direction, for example the shortage of industrial workers in Japan and the deficit in certain professions like nursing and engineering in Australia and the United States.[39] The mass immigration of Muslims to Europe was in part an unintended consequence of post-World War II guest-worker programs in countries like Germany.[40] In other cases, the cause of this scarcity is the culturally conditioned resistance of native-born workers to accept low-paid menial jobs such as domestic or personal services,or restaurant or kitchen work, which have been commonly performed by immigrants in

36 See Sheffer, 2002, p. 201.
37 See Sheffer, 1997, pp. 4–5.
38 See Basch, Glick Schiller, and Blanc-Szanton 1994, p. 6.
39 See Portes, 1997, p. 5.
40 See Portes, 1997, p. 5.

the past.[41] This phenomenon was significant enough to influence the demographics of some wealthier countries. By 1990, the foreign-born population of the United States had reached almost 20 million, the largest absolute total in the 20th century.[42] In 2011, the US Census Bureau recorded the same demographic at 38.5 million or 12.5% of the US population.[43] Toward the end of the 20th century, Germany had a foreign population of 7 million, or roughly 9% of its population.[44] Even in ethnically homogeneous Japan, labor scarcity has prompted a variety of legal subterfuges, including the use of foreign company "trainees" and visa overstayers to perform line industrial jobs. By 1990, the foreign-born population of Japan numbered about 1.1 million. Although this is still an insignificant number compared with Japan's total population of 125,000,000, the constant growth of the foreign-born population (half of which is of Korean descent) is beginning to make its mark on Japanese society.[45]

Transnational communities maintain many kinds of close contacts with their kin countries. They consume kin-created culture (in the form of books, newspapers, and television programs), and as they develop they begin to generate diaspora-made culture, which includes locally produced newspapers, Internet sites, and cable or satellite channels. Moreover, many migrant line workers send some of their income back to family members in their country of origin; but as some diasporas have become financially successful, economic involvement of transnational communities has deepened. Growth of Asian communities in the United States, and the Chinese community in particular, has created opportunities for entrepreneurs from Taiwan and Hong Kong to invest profitably in the United States and, in the process, become part of the transnational community themselves.[46] Smith and Zhou explain how new Chinese banks, established with the help of Taiwan and Hong Kong, have largely financed the rapid growth of Chinese homeowners in the New York suburb of Flushing. They contend that the rapidly growing

41 See Gans, 1992; Guarnizo and Portes, 1990 and Sassen 1989.
42 See Fix and Passel 1991; Rumbaut 1994.
43 See Kandel, 2011, p. 3.
44 See Bade 1995; Münz and Ulrich 1995.
45 See Cornelius 1992, and 1994.
46 See Portes, 1997, p. 14.

Chinese population in Flushing and adjacent cities solely in the borough of Queens is related to the lack of knowledge of English and lack of credentials which otherwise would enable credit from US-based institutions. To meet the burgeoning demand for housing loans processed in their own language, local entrepreneurs have gone to Taiwan and Hong Kong to pool capital for new banks, while new immigrants came to the United States bearing the necessary resources.[47]

As a result, Chinese-owned banks in Flushing have thrived. Though small by conventional standards, they serve the economic interests of both the immigrant community and their overseas investors. Three thousand miles to the west, the city of Monterey Park, California, has been transformed into what Fong has called the "first suburban Chinatown." Many Taiwanese and Hong Kong entrepreneurs have established businesses in the area less for immediate profit than as a hedge against political instability and the threat of a Chinese communist takeover. Opening new businesses in the United States has helped them acquire permanent residence status, which acts as a financial insurance policy against political instability. Many of the owners have brought their families to live in Monterey Park, while they themselves continue to commute across the Pacific for business.[48]

Of particular concern to this book is the political involvement of migrants and exiles in the affairs of their kin countries. This sort of involvement is not particularly new to migrant communities. Historical studies indicate that diasporas have engaged in a considerable amount of political activity from afar for the last one hundred years at least.[49] As the pace and scale of globalization has increased, so have the political activities which accompany it, even when these activities have moved beyond the sovereign territory of a given state.[50] Transnational politics in recent years has led, for example, to Mexican politicians campaigning for votes and financial support in southern California and Israeli political candidates raising money in Jewish communities around the world. Croatians in the Croatian diaspora reportedly provided $4 million towards Franjo Tudjman's electoral

---

47 See Smith and Zhou, 1995.
48 See Fong, 1994.
49 See Vertovec, 2005 p. 3.
50 See Lyons, 2004 p. 2.

campaign of 1990, and were rewarded 12 of 120 seats in recognition of their key electoral role.[51]

In 1975, Glazer and Moynihan asserted that ethnic groups were "the single most important determinant of [US] foreign policy."[52] The political involvement of a particular diaspora may intensify in the case of "conflict-generated diasporas," which emerge as the direct result of conflicts in their homelands.[53] Such diasporas are characterized by the source of their displacement (which is usually conflict-driven rather than the voluntary or individual pursuit of economic incentives), and by the nature of their ties to the homeland (which emphasize symbolically valuable territory and an aspiration to return there once the homeland is free, rather than a situation of narrower kinship and remittance relationships). So the identity and social mobilization of conflict-generated diaspora groups are tied to a very specific, symbolically important, and territorially defined "homeland."

Some scholars have suggested that globalization and the development of diaspora identities will make territory and boundaries less salient as "supranational" identities develop and as political, social, and economic life becomes de-territorialized. Appadurai, for example, writes "ethnicity, once a genie contained in the bottle of some sort of locality (however large), has now become a global force, forever slipping in and through the cracks between states and borders."[54] However, in many cases, conflict-generated diaspora groups largely define their identity in terms of their strong attachment to a homeland defined as territory.[55] Rather than seeking to build a transnational virtual community, many diaspora groups retain the territorial aspect of their identity even if they are physically distant from that territory and unlikely to travel there. When a territorially defined community is geographically distant from its homeland, a sense of solidarity and of attachment to that territory can generate a common identity even though it is far away.

51 See ibid, pp. 2–3.
52 See ibid, pp. 23–24.
53 See Lyons, 2004, p. 5.
54 See Appadurai, 1996 p. 6.
55 See Lyons, 2004, p. 8.

As the intrinsic value of territory diminishes, and as daily life focuses on the new place of residence, the homeland's symbolic importance may even grow.[56]

3.4 Conflict Generated Diasporas

Conflict-generated diasporas are specific diaspora groups that emerged due to an ongoing conflict or a surge in an existing conflict. Clear cases of conflict-generated diasporas include the Oromo and Eritreans from Ethiopia, the Kurds from Turkey, Tamils from Sri Lanka, Armenians, Croats (pre-1991), Irish, Lebanese (mainly Christians), Albanians from Yugoslavia, Iranians following the 1979 revolution, Iraqis, Palestinians, and more recently the Syrians (post 2011).[57] Each of these groups has a large number of members who were displaced either by war or as a result of it, and each of these groups plays an important role in organizations which seek to build and reinforce links from the host countries back to the homeland in conflict. Such conflict-generated diasporas follow different patterns of behavior with regard to homeland conflict than those who may have fled conflict or political repression as seen in Central America, Iran, or Vietnam. They also differ from the much larger populations of migrants who cross borders more or less voluntarily in pursuit of economic opportunity.[58]

Paul Hockenos' study on the effect of diasporas in the war which took place in Yugoslavia in the1990's reveals that diasporas' involvement goes far beyond lobbying for foreign policy support in host nations. The success of the Albanian diaspora in realizing its nationalist agenda stands out among the several cases in the region. In addition to raising hundreds of millions of dollars and advancing a strong lobby in the US, émigré Albanians maintained a shadow government for over a decade and fielded a guerrilla army, which eventually led to NATO intervention and the removal of Serbian troops from Kosovo in 1999. The possibility of such groups creating extra state bodies by drawing on the resources of host countries gives new importance to diasporas in the international arena.[59]

---

56 See Lyons, 2004 p. 9; Shain, 2002 p. 134.
57 See Hockenos, 2003 p. 15; Lyons, 2004 p. 10.
58 See Ibid.
59 See Hockenos, 2003; Wald and Williams, 2005 p. 7.

The anti-Marcos campaign of Filipinos abroad is considered one of most successful and multifaceted diaspora-initiated efforts to unseat a non-democratic regime. in an attempt to clear his name shortly before his death, Marcos published an essay in which he maintained that the chief reason for the shift in the US-friendly posture toward his regime was "the contrived image of the Philippine reality" cultivated "by the articulate and well-financed representatives of the anti-Marcos expatriates residing in North America." He further argued that, "the committee hearings in the U.S. Congress were given the widest circulation by the American press; [and that] the wildest charges [against him] were given credence."[60]

Activities of political diasporas have taken shape in other forms as well. The American Israel Public Affairs Committee (AIPAC), a mostly Jewish lobby and advocacy group for Israel, became involved in an espionage scandal following accusations that were made in 2006 regarding certain information about Iran which was later delivered by AIPAC to Israeli officials. (The charges were dismissed in 2009). NIAC, the National Iranian American Council, a "nonpartisan, nonprofit organization dedicated to advancing the interests of the Iranian-American community," was accused of being a "foreign agent" of the Iranian government as well as being engaged in lobbying efforts that contradicted their tax-exempt status.[61]

Bernal notes that the Eritrean diaspora could be conceptualized as an offshore citizenry or as an extension of the nation in which financial havens and exported jobs serve particular purposes and take on particular characteristics by virtue of their offshore locations. Eritreans' participation in the politics of their homeland from overseas locations shows how citizens are not simply subjects or receivers of state power, but are active consumers and producers of state power. This voluntary engagement in relation to the sovereignty of the Eritrean state from overseas suggests a dimension of citizenship, which might best be understood as "emotional citizenship." That is, Eritrean diaspora groups in North America and Europe are for the most part legally citizens of the countries where they reside and earn their living, but they are emotionally pushed and pulled into Eritrea's national politics.[62]

---

60 See Shain, 1994, p. 813.
61 See NIAC's web site; See Lake, 2009.
62 See Bernal, 2006, p. 164.

Conflict-generated diasporas (hereafter referred to as political diasporas) characteristically develop networks that are based on solidarity, which emphasize identity and work ethic to keep nationalist hopes alive from abroad. These organizations and networks often engage in political activism in support of political struggles back home, including lobbying the host country or international organizations for support, both in the issues of advocacy and funding.[63] It is often noted that migrants and refugees may be at the forefront of political innovation and social change.[64]

As diaspora communities grow and become more established, their ability to influence policy increases as well. Vertovec estimated that more than a half-million children born in the United States each year (American citizens by birth) have at least one additional nationality. This phenomenon significantly increases the lobbying power of expatriate communities.[65]

In a similar fashion, symbolic dates associated with events in the homelands are used by political diasporas to further invigorate their host country communities, to strengthen the ethnic identity and to make a statement about their political agenda. For example, Martyrs Day (November 27) is an important day for community mobilization among the Tamil diaspora. Annual events such as the Ethiopian soccer tournament in North America bring thousands together not only to compete and socialize but also to talk politics.[66] The celebration of national holidays is a particularly important way to maintain links with the homeland and reaffirm borders between the diaspora community and the surrounding host country population. Iranians in the diaspora celebrate Nowruz, the Iranian New Year held annually on the Spring Equinox. Celebrating Nowruz, notes one member of the Iranian Diaspora, "allows practice of nostalgia and defiance of the unfamiliar Christian calendar simultaneously."[67]

The activity of political diasporas has long been institutionalized by various NGOs, advocacy groups, and lobbying groups that were initiated by

63 See Lyons, p. 11.
64 See Bernal, 2006 p. 163.
65 See Vertovec, 2005, p. 6.
66 See Ibid, pp. 11–12.
67 See Khalili, 1998 p. 3.

diaspora communities.[68] Aside from community organizations whose goal it is to strengthen the transnational identity by providing cultural, welfare, and community services, the political groups have a distinct mandate of advocacy which is often aimed at influencing the foreign policy of the host country. There are many examples of diaspora political activity. Following the 1999 capture of Kurdish leader Abdullah Ocalan by Turkish forces, Kurdish groups demonstrated in dozens of localities around the world, bringing Kurdish issues to worldwide attention. As mentioned above, diasporic Iraqi groups and individuals played crucial roles in encouraging American military intervention in Iraq in 2003. The Iranian opposition, which has been instrumental in providing information about the Iranian nuclear program, maintains a very visible profile throughout the world by holding political events, mass demonstrations, and maintaining an active media presence.

Small or midsize diaspora communities can form a wide (and often active) network of communal groups. Indian Americans, for example, with an estimated number of 1.2 million, maintain a wide network of community and policy organizations. On the national level, these include the American Association of Physicians from India (AAPI), the National Association of Americans of Asian Indian Descent (NAAAID), the Federation of Indian American Associations (FIA), the National Federation of Indian American Associations (NFIA), the FHA (Federation of Hindu Associations), the Indian American Council (IAC), and many others.[69] The Jewish community in the United States also has an impressive profile, which lists hundreds of community and political organizations.

The trends described in these sections point to a strengthening of diasporas that have increased their communal, cultural and political activity. As political diasporas become more stable and established, they appear to increase their political involvement with the aim of influencing the foreign policies of their host countries (and, in a number of cases, directly impacting the relations with their kin countries). It appears that the overall trend is one of growing influence where political diasporas often find themselves engaged in the policy process (often on both sides of the isle). The influence of

68 See Bernal, 2006 p. 162.
69 See Vinay, 1999 pp. 42–48.

these groups within their kin countries is often connected to their influence within their host countries, a link that helps explain attempts by diaspora groups to build relations with political candidates and government officials.

3.5 Diasporas of Middle Eastern Descent

The centrality of the Middle East to humankind from ancient until modern times coupled with the involvement of a number of old, new, and colonial empires have helped contribute to the migration and creation of a number of large diaspora communities. Geo-political changes in recent history have further escalated the creation of diaspora communities, mainly made up of Arabs (especially Palestinians), Armenians, Jews, Kurds, Iranians, Iraqis, Turks, and Syrians. There is a substantial body of literature on Middle Eastern ethnic minorities; however, neither Middle Eastern diasporas outside the region nor ethno-national diasporas inside the region have been fully examined.[70]

Middle-Eastern diasporas include both stateless people (Kurds and Palestinians) and state-based diasporas (Egyptians, Lebanese, or Jordanians). In the Middle East itself, there are large numbers of guest workers from foreign countries. Among these foreign workers are many Asians and Arabs in the Persian Gulf as well as in Israel. Their age, organization and connection, or lack thereof, to their respective home countries play a role in a given diaspora's level of activism at the host government level.[71]

Among established veteran diasporas, Armenians have a homeland while Kurds, Druze, and Palestinians are stateless. In a number of Middle Eastern states, we can find incipient diasporas from the region: Palestinians in Lebanon, Jordan and Syria, Egyptians in Saudi Arabia and Iraq, Jordanians in Saudi Arabia and the Persian Gulf states, Syrians in Lebanon and Jordan as well as foreign workers from Asia in the Gulf States and Asians and Eastern Europeans in Israel.[72]

---

70 For more on Middle Eastern ethnic minorities see Esman, 1988; Hudson, 1977; Sheffer, 1997, 2002.

71 See Kelass, 1991.

72 See Ibid.

Before the Arab Spring the region hosted 5,367,400 refugees out of which 2,975,000 were Palestinians.[73] Other major populations of refugees include Afghans mostly located in Iran; Iraqis in Jordan, Turkey, and Iran; Somalis in Egypt and Yemen, and Sudanese in Egypt. The Islamic Republic of Iran used to be recognized as the country that was hosting the largest refugee population in the world. In 1999, Iranian officials reported that there were over 1.8 million refugees in Iran. Afghans made up the largest group (about 1.3 million), and there were about half a million Kurdish Iraqis.[74] The Syrian conflict has challenged these numbers. At the end of 2014, the United Nations High Commissioner for Refugees (UNHCR) reported 3.2 million registered Syrian refugees while other country reports (mainly from Turkey, Jordan and Egypt) have estimated the number to total of over 5 million refugees (in addition to seven million internally displaced). These refugees have relocated mainly to Jordan, Turkey, Lebanon and Iraq. Iraq, a country that generated a significant number of refugees due to the recent wars within its borders, also found itself absorbing great numbers of Kurds and Iraqi refugees who had returned to their homes as well as a large number of Syrians, a number totaling 500,000 in 2014 alone.[75]

The main destinations of other ethnic migrants from Middle Eastern states have been European and Western Hemisphere host countries, where the Palestinians, Israelis, Syrians, Lebanese, Armenians, and Iranians have large diaspora communities. These communities extend financial and non-tangible support to their brethren in the Middle East. Most of these communities have been established in their host countries either on the basis of family connections or as *landsmanshaften* (mutual help associations for those originating from the same places in the old homeland). Armenian, Christian Lebanese, and Christian Palestinian groups are known to be some of the more established diaspora groups.[76]

Having said this, some Middle Eastern diaspora communities are dwindling. Many Middle-Eastern Armenians are migrating to the United States and Canada, and some are returning to the independent Republic

73 See Al-Ali, 2004, p. 6.
74 See Al-Ali, 2004; Zohry and Harrell-Bond. 2003.
75 See UNHCR, 2014; Metin, 2014; Maclucas, 2014.
76 See Sheffer, 1997 pp. 4–5.

of Armenia. The Armenian migrants tend to be younger, more skilled and more affluent, factors which take a toll on their greater diaspora communities. Similar processes are at work among Israeli Druze in Israel and the West Bank. In these regions, signs of a diaspora decline have been influenced by modernization and integration into Israel's political and economic systems. Such trends cannot happen among larger stateless diaspora groups, like the Kurds or Palestinians.[77]

3.6 The Syrian Diaspora

Despite the visibility of the recent Syrian conflict, little research exists on the subject of the Syrian diaspora nor is there readily available basic information such as facts about its size, distribution, and affiliation. With over 10 million Syrians that have become internally displaced refugees as a result of the 2011 uprising, the Syrian diaspora is quickly changing and reforming. Some historical data points to a number of immigration waves that created a dispersed Syrian diaspora with centers across all five continents of the world. The first record of Syrian expat communities appears at the end of the 19th century, at a time in which Syria was under Ottoman rule. Records of Syrian immigration to Latin America can be traced to 1860, following a series of anti-Christian riots in Damascus and Lebanon.[78] The Victoria Museum in Australia holds a census from 1891, which records the presence of Syrian immigrants in the country. In the US, Syrian migration was first recorded in 1880 although it might be the case that Syrians came to the US prior to this year, classified as Turks from the Ottoman Empire.[79] It is important to note that the designation "Syrian" at that time referred to *Bilad a-Sham*—a much larger territory that included the semi-autonomous region of Lebanon, also ruled by the Ottoman Empire at the time.

This concept may help explain the estimates of the Syrian Ministry for Expatriate Affairs which has recorded claims of a Syrian diaspora numbering over 15 million people who emigrated to North America, Europe, South America (mainly Brazil, Chile and Colombia) and Australia. The Syrian

77 See Ibid.
78 See Kuneralp, 2009, p. 4.
79 See Jones, 2009.

government set up the Ministry of Expatriate Affairs in April 2002 with the aim of encouraging Syrians to return to their homeland and re-establish links with Syrian associations all over the world. In an attempt to reengage the large diaspora, new regulations provide for sons of Syrian citizens born and raised abroad to pay $500 in lieu of the mandatory military service. A tax of $100 per year levied on expatriates at the time of renewal of their Syrian passports has been cancelled in light of this new policy.[80] The estimate of 15 million can be partially explained by the answer to the question, "Who is a Syrian?," The answer, in this case, includes all Lebanese and some Turkish immigrants. But even with this in mind, the actual number of Syrian ex-patriots appears to be much smaller.

Verifiable estimates are hard to find, but some existing data may help shed a little light on the broader diaspora dynamic. Since the US keeps good immigration records, the picture regarding the size of its Syrian community is slightly clearer. Some data indicates that nearly 90% of all Arabic speaking immigrants who arrived to the US prior to 1924 were Syrian, predominantly Christian from Mount Lebanon.[81] The US census, which asks about ancestry, put this number at 155,718 in 2006. This number indicates those who self identify as Syrian or of Syrian decent.[82] These more accurate numbers (which include the Syrian-American Jewish community numbering about 75,000) seem to indicate that the official Syrian estimate is exaggerated.

The American Syrian community has been known to be rather active with a number of political, cultural, and media institutions that were founded starting in the early years of the 20th century. These include the Syrian American Club with branches in Washington D.C and Houston Texas; the Association of Young Syrian-American Professionals (AYSAP); the Chicago based Syrian-American Relations Council, the Syrian Studies Association and the Syrian-American Cultural Council among others. These various groups address the question of "Who is a Syrian?" and, for example, the AYSAP Facebook page offers the following remarks in the section dedicated to membership:

80 See Singh, 2008.
81 See Kayal, 1973, p. 409.
82 See U.S Census, 2006.

and nightclubs thus establishing a morality police like the one found in Saudi Arabia. In May 1944, al-Gharra held violent protests against a charity ball held in Damascus where wives of the ruling elite were planning to attend unveiled. Demonstrators took to the streets carrying revolvers and knives, stoning cinemas that welcomed women and burning nightclubs. The riots were successfully tackled by the government, which eventually won the sympathy of the masses. But those events served as an omen of things to come.

From its foundation and until the Ba'ath takeover in 1963, the Syrian Muslim Brotherhood (or the Ikhwan) saw itself as a reformist social and political movement that sought to preserve the Islamic character of Syria. It stood for bringing about the application of Islamic law (*sharia*) through peaceful means, which also meant participation in parliamentary elections.[88]

After 1963 and following the rise of the secularist Ba'ath regime, the movement gradually became a fierce opponent to what it perceived as a secularist and corrupt regime. Secret cells of Islamic groups were formed, and a younger generation of leaders highly influenced by the writings of Sayyid Qutb (and later on by the Iranian Revolution), led the movement toward a strategy of full-blown struggle against the Ba'ath regime. This dynamic developed into a revolutionary organization seeking to overturn the Ba'ath regime and set up an Islamic state through armed struggle—a strategy that eventually led to a military revolt that was brutally crushed by loyal factions of the military in the city of Hama in 1982.[89] Since membership in the Brotherhood is punishable by death in Syria, members have concealed their traditional opposition activities, making them hard to track.[90]

Since then, the Brotherhood has ceased to be an active political force inside Syria with its leadership in exile in Western Europe. Nevertheless, it retained a support network in the country while transforming itself into a non-violent Sunni reform movement with a democratic Muslim agenda. Since its departure from Syria, the leadership of the Muslim Brotherhood has been largely based in London under the stewardship of Aleppo-born

88 See Altman, 2009, p. 24.
89 See Altman, 2009, p. 25, Moubayed, 2005, p. 3.
90 See WINEP, 2011, p. 4.

Sadr al-Din Ali al-Bayanuni, who was elected to office in 1996 and replaced by Mohammad Hekmat Walid in 2014.

While in exile, the movement worked on a strategy to create conditions that would enable its exiled leaders and activists to return to Syria and once again engage in Muslim Brotherhood activities. This strategy involved indirect contacts with the regime, which led to the release of several hundred Muslim Brotherhood members from jail by Bashar al-Assad shortly after assuming power, and within the context of the political openness he initiated. This openness ceased, however, when Bashar ended the "Damascus Spring."[91]

In 2006, following a meeting in Brussels, Bayanouni announced (to the surprise of many) that he was joining forces with former Syrian Vice President Abdel Halim Khaddam, who had formed the National Salvation Front together with a number of other liberals, Communists and Kurdish groups. This alliance was short lived and the Brotherhood withdrew from the Front in April 2009.[92] Within the country, Bayanouni's announcement created another split that was led by Issam al-Alatar, a Brotherhood leader from Damascus who called for a harder ideological line and rejected Bayanouni's efforts at engagement. This dynamic has caused a number of prominent brotherhood members such as Mohamed Farouk and Adel Fares to challenge Bayanouni's leadership. The Syrian Muslim Brotherhood has taken a central role in the wake of the Syrian uprising of 2011 and was visibly active in the waves of protests. The Muslim Brotherhood was also represented in the main gatherings of Syrian opposition parties beginning with the Antalya Conference. This was the first conference to organize Syria's political opposition. Molhem Droubi, a senior official, became a member of the conference's executive bureau that was held in May 2011. A month after the meeting in Antalya, the movement sent 200 activists to Brussels in an attempt to revitalize the Islamist block within the framework of the Syrian National Council. The Brotherhood subsequently organized several conferences that formed opposition groups to serve as fronts for the movement, allowing it to beef up its presence in political bodies. The Brotherhood continued the process of participation in conferences leading

91 See Altman, 2009, p. 24.
92 See Ashark Al-Awsat, 2009; Landis, 2009 (2).

to the establishment of the National Coalition for Syrian Revolutionary and Opposition Forces (NSC, later the National Syrian Coalition). This body emerged as a significant force within political circles and front groups created later on such as the National Union of Free Syria Students; the Independent Islamic Democratic Current, led by Ghassan Najjar; the Syrian Ulema League, the Civil Society Organizations' Union, and others.[93]

By the winter of 2011, the Brotherhood appeared to have greatly expanded its influence. It was not only strong within NSC circles but it also won support within the ranks of military defectors and the local coordination committees inside Syria. Aside from its political activity, the Brotherhood was able to provide material support as well as equipment, media and training to loyalists inside Syria. A number of units in the Free Syria Army, like the Tawhid and Farouq Brigades, Ansar al-Islam; Euphrates Shield; the Capital Shield, and the Aqsa Mosque Shield received significant direct funding support from the movement to form their military wings.[94]

This increased visibility triggered internal debates within the movement and its main political wings (known as the Hama and Aleppo factions). For example, some in the movement did not like the Brotherhood's position of backing an expansion of the National Coalition and supporting the reelection of its president, Ahmad al-Jarba, who was closely aligned with Saudi Arabia.[95] Other activists published a manifesto in January of 2014 challenging the leadership of the movement that "tends to ally with personalities and groups that seek a political settlement with the regime and that have strong ties to regional and international powers, while it reduces its interaction and work with those revolutionary forces that are working to overthrow the regime using all means."[96]

---

93 See Hassan, 2013, p. 2.

94 Ibid.

95 See Lefèvre, 2014; Weiss and Stuart, 2011, p. 18.

96 Statement by anonymous Muslim Brotherhood leaders posted on January 2014 <https://www.facebook.com/riaddrar/posts/337902093014536> and quoted in Lefèvre,2014.

The Radical Islamist Opposition

Radical Islamist movements operated in Syria before the more recent rise of ISIS and Jabhat al-Nusra. The groups known as *At-Tali`ah* (the Combatant Vanguard), a radical offshoot of the Syrian Muslim Brotherhood, has been active already since the 1960's and 1970's. In 1979, the Combatant Vanguard defected from the Brotherhood to take up arms against the regime. In the same year, they launched an attack in which 83 Alawite student officers were killed at the military artillery school in Aleppo. These events prompted President Hafez al-Assad to issue Law 49 in 1980, banning the Muslim Brotherhood and imposing the death penalty on its members.[97] Following the events in Hama and the massacre that followed, the Islamists and the Brotherhood became more withdrawn from political life in Syria, and their center of gravity shifted Europe. This situation has again changed in light of the Syrian uprising that has attracted many radical Islamists from Syrian exile and beyond. Like elsewhere in the Middle East, the relatively well-organized Islamist groups were able to utilize the weakening grasp of the Syrian government.

An additional trigger to the rise of Islamists in Syria came at the beginning of 2012 when the Syrian regime decided to release a group of radical activists including Abu Musab al-Suri, a well-known Al-Qaeda activist that was arrested by the CIA and handed to Syria in 2009.[98] Some of these political prisoners began to mobilize and joined existing structures such as:

1. ***Ahrar ash-Sham***, (the Islamic Movement of the Free Men of the Levant) that quickly became one of the strongest groups fighting Assad with over 10,000 men including a significant foreign fighter's contingency[99]. It serves as an umbrella organization of Sunni Islamist militants who are fighting the Assad while seeking to replace the regime with an Islamic government. The group was founded in late 2011 and it first emerged as a significant force on the Syrian battlefield in January 2012. Most of Ahrar al-Sham's founding members, including commander Hassan Aboud, were former political prisoners that the regime that released in

97 See Carnagie, Syria Resources, 2012, p. 1.
98 See O'Bagy, 2012, p. 15.
99 See ibid, p. 27.

the May 2011 amnesty deal in an attempt to placate religious protestors when the Arab Spring began to threaten regional governments.[100]

2. **Al-Nusra Front** (also known as *Jabhat al-Nusra or* the resistance front) was formed in late 2011, when the Emir of Al Qaeda in Iraq (AQI), Abu Bakr al-Baghdadi, dispatched Abu Muhammad al-Julani to Syria to organize jihadist cells in the region. Al-Nusra quickly rose to prominence among rebel organizations in Syria for its reliable supply of arms, funding, and fighters from a combination of foreign donors and AQI. Al-Nusra units are considered to be well-trained, professional, and relatively successful on the battlefield.[101]
3. **The Islamic State of Syria and Iraq (ISIS)** (*Jama'at al-Tawhid wa'l Jihad*) was formed by Abu Mus'ab al-Zarqawi in 2002 as a militant group in Jordan. Shortly afterwards, the group entered Northern Iraq, pledging allegiance to al-Qaeda and changing its name to al-Qaeda in Iraq (AQI) in October 2004. By 2010, Abu Bakr al-Baghdadi had taken control of AQI, and in 2014 al-Baghdadi announced that AQI had begun operations in Syria. Baghdadi said that AQI would soon merge with al-Nusra Front, changing its name to the Islamic State in Iraq and Syria (ISIS). Al-Qaeda leader, Ayman al-Zawahiri, publicly rebuffed al-Baghdadi's statement and ordered that the group limit its operations to Iraq. After al-Baghdadi spoke against al-Zawahiri's statement, al-Zawahiri renounced all official connection between ISIS and Al-Qaeda Central.[102] By the beginning of 2015, ISIS appeared to have established a semi-functioning state, controlling over a third of Syrian territory as well as significant territory in Iraq.[103]

The Kurdish Opposition

The Kurds are the largest of any minority group in Syria, representing 2.2 million people or close to 10% of the population. This number includes an estimated 250,000–300,000 Syrian Kurds who are denied official citizenship. Under Ba'ath Party leadership, the Kurds found themselves

100 See Stanford, 2015.
101 See Stanford, Mapping Militant Organization Project, ibid p. 31.
102 See Stanford, Mapping Militant Organization Project.
103 See Mek and Youseff, 2015.

consistently discriminated against. Their language was banned, their rights denied, and their lands confiscated.[104] In the late 1990's, inspired by the establishment of Kurdish autonomy in northern Iraq, roughly a dozen distinct Kurdish political factions began publicly organizing. Most agreed to a list of cultural demands (such as recognition of Kurdish as an official language, freedom to celebrate Kurdish holidays) and some, such as the Yakiti party, called for strong federal autonomy for Kurdish territory. This trend was further strengthened after 2000, when Syrian President Bashar al-Assad permitted Kurdish activists to operate more freely, easing the enforcement of restrictions on Kurdish linguistic and cultural expression (though he did not formally lift them). In August 2002, Assad made the first visit by a Syrian president to the Kurdish province in over 40 years, but this landmark visit did not lead to government concessions.

Kurdish political activists continued to be intimidated. Kurds were again denied freedoms of association and assembly, and a number of Kurdish forums and associations were again banned and closed.[105] The new crackdown led to an unprecedented wave of public demonstrations calling for cultural and linguistic rights, including a sit-in outside parliament in December 2002, which was quickly disbanded. Dozens of Kurdish activists were arrested over the following year, while the regime continued to step up its efforts to arm Arabs in the northern border region and to incite violence against Kurdish demonstrators.[106]

These dynamics along with developments in Iraq, where control over the Kurdish region was given to the Kurds, helped trigger the events of March 2004 when Syrian security forces opened fire on an unarmed Kurdish crowd chanting pro-Bush slogans at a soccer match in the northeast Kurdish city of Qamishli. This sparked eight days of Kurdish rioting, which ended with 40 people dead (33 Kurds and seven Arabs), hundreds injured, over 2,000 arrested, and hundreds of millions of dollars in property damage. Though the aftermath of the riots presented an opportunity for the regime to make concessions to the Kurds and split them off from the predominantly Arab opposition front, it failed to take advantage of this opportunity. The June 2005

104 See Badran, 2006; Lowe, 2006 p. 2; Ziada, 2009, p. 2.
105 See Gambil, 2004, Ziada, 2009, p. 4.
106 See Badran, 2006 p. 3.

Ba'ath Party conference not only failed to grant citizenship to stateless Kurds, but reiterated the ban on ethnic political parties, giving the fractious Kurdish groups common cause to join the secular Arab opposition's demand for regime change.[107] In March 2008, Syrian security forces opened fire on Kurds celebrating the Festival of Fire, killing at least three people and wounding others. The government completely ignored this event, failing even to launch a formal investigation.[108] Since the start of the Syrian uprising in mid-March 2011, young Kurds from Qamishli, Amouda and other Kurdish populated centers have been participating in anti-regime demonstrations. They raised the Kurdish flag next to the Syrian national flag and called for freedom, for the fall of the regime and the unity of the Syrian people while demanding national rights for the Kurds. Kurds have also been involved in the fighting with both Assad's government forces as well as with Islamist and other rebel forces over control of North and Northeast Syria.[109] Like the Islamist militant groups, the Kurds were unable to organize a united front against the Syrian regime. While some Islamist Kurds have risen to leadership roles in Islamist factions such as al-Nusra Front, the main Kurdish opposition group, PYD (Democratic Union Party), and its armed branch, YPG, have been battling al-Nusra Front and the Islamic State since 2012. Committees for the Protection of the Kurdish People expelled al-Nusra Front and ISIS members from the strategic town of Ras al-Ain in Hasaka province and also fought them in Northern Raqqa province in 2013. At the end of 2014, Syrian Kurds were once again on the front lines fighting the forces of the Islamic State in the battle for Kobane.

Kurdish Opposition Groups

Ever since the founding of the first Kurdish party, the Kurdistan Democratic Party in 1957, the movement has been plagued by divisions. The Kurdish opposition appears both active and fragmented, with over 20 active political parties in Syria and abroad.[110] There are four main coalitions that appear to embrace most of the parties, but even Kurdish political leaders seem

107 See Gambil, 2004 pp. 4–5; Badran, 2006 p. 5.
108 See Lowe, 2006, pp. 5–6.
109 See Sidki, 2014, p. 2.
110 See Badran, 2006, p. 3.

uncertain of these coalitions' names and compositions.[111] The continual divisions that undermine Kurdish opposition efforts are principally due to rivalries among its leaders, but they should also be viewed in the light of their differences of opinion over the question of whether Kurds should be independent or part of a federated Syria. This hinders the emergence of a unified platform, and of clear demands that would receive an international profile.[112] The four coalitions were as follows:

1. **The Kurdish Democratic Front** (*al-jabha*) led by Abdul Hamid Darwish, brings together three Kurdish parties.
2. **The Democratic Kurdish Alliance in Syria** (*attakhafuf*) unites four parties but has no leader.
3. A small alliance of three independent parties, *Yekiti* (united), *Azadi* (liberty), and the Movement of the Future under the Kurdish Popular Union Party in Syria
4. A fourth component that has distanced itself from the PKK (Workers Party of Kurdistan), and brings together the **Democratic Union Party** and the **Democratic Kurdistani Party.**

Other groups include the United Kurdish Democratic Party in Syria; the Kurdish Democratic Front in Syria; the Kurdish Democratic Party in Syria; and the Kurdish Future Movement in Syria.[113]

Several Syrian Kurdish groups became signatories of the Damascus Declaration signed on October 16, 2005, which called for the "complete equality of Syrian Kurdish citizens with the other citizens on the basis of the unity of the Syrian land and people."[114] However, three leading Kurdish groups (Yakiti, Azadi, and the Kurdish Future Movement) declined to join since the declaration implicitly rejected federalism and did not recognize a Kurdish national identity or national rights.[115] Kurdish groups participated in other coalitions as well, such as the Syrian Democratic Coalition of Farid

111 See Allsopp, 2014, p. 28.

112 See Badran, 2006, p. 5.

113 For more on the United Kurdish Democratic Party in Syria See <http://en.wikipedia.org/w/index.php?title=Kurdish_Freedom_Party&action=edit&redlink=1>

114 See Lowe, 2006, p. 4.

115 See Badran, 2006, p. 5.

Ghadry or the National Salvation Front. The last significant change for the Kurds occurred on July 19, 2012, when the depleting Syrian military was abruptly pulled out of the major Kurdish areas, leaving the Kurds with a chance for a new beginning. These changes have shifted Kurdish political dynamics once again and consolidated two major camps among the Kurds.

On one side stood the Party of Unity and Democracy (PYD), which collaborated with both the Bashar al-Assad regime and with the anti-Turkish, Kurdistan Workers Party (PKK). When the Syrian revolution first broke out in Deraa, a deal was struck between the leadership of the PKK (whose founding leader, Abdullah Öcalan, had been based in the Syrian capital Damascus until 1999) and the Syrian regime, in which the PKK pledged not to join the revolution in return for the regime allowing the party to operate freely in Kurdish areas.[116]

On the other side stood the Kurdish National Council of Syria (KNC), an amalgamation formed in October 2011 comprised of 15 local parties opposed to both Assad and the PKK.[117] The council comprised of both individuals and representatives from 10 established Kurdish groups, organized a conference to elect an executive committee and general secretariat. In its closing statement, the participating groups demanded both "the right to determine the destiny of the Kurdish people in the framework of a unified Syria," and "changing the security-based dictatorship and instituting a plural democratic state."[118] Subsequently, the Kurdish delegation withdrew from the Istanbul Conference (the effort to unify the Syrian opposition) after the Syrian National Council refused to include Kurdish demands in the conference's "National Pledge" document.[119]

Kurdish politics is also influenced by other actors such as Turkey, which shares a border with Syria and is home to half of the global Kurdish population. The Kurdistan Regional Government (KRG) is also located in Turkey, which serves as an inspiration to many Syrian Kurds seeking independence.

Other Minority Groups – In addition to the Kurds, there are also Assyrian (Christian) opposition groups that maintain some activity in Syria and

116 See Hasan, 2013, p. 4.
117 See Pollock, 2012, p. 2.
118 Ibid, p. 6.
119 Ibid, p. 7.

the diaspora. Though the small Christian minority is largely integrated and does not usually form Christian-only organizations, some activity exists among the Assyrian community, a non-Arab minority, which is organized under the German-based Assyrian Democratic Organization (Mtakasta) and the Assyrian Democratic Party (ADP). The ADP operates as an underground movement and is forbidden in Syria while the Asyrian Democratic Organization (ADO), founded in 1957, is its largest Assyrian organization. ADO strives to gain minority status to promote the Assyrians' own cultural heritage and language. The Syrian government generally tolerates this organization, although in a few instances (namely in 2004 and 2010) the Syrian security authorities banned the organization from marking the anniversary of an Iraqi government crackdown on Chaldean-Assyrians in Northern Iraq.[120]

"Old Guard" Opposition

A number of former officials and exiled members of the Assad administration have become engaged in opposition-related work. These include former officials in the Syrian regime and even members of the Assad family who, as a result of internal disputes, have found themselves in exile. Despite their rhetoric, which often appears moderate and liberal, their regime-related past and the complex relations they still maintain with Damascus, shed some doubts on their true "opposition standing."

Abdul Halim Khaddam and the National Salvation Front

On December 30, 2005, following six months of silence, Abdul Halim Khaddam in an interview with al Arabiya stated that the Syrian President had harshly threatened former Prime Minister Hariri before the assassination, and that the operation could not have been carried out by Syrian intelligence officials without his knowledge. This dramatic announcement, which was greeted with surprise by many in the opposition, led to the establishment of the National Salvation Front, an umbrella group of

120 Associated Press, 2004.

expat opposition leaders who have sought to offer an alternative to Bashar al-Assad's rule in Syria.[121]

Abdul Halim Khaddam, a Sunni Muslim, was born in the Northern Syrian seaport of Banias in 1932. He was a close high school friend of the late Hafez Assad, and became a member of the nationalist Ba'ath Party at age 17. He assumed a series of provincial governorships, being named Attorney General from 1968–69, and the Minister of Economy and Foreign Trade from 1969–1970. After Assad assumed the presidency in 1970, Khaddam was appointed Foreign Minister, which meant he was chiefly responsible for Syria's policy in Lebanon. In 1984 he was appointed to be one of Syria's three vice-presidents, but continued to carry out special diplomatic missions abroad. His power in Syria was weakened following the death of President Hafez al-Assad in June 2000. It was later rumored that Khaddam had voiced objections to other senior regime figures within hours of Hafez al-Assad'sdeath, and was sharply rebuked.[122] Bashar al-Assad, who began to assemble a new team of advisors loyal to him, sought to limit the influence of the old guard and assert his control as the new leader of Syria. Under the new Syrian President, Khaddam's influence was fading quickly and many of his allies including Gen. Ghazi Kanaan, were removed from power. Between 2000–2005 Khaddam continued to lose power and influence, and the assassination of his longtime friend and ally Rafiq Hariri in February 2005 made his future in Syria untenable. Khaddam found himself and his family under constant government surveillance.

At the opening session of the 10th Ba'ath party regional conference in June 2005, he delivered a lengthy speech criticizing Syria's foreign policy and the governments handling of foreign policy with Lebanon, which lead to a heated exchange with Foreign Minister Sharaa. He then stunned the more than 1,000 delegates in attendance by announcing his resignation from all government and party posts. He left for Paris shortly thereafter, and his family members followed soon afterwards.

Following his Al Arabiya interview, Khaddam established the National Salvation Front with offices in Belgium, France, Germany and the United States. Using his regional stature, Khaddam was able to assemble a significant

---

121 See Salhani, 2005; Gambil, 2006.

122 See Gambil, 2006.

group of partners. During a 2007 meeting in Berlin, there were reports that some 140 opposition figures were in attendance. His most significant alliance was with the Muslim Brotherhood in Syria and its exiled leader Bayanouni. This ended up being short lived and officially ended on April 6, 2009, following differences of opinion over the Brotherhood's support of Hamas. (oOther alliances and agreements with opposition figures, minority groups, and regional representatives were short-lived as well).[123] Supported by allies in Saudi Arabia and Lebanon, Khaddam was able to gather together a number of groups including Kurds and some liberal figures such as Ammar Abdulhamid of the Tharwa Foundation. However, internal disputes quickly led to the closing of the National Salvation Front's DC and Belgium offices in early 2009, and later led to the end of the alliance with the Muslim Brotherhood.

For a short while, starting on August 17, 2008, the NSF was able to open a TV channel, Zenobia, which aired from Brussels via EuroSat's Hotbird network. However, these broadcasts were often interrupted. Later on, the director of programming for the station, Bashar Elsbihi, found himself back in Syria following an "agreement" reached with the government.[124] Without the funding promised by the Saudis and the backing of Bayanouni, Khaddam was unable to fulfill many of the promises made to his allies, which caused the NSF to become far less active and relevant. As of the beginning of 2010, the NSF appeared to be dormant.

Rifaat al-Assad

Rifaat al-Assad, the younger brother of the late Syrian president Hafez al-Assad, was forced to leave Syria after a failed attempt to take over Damascus. Trying to take advantage of Hafez al-Assad's heart problems, which worsened at the end of 1983, Rifaat mobilized loyalist forces to advance toward Damascus while distributing posters and banners of the "new" leader of Syria. Using a large portion of the army, numbering over 50,000, he began asserting control in Damascus in an attempt to succeed his brother. Hafez al-Assad, who regained his strength as well as the loyalty of his

123 See Landis, 2009, p. 1.
124 See Landis, 2009b.

officers in early 1984, brought an end to this unsuccessful coup d'état. As a result, Rifaat was stripped of his power and influence, though officially he still carried the title of Vice President. His closest supporters, and others who had failed to prove their loyalty to Hafez, were purged from the army and the Ba'ath Party in the years that followed. In 1984, he was sent on "an open-ended working visit" abroad, and in April of 1988, Rifaat resigned all his official positions. He left Syria to spend most of his time in France and Spain. Rifaat was able to maintain ties inside Syria, including a significant business network and an active group of loyalists, but his tense relations with his brother continued to play a role, including a 1999 crackdown marked with armed clashes in Lattakia. This destroyed much of Rifaat's remaining network in Syria. This crackdown was thought to be connected to the issue of succession, since Rifaat had begun to position himself to succeed the ailing Hafez, who in turn wanted to eliminate all potential competition for his designated successor, his son Bashar al-Assad.

Positioning himself as an alternative voice, Rifaat protested the succession of Bashar and gave public statements about his plans to return to Syria. While he intended to rule benevolently and democratically, he would do so with "the power of the people and the army" behind him. While in Paris, he established the Arab News Network (ANN), an Arabic news satellite channel based in London that supported his political aspirations. The channel was managed by Samar al-Assad and (as of 2008) by Ribal al-Assad, who attempted to assume a position of leadership within the opposition. The station broadcast daily English news from November 2004 to March 2006, but since then it has been broadcasting solely in Arabic. Ribal al-Assad, who has continued with his attempts to pursue a position of leadership in the opposition, has also created the "Coalition for the Promotion of Democracy and Human Rights," which is based in the US.

Mustafa Tlas

Mustafa Tlass is a senior Syrian military officer and politician who was Syria's minister of defense from 1972 to 2004. Born in a Sunni Muslim family, he joined the military academy where he met Hafez al-Assad and later struck a lifelong friendship with him which helped in establishing him as a dominant military officer as well as an influential politician in later years. He was part of the four-member Regional Command during the Hafez al-Assad era and considered a close confident of the late president. Tlass helped the post-Assad transition and was a member of the committee formed to oversee the transition period; however, he was asked to leave his post as Minister of Defense in 2004 and in 2005 he left his last military position and published his two-volume memoir titled *Mirat Hayati* (Reflections of My Life). Mustafa left Syria in 2011, allegedly for medical treatment, but remained in France. His two sons, Firas and Manaf, have taken a more visible position with the opposition. Firas Tlass, a Syrian Tycoon announced in 2012 that he "pledged his fortune to the revolution" and to "build a democratic society in Syria."[125] Manaf Tlass, who was a confidant of Bashar al-Assad's, a member of the central committee of the Ba'ath Party, and a one-star general in the Republican Guards likewise defected in May of 2012.[126] The family increased its activity in opposition circles and Manaf's name is mentioned as a man who could have a possible role in a Syrian transition.

"Newcomers"

1. The Reform Party of Syria (Hizb al-Islah al Suri)

The Reform Party of Syria (RPS) is a US-based opposition party that emerged in 2002 as a result of the attacks on September 11, 2001. The party defines itself as being governed by "secular, peace-committed American-Syrians, Euro-Syrians, and native Syrians who are determined to see a New Syria which embraces real democratic and economic reforms."[127] Farid Ghadry, the founder of the party, is a Syrian-American businessman who left Syria at a young age and spent most of his life in the United States. From its inception, the RPS adopted a secular, pro-Western line, calling for strong American intervention in order to help change the regime in Damascus. It has worked to promote the Syria Accountability Act, and supported US candidates such as Rep. Elliot Engel and Iliana Ross-Lehtinen, who have

---

125 See Sherlock, 2012.
126 See Landes, July 5th, 2012.
127 From party web site.

advocated for a stronger American policy against Assad's regime.[128] In the following year, Farid and a Kurdish colleague traveled to Israel, where Farid spoke at the Knesset as a guest of the Foreign Affairs and Defense Committee.[129]

In 2003 the RPS created the Syrian Democratic Coalition (SDC), which was comprised of 7–8 Syrian and Kurdish groups including the Syrian Democratic National Gathering (SDNG), a political organization formed in 1986 in Syria, led by Marwan Hammoud; the Solidarity Council, a Kurdish organization whose leadership is inside Syria; the Kurdish Yakiti party; and the Assyrian Movement. A number of other parties in the SDC chose to stay anonymous. The coalition remained active until 2006, when it disappeared due to lack of activity and disagreement amongst its members.

In March of 2009, Farid Ghadry resigned as president of the RPS without announcing a successor. The party continues to maintain an active web site, but little else in the way of activity was being pursued until the beginning of the "Syrian Spring." During the uprising, Farid kept up with his writing and speaking activities, but without any mention of political aspirations. His role, like those of other expat groups, became even more marginal facing the growing presence of opposition from within.

2. *Movement for Justice and Development in Syria (Haraqat al-Adala wal-Bina'a fi Syria)*

The Movement for Justice and Development was established in London in 2006 as an expat movement modeled after the Turkish AKP. Its claimed mandate was the expat representation of the Damascus Declaration process. In a 2004 interview at the Turkish newspaper *Hurriyet*, the movement's founder, Damascus-born Anas al-Abdah, said that its leaders have "studied" AKP press releases, reports, and publications in order to help mold their own party, formed in late 2004, but which due to political circumstances was not announced until the middle of 2006. Al-Abdah, spoke about a "democratic Islamic path," or a "third path," which would represent the new face of the Syrian opposition. The movement gained traction in

128 See Landis, 2006.
129 See Meranda, 2007.

2008–9 and was able to initiate a good number of activities in Europe and the US, including a TV station (Barada TV), which operates from the UK. The channel attracted some attention following a phone interview given by lawyer and activist Haytham al-Maleh from Damascus on October 12, 2009, focusing on the tightening grip of the country's security and intelligence forces as well as the recent clampdown on dissidents. Al-Maleh was arrested two days later. Soon after, Barada's TV station, just like many other satellite channels, was blocked by the Syrian government and ran out of money in February of 2010. Al-Abdah's deputy, Ossma Monajed, resigned in March 2010 after publicly criticizing the leadership of the movement. Nevertheless, the station continued to broadcast as of November 2010.

3. *Damascus Declaration in Exile*

Since its publication on 16 October 2005, the "Damascus Declaration for Democratic National Change" has become the most significant voice of the Syrian opposition inside the country. In response to this clear call for political change, the Syrian regime has arbitrarily detained hundreds of political and human rights activists in an attempt to silence the growing support for the declaration. A few of its original signatories were able to leave Syria and continue their work from abroad, while other activists have adopted the declaration for their own purposes. With the opposition's leadership behind bars, it's difficult to speak of a real "representative structure" but a National Council comprised of 250 leading opposition members who represented local constituencies was formed and continues to function by relying on those members who are free to speak and communicate. A number of committees affiliated with the Damascus Declaration were established in Europe and the US. Active committees exist in Canada, the US, France, the UK, Spain, Belgium, Holland and Germany. These committees are meant to support the work of the National Council, but disputes over leadership and strategy have developed, and the coordination between domestic and exile committees does not appear to work well.[130]

---

130 See interviews, Bitar, Abdulhamid.

4. *Alentefah Party*

Dr. Hasem Sultan, a Syrian physician who resides in Miami, Florida, established the Alentefah Party in 2005. According to its founder, the party was born as a "response to the ever-growing deterioration of Syria's living conditions, its political and economic isolation, and the inclination of driving Syria's future into an endless labyrinth." It is a secular party that consists of a few hundred members. One of its key people was previously mentioned Bashar Elsbihi, who managed Zenobia TV for a short while and ended up returning to Syria where he began to work for the regime.[131] The party appears dormant since 2010.

5. *The Syrian National Council (US)*

The Syrian National Council (US) is an umbrella group of US-based dissidents that was established in 2005 by Mohammed Khawam and Hussam al-Dairi.

The Washington-based council seeks to "coordinate with opposition groups inside and outside Syria to promote democratic change in the country."[132] Najib al-Ghadban, Hussam al-Dairi, Mohammed al-Khawam, Iyass al-Maleh and Abd al-Muhaymen al-Sibai were selected as members of its executive committee. The council was announced following a conference that brought 30 US-based Syrians to Washington in June 2005, and sought to position itself as an umbrella group rather than a political party. The SNC's activities consisted of holding meetings between different opposition activists, working on human rights and democracy campaigns, and organizing US-based activities for the opposition. The group continued the annual meeting of activists, and similar meetings took place in 2007. Just like the rest, this coalition also saw its own share of internal divisions: Mohammed al-Jbaili, a former speaker of the party, and Farid Ghadry the president of the Reform Party of Syria, were not invited to the 2007 meeting because of their position that stated the inclusion of other Ba'athist activists in the coalition structure. Following the meeting, a decision to ally with the National Salvation Front caused another split among the remaining group members. No activity was listed after June 2007.

---

131 See Landis, 2009b.

132 Taken from organizational brochure.

New Structures of the Syrian Opposition

The Syrian wave of protests that began in January 2011 have mobilized the ranks of the Syrian opposition and quickly altered dynamics among new groups, new players, and a number of new umbrella groups that were established in order to coordinate the work of the opposition at large. These new structures are forming and changing as I write while events continue to unfold. In August 2011, the Washington Institute for Near East Policy produced a working model for the Syrian opposition with 12 key players. As noted in Chart 3.1, many of these new players have little to do with old oppositional structures (although some of the opposition leaders have found their personal place within these new structures). Some of the newer groups include:

1. Local Coordination Committees (LCC)

This is a grassroots activist organization with chapters throughout Syria. It is considered to be the main united force engaged in planning nationwide protests. As the uprising began, local committees were formed in various cities and villages to organize protests. These committees then joined to coordinate protests and issue public statements. The LCC is composed of committees in Deraa, Homs, Banias, Saraqeb, Idlib, Hasaka, Qamishli, Deir Ez Zour, Hama, Raqqa, Swaydda, Damascus, the Damascus suburbs, and on the Syrian coast. The LCC has put forth a political vision that has garnered public acceptance by the leading opposition activist Burhan Ghalioun (who was later elected as president of the Syrian National Council) and the Committee of Kurdish Youth. This vision calls for a national conference to lead the transition to a democratic and pluralistic state, with a transitional period lasting no longer than six months. The transitional council, according to the LCC, would implement reforms and would be made up of military personnel and civilians. Omar Idlibi serves as one of the LCC's spokesmen inside Syria. The LCC boycotted the June 27 "Syria for All" Conference (see below).

2. Union for the Coordination of the Syrian Revolt (UCSR)

Not much is known about this organization, but it serves the same primary function as the LCC. The USCR also denounced the "Syria for All"

Conference, and publicly announced its refusal to negotiate with the regime. Some UCSR members feel that the LCC "hijacked" the revolution that they themselves launched.

3. Conference for Change in Syria (Antalya Gathering)

This conference was held May 31-June 2, 2011 in Antalya, Turkey and was titled, The Syria Conference for Change. Its stated goals were to create a support group to lobby internationally on behalf of the Syrian revolution as well as for the ouster of President Bashar al-Assad and the dismantling of his regime. The conference was attended by dissidents of various political backgrounds and included Kurdish, Muslim Brotherhood, Assyrian, and tribal representatives. A 31 member consultative council was elected, as well as a full-time, nine-member executive council. The conference's final statement called for "President Bashar al-Assad to resign immediately from all of his duties" and to hand over power to Syrian Vice President Farouk al-Sharaa until the election of a transitional council that would draft a new constitution and oversee Parliamentary and Presidential elections "within a period not to exceed one year."[133] Controversy surrounded the sparse Kurdish representation at the conference, which consisted, according to one source, of a single figure, Muhammad Ammo of the Kurdish Future Party. However, as seen on Chart 3.1, two individuals from the independent Kurdish community were elected to the conference's consultative council.[134] Like other similar platforms, the group ended up existing as a loose alliance between activists who have found their place within more established structures.

4. National Initiative for Change

This group identified itself on April 29, 2011 about six weeks after the revolution began. It sought to keep the identity of most of its members secret, but provided some names to The *New York Times*. The group claimed that its 150 members in Syria "represent a broad spectrum of groups opposing...Bashar al-Assad" and also include "most of Syria's diverse ethnic

133 See WINEP, 2011.

134 See WINEP, 2011, Weiss and Stuart, 2011, p. 18.

and religious communities."[135] The group identifies the military as the only force within Syria that would be capable of leading the transition to a democratic system. Some leading members of the coalition who have been named are Radwan Ziadeh, a signatory to the Damascus Declaration and Najib Ghadbian, who is on the consultative council of the Antalya Gathering (see above). Khawla Yusuf is another leading member of the group who is on the executive committee of the Antalya Gathering and the wife of Ammar Abdulhamid of the Thawra Foundation. Ausama Monajed one of the organizers of the National Coalition to Support the Syrian Revolution Conference, in Brussels was another leading member of the National Initiative for Change. Like other similar platforms, the group ended up existing as a lose alliance between activists who have found their place within more established structures.[136]

5. National Coordination Body for Democratic Change

This entity was formed on June 30, 2011 and it is led by Hassan Abdel Azim, the Secretary-General of the Democratic Arab Socialist Union and spokesman for the National Democratic Gathering. Members reportedly included individuals from leading opposition groups and six Kurdish organizations, as well as individuals such as Michel Kilo, Haytham al-Maleh, Burhan Ghalioun (who later emerged as the head of the Syrian National Coalition), and Rami Abdel Rahman. The body supports "overall national dialogue" to solve the Syrian crisis; it called for the release of political detainees, and the formation of a new constitution that excludes Article 8, which stipulates that the Ba'ath Party is Syria's ruling party. It declined to participate in the Syrian regime's national dialogue meeting, which was held on July 10, 2011.

6. National Movement of Kurdish Parties

This twelve-party coalition led the boycott of the Antalya Gathering. Comprised of the General Council of the Democratic Alliance in Syria, the Kurdish Political Council, and the Democratic Union of Syria (the Yekiti

135 See Winap, 2011.
136 See Landas, 2011.

Party), the group launched its own initiative on May 15, 2011. It aligned itself with the National Democratic Movement and demanded an end to discrimination against the Kurdish people. After being asked by the Assad regime to engage in dialogue, the coalition ultimately refused on June 8, citing regime-initiated violence against the Syrian population. The coalition did, however, call for a national conference as a platform for dialogue between all opposition parties and the regime.

7. *National Council for the Revolution*

On June 19, 2011, before President Assad made his second speech to the Syrian people, the National Council publicly announced its existence in a village near the Syrian-Turkish border. Spokesman Jamil Saib identified the group as consisting of "all communities and representatives," both inside and outside Syria, who support the revolution. Correspondingly, the group called on protestors around the country to work to bring about the fall of the regime. Notable members include Abdullah Trad al-Moulahim, Haytham al-Maleh, Suhair al-Atassi, Aref Dalila, Sheikh Khaled al-Khalaf, and Mamoun al-Homsi. Since its formation, the National Council has made no announcements, and taken no public actions.

8. *The Cordova Group*

The Cordova group was established in 2012 by Mohammad Barmo, a former member of Syrian parliament that left Syria at the beginning of the uprising. The Cordova group was able to gather members of various moderate groups including representatives from the National Coalition, the Syrian National Council, the National Development Party, minority and ethnic groups, think tanks and civil society movements. Since 2012, the group convened ten conferences while creating one of the more active Syrian civil networks. Unlike other groups that were quick to disappear, the Cordova group increased its presence in various Syrian political circles, and by the end of 2014 it had established itself as one of the most active opposition networks.[137]

---

137 The author attended a number of Cordova events and interviewed a number of its members.

9. *Regional Sheikhs*

A number of sheikhs have emerged as leading local opposition figures. One of these, Imam Sheikh Anas el-Airout, was a preacher at the main Rahman mosque in Banias before Syrian security forces arrested him in early May 2011. El-Airout had addressed groups of two to three thousand protestors, during which time he emphasized the importance of peaceful protests. Another notable local figure is Imam Sheikh Ahmad Sayasna of the Omari mosque in Deraa, who is currently in hiding. In an interview, Sayasna, who is blind, complained of the regime's neglect of Deraa's needs. Security forces raided his home on April 30, 2011 searching for him, and killed his son. A third leader, Sheikh Muadh Raihan, was based in Hama and as of May 19th had been missing for three weeks. In Deir Ez Zour, Sheikh Nawaf al-Bashir, a member of the Secretariat General Head Office of the Damascus Declaration, has frequently spoken out against the regime's violence and has accused Hezbollah of attacking protestors during the demonstrations.[138]

Chart 3.1: Working Model of the Syrian Opposition

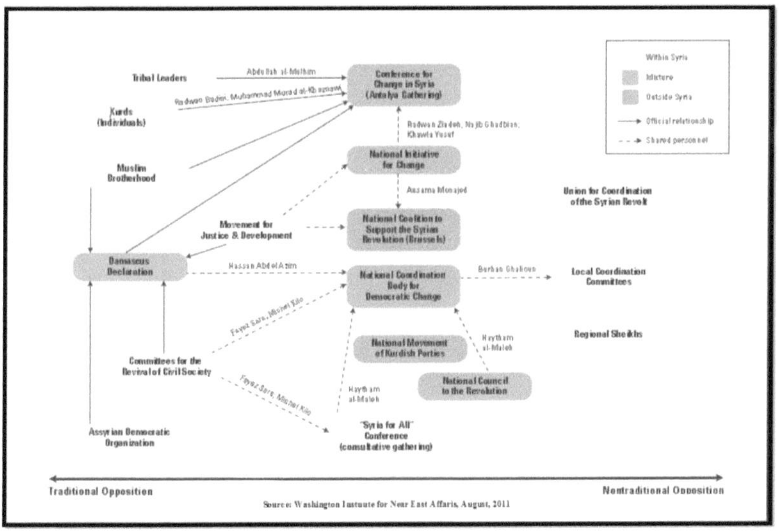

Source: Washington Institute for Near East Affairs, August, 2011

---

138 See WINEP, 2011, Weiss and Stuart, 2011, p. 18.

3.8 The Iranian Diaspora

The size of the Iranian diaspora is estimated at somewhere between 3 and 4 million, with large centers in the US, Europe and the Persian Gulf. Despite its size, its visibility and its importance with increasing global attention directed towards Iran, it has not been studied or mapped in great detail. The phenomenon of diaspora in Iran is itself relatively new. Sohamanesh notes that with the exception of sporadic ancient migrations caused by Alexander Macedon's invasion of Persia in 331 BCE, the Arab conquest of 633 CE and the Mongol devastations which commenced in 1219, Iranians have had until recent times little cause to leave their country en masse. Nevertheless, Iran did experience some early waves of immigration following the Arab conquest in 936 CE. Zoroastrians, whose faith was threatened, fled to western India. Also, in the mid-19th century shortly after the founding of Bahai'ism, followers of that faith sought refuge in the Ottoman Empire because of persecution in Iran. In the later part of the 19th century and the early 20th, high-profile Iranian intellectuals left the country due to their agitation with political changes during the period leading up to Iran's Constitutional Revolution from 1905–1911.[139]

It was the establishment of the Islamic Republic, and Iraq's invasion of Iran less than a year later (in 1980), that created the first significant wave of modern immigration out of Iran. Unlike previous waves, these new exiles came from all classes of pre-revolutionary Iranian society. Secularists and liberals, communists, opposition groups and ordinary Iranians feared the changing face of Iran that now included restrictions on civil rights, gender inequality, hijab laws, and similar edicts issued by the new government, led by Khomeini. The exiles also included many representatives of Iran's intellectual and economic elite.

Hakimzadeh describes three modern immigration waves beginning in the 1950's:

The First Wave: 1950–1979

The first modern immigration wave, which began in 1950 and lasted until the 1979 Islamic Revolution, was triggered by Iran's slow economic recovery and the resumption of oil production after World War II.

139 See Introduction in Hakimzadeh, 2006, Sohamanesh, 2009.

Revenue from oil exports permitted a relatively sudden change in Iranian society from traditionalism to modernization, motivating middle and upper-class families to send their children abroad for higher education as a means of ensuring their socioeconomic security and giving them political access upon their return. In the 1977–1978 academic year, about 100,000 Iranians were studying abroad, of whom 36,220 were enrolled in US institutions of higher learning; the rest were mainly in the United Kingdom, West Germany, France, Austria, and Italy. In the 1978–1979 academic year, the number of Iranian students enrolled in the United States totaled 45,340, peaking at 51,310 in 1979–1980. According to the Institute of International Education, more Iranian students were studying in the United States at that time than students from any other country. Many of these foreign students opted to stay in the West, while many of their relatives attempted to join them. Also included in this first period were families who were closely associated with the monarchy as members of the government, military personnel, or bankers. These royalist sympathizers fled during the early stages of the revolution, often with significant liquidated assets in hand. Finally, members of religious minorities such as the Baha'is, and ethnic-religious groups such as Jews, Armenians, and Assyrians, chose to flee in this initial phase. Anticipating persecution, a disproportionate number of these marginalized populations left as soon as cracks appeared in the Pahlavi regime.

The Second Wave, 1979–1995

Following the revolution, a larger second wave began. Socialist and liberal elements were the first to leave, followed by young men who fled military service, and as a result the Iran-Iraq War. Young women and families followed, escaping overly confining gender restrictions. Having a daughter was a decisive factor in a family's decision to flee since the post-revolution era forced women to wear the hijab, offered fewer educational possibilities, and enforced obedience to male kin. Because the second wave included large numbers of professionals, entrepreneurs, and academics, it accelerated the country's "brain drain."

According to Iran's Ministry of Culture and Higher Education, just before the revolution and the subsequent closure of all the universities in

1980, there were 16,222 professors teaching in Iran's institutions of higher education. When the universities reopened in 1982 this figure had plummeted to 9,042.[140] Similarly, the *Iran Times* estimated that 5,000 physicians and dentists (about a third of the total) left after the revolution. In addition to this reduction of manpower, studies estimate that the flight of capital from Iran shortly before and after the revolution was in the range of $30 to $40 billion.[141]

It' is important to note that many members of both the first and second emigration waves did not consider their departure permanent. On the contrary, many merely locked up their homes and packed a few suitcases because they viewed leaving as a temporary departure from their lives back in Iran, which they thought would resume when the revolutionary government was overturned. Sohamanesh describes an abrupt exodus, with thousands leaving their possessions and properties behind, thinking that they would be gone only temporarily and not imagining that they would never return. Many had their life-long savings and real estate confiscated by the Iranian authorities, and others fled out of fear of having to undergo military service and being sent to their deaths in the eight-year war with Iraq. For most of them, the likelihood of a permanent return has grown increasingly unlikely.[142]

Third Wave, 1995-Present

Finally, a more recent third wave of emigration has surfaced over the last two decades, roughly from 1995 to the present. This wave consists of two very distinct populations: on the one hand there were the highly skilled individuals who left universities and research institutions in a continuation of a previous trend. On the other hand there were working-class migrant laborers and economic refugees, who commonly have lower education levels and less-transferable skills than previous emigrants. This wave was also characterized by a significant number of asylum seekers, refugees and internally-displaced persons, totaling over 100,000 to date, who have

140 See Hakimzadeh, 2006, p. 2.
141 See Hakimzadeh, 2006, p. 3.
142 See Sohamanesh, 2009, p. 5.

fled Iran on account of the government's poor human rights record and its crackdowns on political dissidents.[143] In the year 2000 alone, Iranians submitted 34,343 asylum applications, the highest rate since 1986. Unlike the two previous waves, this one was caused by Iran's economic crisis, its deteriorating human rights record, diminishing opportunities, and the enduring tensions between reformist and conservative factions.[144]

At the end of 2005, the United Nations High Commissioner for Refugees (UNHCR) estimated that there were 111,684 refugees, asylum seekers, internally displaced persons (IDPs) and other persons of concern from Iran. The countries hosting the largest populations of Iranian refugees were Germany (39,904), the United States (20,541), Iraq (9,500), the United Kingdom (8,044), yhe Netherlands (6,597) and Canada (6,508).[145] In 2004, Iran ranked tenth among the countries of origin of asylum-seekers across Europe. In the year 2000, 55% of all Iranian asylum applications were submitted in Western European countries, including the United Kingdom, Germany, Belgium, Austria, and the Netherlands.[146] In 2001 alone there was a 300% increase in the number of Iranians seeking asylum in Britain. Furthermore, in 2004 Iranians were the most common asylum seekers in the UK, accounting for 10% of all applications. Preliminary observations suggest that these recent migrants often come from smaller provinces outside of Tehran, and that they face greater obstacles to integration in their host societies, especially in comparison to the relative successes of their more urban predecessors in those same countries.[147] Given that countries of the European Union have made it difficult to obtain asylum, Iranians who are not recognized as refugees will often go to another country, remain illegally in the country where they applied, or return to Iran.[148]

---

143 See Sohamanesh, 2009, p. 6.
144 See ibid.
145 See Hakimzadeh, 2006, p. 3.
146 See Table 3.1.
147 See Hakimzadeh and Dixon, 2006, p. 3.
148 See Hakimzadeh, 2006, p. 4.

Table 3.1: Iranian Asylum Applications, 1995 to 2004

	1995	1996	1997	1998	1999	2000	2001	2002	2003	2004	Total
Germany	4,314	5,264	4,490	552,9	3,407	4,878	3,455	2,642	2,049	1,374	34,828
Turkey	936	1,454	1,654	1,979	3,843	3,860	3,385	2,505	3,092	—	22,708
United-Kingdom	520	615	585	745	1,320	5,610	3,415	2,630	2,874	3,976	22,290
Nether-lands	6,075	2,698	1,521	1,679	1,527	2,543	1,519	663	555	450	19,230
Austria	485	656	502	950	3,343	2,559	734	760	979	347	11,315
Canada	1,901	1,728	1,210	880	794	767	768	381	329	342	9,100
United States	498	468	811	746	778	870	944	880	503	421	6,919

Source: Governments, UNHCR. Compiled by: UNHCR, Population Data Unit.
Note: Only includes industrialized asylum countries (Hakimzadeh, 2006, p. 4).

The Spread of the Iranian Diaspora

Today, the largest concentrations of Iranians living abroad can be found in five regions, the Middle East, Europe and North America. The US hosts over a million Iranians, the largest Iranian emigré population in the world. The United Arab Emirates, which is a convenient hub for Iranian business and tourism because of its proximity to Iran, hosts some 400,000 Iranians. Canada is third with 120,000 Iranians (Toronto is affectionately called "Tehranto" by some Iranian-Canadians), followed by Qatar and Germany, with numbers fast approaching 100,000 each. Other countries with large concentrations include Sweden, with approximately 54,000; the UK with about 43,000 Iranian exiles; and Israel, home to 48,000 Persian Jews.[149] Table 3.1 provides some additional numbers for Iranian communities in the diaspora, though it should be noted that these numbers should be treated as estimates since no reliable studies exist to date.

Notwithstanding the hardships of immigration and the thousands of harrowing accounts of the struggles that followed it, the story of the Iranian diaspora is one of success and achievement. Today, Iranians are a successful immigrant group with accomplished engineers, healthcare practitioners,

149 See Sohamanesh, 2009, p. 6.

artists and entertainers as well as journalists, scientists, academics, business owners and entrepreneurs. Iranian exiles have been quick to embrace the hospitality of their adopted nations and have, in a relatively short span of time, achieved the ability to give in return as productive citizens.

The Iranian Community in the US

In the US, where more accurate census data exists, it appears that approximately 330,000 Iranians arrived between 1978 and 2006. Interestingly, the majority of Iranian immigrants were members of religious and ethnic minorities, such as Baha'is.[150] Other studies using alternative statistical methods have estimated the actual number of Iranian Americans in the range of 691,000 to 1.2 million.[151] From 1980 to 2004, more than one out of four Iranian immigrants was a refugee or asylee.[152] Nevertheless, the profile of these political refugees was different than that of other such groups from Middle Eastern or African countries in terms of their level of education, motivation and employability. Iranian Americans seem to feel integrated and increasingly secure in the United States.[153] According to a study published by the Iranian Studies Group at MIT, apart from occupying senior leadership positions at many of the Fortune 500 companies, Iranian-Americans are teaching in a wide array of disciplines as tenured professors in elite American universities, such as Berkeley, MIT, Harvard, Yale, Princeton, Stanford and Columbia, to name but a handful. This trend largely repeats itself in every country inhabited by a critical mass of diaspora Iranians.[154] The Iranian-American community also appears to be doing well in economic terms. By 2006 estimates, Iranian expatriates were worth a net US $1.3 trillion.[155] By the year 2000, diaspora Iranians had invested close to $400 billion outside of their country, albeit with very little investment in Iran itself. These figures are much higher today and it is estimated that the flight of human capital costs Iran about $38 billion annually. The exodus of

150 See Hakimzadeh and Dixon, 2006.
151 See Hakimzadeh, 2006.
152 See Hakimzadeh and Dixon, 2006.
153 See PAAIA Survey (2015), p. 2.
154 See Sohamanesh, 2009, p. 5.
155 Ibid.

brainpower and capital currently continues, and will likely only increase in view of recent government purges and the suppression of voices of dissent.

The American-Iranian diaspora appears to maintain a high level of involvement with events taking place in the home country. Most Iranian Americans (more than 8 in 10) have close family still in Iran, with one-third having parents in Iran and more than one-half having siblings there. While most Iranian-Americans do not travel to Iran to visit family, they do remain in close contact, with 6 in 10 reporting that they communicate with family and friends in Iran at least several times each month.[156]

Iranian-Americans have established a large network of non-governmental organizations, charities, and other non-politically aligned entities charged with countering the social ills of Iranian society (such as poverty, narcotic addiction, gender inequality, human rights abuses, and discrimination), promoting civil society in Iran, encouraging the sharing of expertise between Iranian professional bodies and academic institutions, supporting Iranian arts, and assisting in the development of the Iranian tourist industry. Iranian Americans have been visible and active in the debate about Iran's nuclear deal and the removal of sanctions. More than two-thirds report that economic sanctions imposed on Iran have had a significant impact on their family and friends in Iran.[157] A poll taken during the week of the congressional vote found that 60% of Iranian Americans support the deal but also that 81% support a political change in Iran with 63% supporting a regime change that will make Iran a secular democracy. At the same time, the survey found that over 70% of Iranian Americans were not familiar with the main Iranian American national groups such as Iranian American Council (NIAC), The Public Affairs Alliance of Iranian Americans (PAAIA), and the Organization of Iranian American Communities (OIAC).[158] This finding may coincide with the lack of communal approach demonstrated by Iranians at large.

---

156 See PAAIA survey (2015) p. 1.

157 Ibid.

158 See Emmerson survey, 2015. pp. 3–8.

Other Iranian Diasporas

Aside from the US, Iranian communities have been established throughout the world with large centers in the Gulf, Turkey and Europe. Table 3.2 provides additional country estimates for these diasporas:

Table 3.2: Persian Diaspora (Estimates)

Australia	22,500*****
Austria	15,000*
Belgium	6,000*
Canada	400,000***
China	10,000*
Cyprus	2,000*
Denmark	10,000*
Eastern Europe	50,000*
Egypt & North Africa	20,000*
Finland	2,000*
France	62,000*
Germany	110,000*
Greece	20,000*
India	60,000*
Iraq	250,000*
Israel	50,000*
Kuwait	20,000*
Lebanon	50,000*
Norway	6,000*
Pakistan	40,000*
Philippines, Korea & Japan	50,000*
Russia & Other Former Soviet Union Countries	50,000*
South Africa	5,000*
Spain & Portugal	15,000*
Sweden	15,000*
Switzerland	43,000***

Syria	50,000*
The Netherlands	31,667 **
The Commonwealth of Independent States (CIS)	50,000*
Turkey	800,000*
United Arab Emirates & Bahrain	400,000***
United Kingdom	67,000***, ****
United States of America	1,560,000*
Qatar	100,000***
Central & South America & Other Parts of The World	100,000*
Total:	4,542,167

Sources: *Iranian Christian International, 1996, ** Netherland Central bureau of Statistics, Den Haag/Heerlen, 2010, *** Sohamanesh, 2009, United Kingdom, Office of National Statistics, 2008 Estimates. *****, Australian National census, 2006

3.9 Iranian Opposition Groups

The Iranian expat community is composed of a large international network of political groups and organizations. It has always been divided from within despite the disproportionately large number of organizations and groups that have similar political visions for their homeland.

The Monarchists

Several monarchist political parties support the restoration of a royalist regime in Iran. With varying degrees of enthusiasm, the monarchists believe that Reza Cyrus Pahlavi, born in 1960 and the eldest son of the last shah and former crowned prince, is the legitimate heir to the throne. In 1980, following the death of his father, Pahlavi proclaimed his willingness to serve as Shah Reza II pending acceptance by the Iranian people. Pahlavi later announced his desire to reign as a constitutional monarch in a role similar to that of the King of Spain.

In the 1980s, the most active monarchist group was the Paris-based National Resistance Movement of Iran under the leadership of Shahpour Bakhtiar, the last royalist Prime Minister. The National Resistance Movement's official position was to restore the 1906 constitution to the form intended by its original drafters, with a "reigning shah" in contrast to a "ruling shah." In 1983, Bakhtiar's group joined forces with the Iran Liberation Front, another Paris-based party led by elder statesman and former royalist Prime Minister, Ali Amini. This short-lived union dissolved after Amini's death in 1992. After Amini's death, the National Resistance Movement became the largest royalist movement. However, by the end of the decade and after the assassination of Bakhtiar in 1991, it too dissolved.

Other monarchist groups, such as the Azadegan and the Constitutionalist Party of Iran (liberal democrat), advocate for the restoration of the constitutional monarchy while endorsing the Pahlavi dynasty. Currently, the Constitutionalist Party of Iran remains the most active monarchist group with an affiliated television station and organized branches in North America, Europe, and the Middle East. Other Monarchist parties include the Iran Democratic Union (IDU) and Rastakhiz: The Imperial Iranian Guards.

These monarchist groups continue activities both inside and outside Iran. Even before the 2009 protests, a number of pro-monarchist demonstrations have been dispersed by tear gas and violence. The UN has further reported Iranian police activities including arrests and imprisonment of monarchist activists as well as attempts to remove satellite dishes to disrupt the pro-monarchist broadcasts from Los Angeles.[159]

Republicans

A significant number of Iranian groups advocate for a new republican or constitutional political structure to replace the old monarchy. Among others, these groups include the Democratic and Secular Republicans of Iran, the Jomhouri, the Jomhourikhahan Melli, the Green Party, Marz-e Porgohar, United Iranian Front for Democracy in Iran, and the United Republicans of Iran (URI).

Democratic and Minority Parties

There are also several pro-democracy parties that support a republican form of government. These groups include the National Democratic Front and the Kurdish Democratic Party of Iran (KDP), which also espouses

159 See UNHCR, 2002.

various forms of socialism. Both the National Front and the National Democratic Front of Hedayatollah Matin-Daftari are headquartered in Paris. Neither the National Front nor the National Democratic Front has engaged in significant political activity since 1982. In contrast, the KDP, which has advocated political and cultural rights for the Kurdish ethnic minority within a federally organized government, has been fighting against the Islamic Republic since 1979. By the beginning of 1986 however, KDP forces had been driven out of Iranian Kurdistan, though they continued their political work and, at times, their military struggle until Pejak, the Party of Free Life of Kurdistan (which is linked to the PKK), adopted a more militant conduct and took the lead on the militant Kurdish struggle. According to the KDP, on July 13, 1989, during negotiations with envoys of the Iranian regime for a peaceful solution to the Kurdish issue in Iran, Abdul Rahman Ghassemlou, the Secretary General of the KDP, along with two of his colleagues, were assassinated in Vienna. Ghassemlou's successor, Sadegh Sharafkandi, was also assassinated on September 17, 1992, in Berlin along with other opposition leaders at the Mykonos Greek restaurant.

Islamic Groups

Without a discernable political structure behind their movements, many prominent Muslim leaders have expressed significant criticism of the Islamic Revolution (*velayet-e faqih*). This includes voices from the senior echelons of the Iranian clergy such as Grand Ayatollah Hosein Ali Montazeri, who lost his post as successor to Khomeini due to his criticism of Khomeini's human rights and treatment of political dissidents. Montazeri was put on house arrest but nevertheless remained a vocal critic of the regime until his death in 2009. His funeral turned into one of the largest anti-regime demonstrations in the holy city of Qom. Before Montazeri, Grand Ayatollah Kazem Shariatmadari, who played a major role in preventing Khomeini's execution by appointing him a Grand Ayatollah in 1963, suffered a similar fate. Shariatmadari was a supporter of the revolution; he led one of the political factions and founded the Islamic People's Republican Party. He also headed the Center for Islamic Studies and Publications, and served as acting Grand Ayatollah in Qom at the time of the Iranian revolution in 1979.[160]

Shariatmadari's interpretation of the revolution differed from Khomeini's. He pushed for a more limited rule for the jurists in administering the affairs of the people along the lines of the 1906 constitution. His views led to a process of marginalization and in 1982 he was blamed for involvement in an attempt to bomb Khomeini's home and overthrow the state. Shariatmadari was eventually neutralized and his party was dismantled. As a final act of disrespect, upon Shariatmadari's death, clerics were prevented from attending his funeral prayer, an act that drew much criticism from Ayatollah Montazeri.

The son of a Grand Ayatollah, an important theologian and a dissenting cleric, Grand Ayatollah Qomi spent most of his life under the Islamic regime under very strict house arrest until his death. Grand Ayatollah Shirazi, also known for his opposition to *velayet-e faqih* or the Islamic Revolution, was unable to get a burial place. His body was snatched during his funeral in 2001 and was buried in secret. Also known for his activist stance, Ayatollah Boroujerdi, the son of Ayatollah Mohammad Ali Kazemeini, was arrested with many of his followers in 2006. Other Ayatollahs who are current critics of the regime include Ayatollah Javadi Amoli, who performs Friday prayers in Qom and resigned in 2010. In his departure statement, he expressed his frustration with the lack of listening on the part of the Supreme Leader. In another recent sermon, Ayatollah Reza Ostadi, a Friday prayer leader in the holy city of Qom, condemned the "extremism in support of the Supreme Leader," or the heavy-handed tactics used by the regime to impose Khamenei's authority. In response, one of President Mahmoud Ahmadinejad's aides launched a verbal attack on the senior cleric. However, in response to this government attack, 19 top members of Qom seminaries issued an open letter in support of their colleague.[161]

In June 2009, shortly after the first peaceful demonstrations were met with violence, Grand Ayatollah Ali Mohammed Dastghaib, the most senior religious figure in Fars, released a YouTube clip openly calling the Supreme Leader an apostate who should be removed from God's mercy. In another

160 See Cohen, 2013, pp. 98–99.
161 See Boms and Arya, 2010.

YouTube clip, Ayatollah Shirazi, son of Grand Ayatollah Shirazi, called Khamenei "worse than Yazid." He was referring to an historical figure who is the embodiment of Satan for Shi'ites, thereby dubbing Khamenei as an enemy of the faith.[162]

The Mujahideen Khalk

The Mujahideen Khalk (MeK) was founded in 1965 by a group of religiously inspired young Shias who believed that armed struggle was the only way to overthrow the Shah. It is an important and a very active group that does not fall into any other category of the opposition. In the early 1970's, the Mujahideen both engaged in armed confrontations with the military and conducted acts of terrorism, including the assassination of six American military advisors in 1971. The Mojahedin was almost eradicated in 1975, but reemerged in early 1979 to oppose the rule of Khomeini.

During the summer of 1981, the Mujahideen's unsuccessful attempt at an armed uprising against the government resulted in over 7,500 MeK fatalities. Massoud Rajavi, the leader of the Mojahedin, managed to escape from Iran to France with Bani Sadr in July 1981. In France, Rajavi reorganized the Mojahedin, and tried to broaden their appeal. From the perspective of the other political parties, one of the Mujahideen's most controversial positions was its public endorsement of direct contact with Iraq, where the Mojahedin still maintain a base (Camp Ashraf), beginning in 1983. This move has further distanced other allies including Bani Sadr. In June 1987, Rajavi announced the formation of the newly reorganized and expanded National Army of Liberation, which was opened to non-Mojahedin members to help overthrow the government of Iran. These acts of violence, along with the "cult-like" leadership style of Rajavi and the National Council of Resistance, have distanced most other Iranian groups from the MeK, who were put on the terrorist list in 1997 by the US and in 2000 by the UK. The organization remains active in Europe and the United States. They have been able to facilitate large-scale events, mainly in Paris, which have drawn

162 See Ibid.

sizable crowds. The group was also active in releasing information related to the Iranian nuclear program.[163]

Marxists

Like the Mujahideen, several other Marxist political parties have maintained clandestine cells inside Iran. Tudeh leaders, who managed to escape the government's mass arrests and the forcible dissolution of their party in early 1983, reestablished the Tudeh in exile in the German Democratic Republic (East Germany). The Fadayan Majority, which suffered the same fate as the Tudeh later in 1983, was decimated by government persecution. Its surviving members eventually joined the Tudeh. The Komala (*Komala-ye Shoreshgari-ye Zahmat Keshan-e Kordestan-e Iran*, or Committee of the Revolutionary Toilers of Iranian Kurdistan), a predominantly but not exclusively Kurdish party, had rejected the Tudeh and Fadayan Majority policy of cooperation with the regime as early as 1979, and continued to fight against central government forces up to the end of 1985 when it was forced to retreat to Iraqi Kurdistan. The Fadayan Minority joined the Mujahideen uprising in 1981, and consequently lost most of its cadres in the ensuing confrontation with the regime. It has party offices in several West European cities and on university campuses in the United States. The Paykar, which also joined the Mujahideen's unsuccessful rebellion, was largely destroyed by the end of the decade. Today these groups are considered much weaker and with limited presence.

The Green Movement

The term "Green Movement" has become the most visible symbol of the opposition inside Iran. The Green Movement generally refers to a series of protests, demonstrations, and arrests inside Iran that has galvanized the international community following the 2009 presidential election. Following a nation-wide conviction that the election was rigged, the Green Movement protests focused on demanding the removal of Mahmoud Ahmadinejad from office.[164] In particular, the movement was affiliated with organizing a mass rally on June 25, 2009, under the title "Where Is My Vote?" calling to change

163 See Sinha and Beachy, 2015.
164 See Dabashi, 2013.

the election process in the country.[165] Many Iranians, especially the younger generation, were more at ease supporting the Green Movement with its general call for democracy, transparency and civil rights than becoming identified with a particular political party inside or outside Iran. Supporters of the movement, who quickly became the most visible symbol of the opposition inside Iran, were affiliated with individuals including bloggers, students, and Iranian activists who were also able to actively participate in carrying the "green message," which often came via Twitter and Facebook. The Iranian authorities were quick to resolve many of these new "green related" structures like the 2010 ruling of an Iranian court banning two leading reformist parties, the Iran Participation Front and the Islamic Revolution Mujahideen that were "dissolved." Both parties supported the Green Movement's leader, Mr. Mousavi.[166] The regime continued with attempts to stop the movement and placed its leaders, Mir Hossein Mousavi, his wife Zahra Rahnavard, and his associate, Mehdi Karroubi, under house arrest and silenced them.

Other prominent figures continued to write and air their demands for change and reform. Some of the more prominent voices were those of Abolfazl Ghadyani, Mostafa Tajzadeh and Mohammad Nouriza, who were all leading Muslim revolutionaries affiliated with the Khomeini circle in leading the Islamic Revolution of 1979. Nevertheless, many of the succeeding leaders–including the abovementioned—were likewise arrested and silenced.[167] The movement was forced to continue operating underground.

3.10 Do Middle East Diasporas Threat Their Host Countries?

During World Refugee day in 2014, the UNHCR, the UN refugee agency, reported that the number of refugees, asylum-seekers and internally displaced people worldwide has, for the first time in the post-World War II

165 Ibid.

166 See Erdbrink. 2010.

167 Ghadyani was first arrested in December 2009 and was sentenced to one year in prison on charges of "insulting the president." He is considered the oldest "Green Movement" prisoner. Mostafa Tajzadeh was arrested shortly thereafter. Mohammad Nourizad, a known filmmaker, was arrested in 2010, released after a hunger strike and arrested again in 2014.

era, exceeded 50 million people.[168] UNHCR's annual Global Trends report shows that 51.2 million people were forcibly displaced at the end of 2013, 6 million more than the 45.2 million reported in 2012. Syria became the world's biggest source of these refugees. Although refugees are not traditional diasporas, they join the broader circle of ethno-national groups in their host countries while bringing a new set of issues, problems and concerns that join an existing framework of dealing with diasporas of Middle East dissent.

Though they are permanently settled in their host countries (and are frequently citizens of these countries), the members of ethno-national diasporas are often regarded as aliens who pose potential or real threats to their host societies and governments. Some of these communities are accused of having dual loyalties or, in some cases, accused of being more loyal to their homelands and brethren abroad, than they are to their host country and its government.[169] This suspicion has been heightened as the events of the 20th century have shown that ethnic minorities including diasporas can establish their own state entities. (Israel, Armenia, Slovenia, the Kurds and the PA can serve as examples of that process). The rising tensions between Arab and Muslim countries and the West at the beginning of the 21st century have triggered a debate about the issue of loyalty in Western countries hosting Muslim migrants. This debate continues to intensify as migrant populations become increasingly involved in political and military affairs, such as fighting in Syria and Iraq and becoming involved in terrorist attacks. The Center for the Study of Radicalization (ICSR) in London estimated that in 2014 there were over 20,000 Europeans fighting in Iraq and Syria, a fifth of them residents or nationals of Western European countries.[170]

Though the establishment of independent states in the former Yugoslavia and USSR has reduced the number of stateless diasporas, some of the remaining ones do undeniably pose some threat to their hosts. Influenced by an ethno-nationalist ethos and awareness that some once-stateless diasporas such as the Jews and the Armenians have established their own independent states, Palestinians and some Kurds have adopted similar goals. In these

168 See UNHCR release, 20th June 2014.
169 See Savage, p. 44.
170 See Neumann, 2014, p. 5.

two cases, it also appears that diaspora groups tend to adopt more militant approaches than those that actually reside in the region.[171]

Today, Muslims constitute the majority of immigrants in most Western European countries, including Belgium, France, Germany, and the Netherlands, and they are the largest single component of the immigrant population in the United Kingdom. In 2005 it was estimated that Europe is home to around 23 million Muslims, who now make up 4 to 5% of the total European population. These numbers reflect a significant growth that has more than doubled the European Muslim population in the last three decades. In 2010 the number of Muslims in Europe was reported at 44 million (about 6% of the population). According to a Pew Survey, it is projected to rise to 58 million (8%) by 2030.[172]

Table 3.3: Muslim Population in Europe

Country Grouping	Number Of Muslims		% of Total European Population		
	1982	2003	1982	2003	2010
EU-15	6.8 mil.	15.2 mil	1.9	4.0	4.5
New EU Members	208,000	290,000	0.4	0.4	0.5
All European States (not incl. Turkey)	15.6 Mil.	23.2 Mil.	3.2	4.5 Mil	44 Mil.

Note: Numbers used from US Department of State, *Annual Report on International Religious Freedom 2003*; Pew Research Center, The future of the Global Muslim Population. 1982 estimates in brackets for comparison, from M. Ali Kettani, *Muslim Minorities in the World Today* (London: Mansell) Publishing Ltd., 1986), 2010 numbers from the Pew report "The Future of Global Muslim Population"

These numbers, according to the Intelligence Council, suggest that Europe's Muslim population will double by 2025.[173] These issues have been made very apparent and urgent by a series of cases in which individuals from these communities were found to be involved in planning and implementing terrorist attacks (in the US, London, Madrid, Tel Aviv, Paris, Syria and

171 See Sheffer, 1997, p. 5.
172 See Savage, p. 25 and Pew, 2011 pp. 4–6.
173 See Leiken, 2005 p. 122.

Iraq), incitement for hate, religiously-motivated murder (the Van Gogh killing), as well as demonstrations that became violent.

These tensions have greatly affected the level of trust and the mutual perceptions of Muslims and Westerners alike. The Pew Global Attitudes project, a series of surveys which encompasses a broad array of subjects ranging from people's assessments of their own lives to their views about the current state of the world, provides a number of measurements that describe this growing rift. Public attitudes reflect a clear perception of an existing divide between Muslims and non-Muslims worldwide, and many in the West see Muslims as fanatical, violent, and lacking tolerance. Meanwhile, Muslims in the Middle East and Asia generally see Westerners as selfish, immoral and greedy, as well as violent and fanatical.[174] According to the Pew survey, the events surrounding the cartoon depictions of Muhammad which were published in a Danish paper and caused a series of demonstrations in the winter of 2006, serve as the strongest example of the existing divide between Muslims and the West. Most people in Jordan, Egypt, Indonesia and Turkey blame the controversy on the disrespect with which Western nations regard Islam, while majorities of those Americans and Western Europeans who have heard of the controversy say Muslim intolerance to different points of view is to blame.[175] In one of the survey's most striking findings, majorities in Indonesia, Turkey, Egypt, and Jordan say that they do not believe groups of Arabs carried out the September 11, 2001, terrorist attacks. The percentage of Turks expressing disbelief that Arabs carried out the 9/11 attacks increased from 43% in a 2002 Gallup survey to 59% in 2010. This attitude is not limited to Muslims in predominantly Muslim countries. 56% of British Muslims say they do not believe Arabs carried out the terror attacks against the US, compared with just 17% who do.[176] This low level of trust can serve as indicator of additional tensions in Europe and elsewhere between Muslims and their Western host countries.

---

174 See Pew, 2006, p. 3.
175 See ibid, p. 6.
176 See ibid. p. 7, and Pew 2011.

Chart 3.2: Relations between Muslims and Westerners (Muslim and non-Muslim respondents)

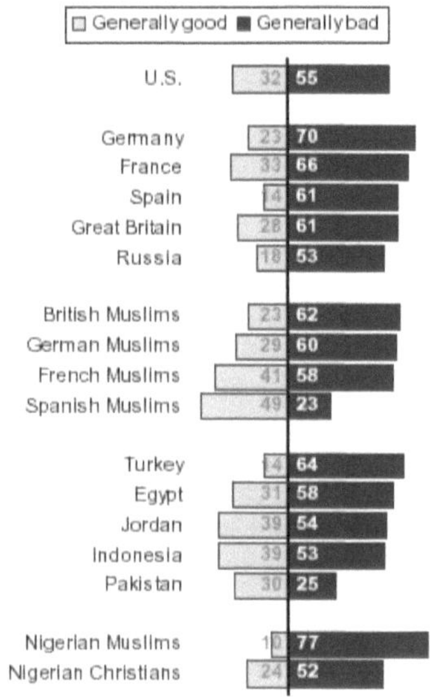

Source: The Great Divide: How Westerners and Muslims View Each Other, Pew Global Attitudes Project, June, 2006.

Local diasporas (diasporas which are located close to their home countries) are often considered a threat to the authoritarian regimes of the Middle East. Regional rulers tend to protect their regimes from what they perceive as potential internal and external threats.[177] The Palestinian diaspora in Jordan, a country controlled by a Hashemite tribe of Bedouin origin, can serve as a good example of the realization of these fears. Over 65% of Jordan's original population is Palestinian, a fact that could by itself pose a threat to the Hashemites. Following the 1948 and 1967 wars with Israel, a new influx of Palestinian refugees entered Jordan. These refugees chose (or were encouraged) not to fully integrate into Jordanian society, but rather to keep their community affiliation as a refugee community. (The UN encouraged this approach by creating UNRWA, the United Nations Relief and Works Agency for Palestine Refugees in the Near East, the

177 See Sheffer, 2002, p. 195.

only global body dedicated to one community of refugees). The Palestinian refugee community has gradually become larger, reaching 1.7 million in 2005, and more politically oriented.[1] Since Abd al-Karim Qassim and Gamal abd al-Nasser called for a Palestinian state and particularly since the establishment of the PLO (Palestine Liberation Organization) in 1964 the tensions between Hashemite and Palestinian Jordanians have become more acute, while the PLO, headed by the vibrant Ahmad Shuqairi, has became increasingly popular in the West Bank.[2] These developments threatened to shake the precarious Jordanian-Palestinian entity, and eventually led to the events of Black September, a Jordanian military move to quash an attempt by Palestinians and PLO organizations to overthrow the monarchy.[3] Similar tensions and sensitivities exist between Palestinians and Egyptians, and between the Kurds and Turkey (and Syria to a lesser extent). The case studies of stateless diasporas that were able to form nation-states, such as the cases of the Jews and the Armenians, have further increased these particular tensions in the Middle East.

Guerrilla and terrorist actions are only the tip of the much larger iceberg of diaspora activities. Diasporas collect and transfer resources needed for the operation of their liberation armies in the homelands and also for acts of international terrorism. They recruit and train cadres, lobby for political and diplomatic support and gather intelligence. Beneficiaries of such efforts include Hamas, Islamic Jihad, Hezbollah, and the PKK in Turkey.[4] These activities often meet the opposition of the region's regimes, which make a great effort to prevent the importation of "improper" ideological and emotional influences, as well as financial and other resources which may lead to subversive activities that, in turn, may destabilize existing regimes and encourage undesired intervention in their affairs from abroad.[5]

Attempts by various governments to cut these links and curb these transfers have generally failed. As mentioned previously, the available means of communication make it virtually impossible to stop the flow of ideas,

1 See UNRWA, 2005.
2 See Nevo, 1998, p. 3.
3 See ibid., p. 4.
4 See Sheffer, 1997, p. 6.
5 See Sheffer, 2002, p. 196.

information, arms, and money, especially as international borders have become more permeable and the diasporas' trans-national organizations have become better organized and adopted more sophisticated technologies.[6] But not all established diasporas in the Middle East pose security threats to their hosts. Whether they do or not depends partly on their structure and goals, and partly on the authoritarian nature of most of the regimes in Arab countries. The least dangerous diaspora in the Middle East appears to be the Druze, who has adopted an "accommodationist" philosophy.[7]

Members of such diasporas are interested in physical and cultural survival, enjoying the same rights as the rest of the population, and gaining some cultural autonomy. Similarly, guest workers pose little or no threat to the region's government. The ultimate interests of guest workers who form diasporas are to earn money to send to their families, receive fair treatment, practice their religion, and maintain their culture. However, even these quieter diaspora communities ate not immune from the changing political circumstances in the region. The recent tensions in southern Syria have brought even this relatively quiet Druze community to demonstrate unrest both in Israel as well as in Lebanon asking for certain degrees of intervention on their behalf and creating a new militia in the Druze Mountain in Syria to protect against a possible ISIS attack.[8]

Despite the fact that in most Middle Eastern countries guest workers are not treated very well, they continue to arrive and usually behave unobtrusively. This can partially be explained by the fact that most workers come from countries that are non-democratic and poor, and also from cultures that stress obedience.[9] Yet clashes stemming from divided or dual loyalties cannot always be avoided, especially during periods of tense relations between homelands and host countries. Since the Khomeini revolution in Iran and the Gulf War, this has been the case for both Iraqi and Iranian communities in the United States and Europe. Consequently, an increasing number of host societies and their governments now oppose the influx of poor migrants, and more Western

---

6 See Sheffer, 1997, p. 6.

7 See Ben Dor, 1979; Hitti, 1982.

8 See a detailed analysis on the Druze militias by Aymenn Jawad Al-Tamimi at Syria Comment, August 8th, 2015.

9 See Sheffer, 1997, p. 8.

countries are trying to prevent the entrance of Middle Eastern refugees and guest workers, as we see in Germany, France, UK, and the United States.[10]

The Civil War in Syria has provided the most recent case study since it has generated a significant diaspora that migrated mainly to the surrounding countries. With over seven million Syrian refugees in neighboring countries, one in five Jordanians is now a Syrian. In neighboring Lebanon, one in four Lebanese is now a Syrian.[11] This mass scale migration—with a majority of poor refugees who quickly become an additional financial burden to their host country—creates both new realities and significant challenges in Lebanon and Jordan (as well as in Turkey although to a lesser extent). The realities of mass refugee cities, unequipped for long stays and lacking basic facilities quickly triggered events such as protests and anti-government demonstrations. The camps, filled with otherwise weak and unprotected populations, quickly turned into crime scenes as well as an extended battlefield for clashes between rival Syrian groups. Clashes between rival groups became routine,: in several clashes Jordanian soldiers even found themselves trapped in crossfire.[12]

Officials in Lebanon describe the flux of Syrian refugees as an "existential problem," one that has great influence on the nation's stability and one that poses a threat to "unravel the country economically, politically and socially."[13] Although Jordan appeared to contain the crisis in a more effective way than Lebanon, voices in the Kingdom have been bolder in criticizing the monarchy for its failing economic policy and for its open hospitality policy that come at the expense of the average Jordanian. Such criticism has also taken the form of leaflets and banners calling for national unity to combat a corrupt government, a rise in the frequency and size of labor protests, university demonstrations, and sit-ins at government offices.[14]

10 See ibid.

11 While estimates of the number of refugees vary, as of 2015 Jordan claims to host 1.4 million refugees (620,000 registered with the UNHCR), while Lebanon claims to host 1.2 million. Turkey claims to host 1.5 million Syrian refugees. See Ghazal, (2015); Lebanon News, (2015). These numbers reflect about one Syrian for every four Lebanese and one Syrian for every five Jordanians.

12 See Associated Press, 2012.

13 Lebanon's Ambassador to the U.S in a Brookings briefing, see Does, 2014.

14 See Satloff and Schenker, 2013, p. 4.

The ever-changing situation in Syria and the growing reach of ISIS has created another problem for Jordan as it finds itself pulled further into the Syrian quagmire. Jordan has participated in anti-ISIS coalition strikes and has taken a number of Syrian prisoners in the process. ISIS succeeded in capturing Mouath al-Kasaesbeh, a Jordanian pilot who was later burned alive. This prompted Jordan to execute two ISIS prisoners and extend its military involvement further into Syrian territory.

The Syrian battles have also moved to neighboring Lebanon where Hezbollah, the Iranian backed pro-Assad militia, holds a home base from which they take a very active role in the Syrian conflict. Events started as early as mid-2011 when seven people were killed and 59 wounded in a fight between gunmen in Tripoli. In May 2012, the conflict spread to Beirut and later to South and East Lebanon. This expansion of hostilities included events such as simultaneous bombs that exploded in two mosques in Tripoli, killing 42 people and injuring over 500 in March 2013.[15] As of December 2013 there have been at least 355 fatalities and more than 2,000 injuries in Lebanon due to a spillover from the Syrian hostilities. These dynamics are only expected to escalate, as a solution to the Syrian crisis is still far from reach. At the end of 2014, the European University Institute estimated that over 150,000 Syrians have already asked for asylum in European countries.[16] Some unofficial estimates point to a significant increase in these numbers and up to 10,000 refugees who seek to enter Europe in a given month. These numbers and the above-mentioned dynamics point to a new emerging crisis that is likely to affect a large number of countries both in the Middle East and Europe. The poorer refugees who left with little in their pockets are likely to pose an additional burden on their host countries and create additional challenges of integration and resettlement. The refugees will likely bring their politics and sectarian divisions with them and will create an additional politicization of the dynamics in their host countries which will be forced to absorb and handle these new issues as well.

---

15 See Holmes and Siddiq, 2013.

16 Numbers from the Migration Policy Centre at the European University Institute, <http://syrianrefugees.eu/>

Chapter 4: Analysis

This book attempts to analyze the influence of Information and Communication Technologies (ICT) on democratization and democracy discourse in the Middle East, with a focus on the work of expatriate groups who utilize ICT to advance political reforms and democratization discourse focused in Syria and Iran. As noted earlier, over 60 in-depth interviews were conducted during the Delphi and pre-Delphi process with relevant area experts, expat leaders, journalists and democratization activists.[1] The research questions deal with the role and influence of ICT on the democratization discourse in the region; with the utilization of ICT by expat groups as a means of communicating messages; with the penetration, reception and influence of these messages; and with the framing of this expat effort as a "civil society" effort. The timing of the research immediately preceded the Arab Spring and hence, some of the statements described need to be understood with this timeframe in mind.

The following questions were asked:

1. What is the role of ICT in relation to the discourse of political reform and democratization in the Middle East?
2. How do democratic expatriate groups utilize ICT in order to deliver and convey political messages?
3. How are these messages perceived, and what is their degree of penetration in the Middle East, specifically Syria and Iran?
4. Can expatriate opposition efforts, and the use of ICT, be placed within the framework of Civil Society theory?
5. What is the overall influence of democratic expatriate groups on democratization in the Middle East?

The analysis below reflects the main findings gathered from the core Delphi process reflecting 50 in-depth interviews.

---

1 See Appendix I.

4.1 The Role of ICT in relation to the discourse of political reform and democratization in the Middle East

As the literature review has shown, ICT is an accelerating factor that is positively related to productivity, economic growth, modernization and other economic indicators.[2] The Internet in particular helps to create new public spaces for political intervention, which in turn, generates new forms of critical media that are considered essential to the process of democratization.[3] Following this logic, the rising penetration of ICT and the Internet in the Middle East (with an internet penetration growth of over 1300% in the first decade of the 21st century, reaching 24% penetration in the Middle East) should be perceived as a catalyst for regional democratic discourse.

As noted before, a rare consensus (48/50) was built on the idea that media has significant potential influence on the process of openness, democratization and liberalization. Media was treated as a very important driver for change, and an equally important factor in the analysis of the region's dynamics (though not as its sole trigger).

The positive influence of ICT on democratic discourse was seen to be dependent on a number of variables, but mainly on the ownership of media; the quality and reach of alternative media; the effectiveness of censorship; and the nature of government response to and interference with this media.

The documented attempts at government censorship, as well as other government-related efforts to establish media outlets aimed at discrediting the opposition, serves as an indicator of the fear shared by the region's autocratic governments over the messages being distributed by the pro-democracy opposition.

ICT enabled the creation of a number of liberal media outlets (such as Elaph, MiddleEastTransparent, allforSyria, Aafaq and others), which provide a strong platform for those advocating liberal agendas. It should be noted, however, that due to the significant presence of Islamists and governmental control agendas within such media outlets, it appears that non-liberal agendas often gain or maintain the lead in influencing public opinion. In this sense, the potential of ICT, especially in conjunction with

---

2 Crafts 2001; Oliner and Sichel, 2000; Triplett, 1999.

3 Kellner, 2000; Habermas, 1989; Mills, 1956.

certain political developments, can be fulfilled in a direct opposite direction to that of a liberal or democratic discourse.

This overall trend can be described as an "intensification" of the discourse in which the media, now consumed by a significantly larger number of people, plays an increasingly critical role as the carrier of new ideas. However, the increased consumption of media and the establishment of new media outlets have generated a growing audience for the advocates of liberal agendas, who are able to participate in the discourse via not only the various Internet forums but also the mainstream satellite channels as well.

Expatriate opposition groups were quick to take advantage of these trends. They contributed to the creation of a democratic discourse by creating new web sites, portals, and Internet forums as well as by initiating satellite TV and radio stations that reach Syria and Iran. The penetration and success of efforts by Syrian and Iranian Expatriate groups have varied, but both have succeeded in making their voice heard, triggering a number of governmental responses that are a clear indication of their reach and their potential influence.

4.2 The Use of ICT by Pro-Democracy Expatriate Groups to Deliver Political Messages

Due to its low cost and relative availability, ICT has become the preferred means of communication by Expatriate opposition groups. Most groups have developed and maintain extensive web sites that feature a number of web applications including newsletters and distribution lists in more than one language. Other forms of ICT such as radio and satellite TV stations have also been used, with a preference for the latter.

The Internet

With its current penetration rate of 40% in the Middle East (see Table 1.1), the Internet serves as the most popular and cost-efficient means of communication. Most Expatriate groups, with the exception of small ad-hoc forums, maintain extensive web sites with a large distribution system aimed at expanding the reach of their messages. Web sites that belong to Syrian and Iranian political groups fulfill a number of roles including:

1. Providing an identity platform that offers an in-depth explanation of the owner's political platform, ideology and opinions
2. Serving as the main (and sometimes the only) platform for distributing leadership statements and opinions on current affairs in closed societies
3. Making resources available on relevant issues including political commentary, historical and intellectual perspectives, human rights, women, regional, local and affiliated networks and more
4. Acting as a primary source for updates on activities, campaigns and other issues of concern to group supporters and sympathizers

A parallel milieu of independent activists' blogs and web sites fulfill a similar function with an emphasis on public discourse, but in most cases without a clear political affiliation.

Satellite Broadcasting

The relatively high cost of satellite systems (which include the maintenance of a TV studio, a satellite link and airtime) has made this medium less accessible to opposition groups when compared to other kinds of ICT. Outside Syria, a few attempts to initiate opposition TV stations such as Zenobia TV, Barada TV and the Kurdish station have materialized but with limited reach and success. In addition, these efforts have been highly dependent on foreign funding (Qatari, American or Saudi), which have made them less independent. A number of independent TV stations, along with opposition-affiliated stations such as Fars1, Azadi TV and RASA TV, broadcast to Iran from abroad, mainly from Los Angeles. A more organized Iranian community, local and foreign funding, as well as the creation of a commercial base for some of these stations, has helped sustain their existence and presence in the opposition arena. Other forms of ICT used by opposition groups include SMS messages, the development of counter-censorship tools (such as anonymisers and proxy servers) and VOIP communications.

In summary, ICT media, led by Internet outlets, are being utilized by a growing number of opposition groups and activists. The penetration of their messages appears to be growing, yet it is still perceived as rather limited in light of poor content quality and successful censorship efforts by the Iranian and Syrian regimes.

4.3 The Reception and Penetration of Expatriate Messages in Syria, Iran, and the Broader Middle East

As stated in Section 4.2, despite that the data indicates a growing penetration of alternative media (with an internet penetration that in 2010 passed the world average for the first time), the character of this penetration remains unclear. Although the reach of this media appears to be growing in both numbers and significance, alternative media appears to be reaching mainly the elites and the younger generation. The lack of survey data poses another obstacle to evaluating the effectiveness of alternative media. Additionally, the effectiveness of successful censorship efforts and the creation of an atmosphere of self-censorship further limit the reach and effectiveness of these media.

Messages delivered by expatriate media (in the broad sense of the term) are largely perceived as important, although far from reaching their potential. Different expatriate media outlets, ranging from semi-independent newspapers to satellite channels to liberal web sites and opposition-related outlets are perceived as a mixed bag, which offer a conceptual contribution that may be important but is often of a low quality. As one interviewee states, "Opposition News network gets about 1–2% ...it's available but the quality is so poor, the news they put out and the programs they have are poor so people do not like what they put out..... Overall, perhaps 10% are listening to the opposition."[4]

In Iran, where both state-sponsored as well as expatriate alternative media has existed for decades, and where other Farsi alternatives hardly exist, the penetration of alternative media appears deeper and more firmly rooted. However, the commercial character of many of the Iranian stations (most of which function as for-profit companies), and the relatively low production quality and partisan nature of their work (which often results in a significant loss of energy to infighting), paint the picture of a divided opposition that is not yet ripe for leadership. It appears that the Iranian government is not making a significant effort to block these broadcasts, since they do nothing to contradict the government's message that the opposition

4 Tariq Al-Hamzawi, political activist, former broadcaster for Arabic News Network.

is immature, disoriented and incoherent. As one of the interviewees summed it up, "Penetration exists. Iranians do know about the opposition stations and they listen to them occasionally, but it does not contribute much to the effectiveness of the messaging."[5]

A similar picture is seen in Syria, where a large portion of the opposition consists of "old guard" figures or expatriate leaders who appear disconnected from the Syrian reality. The rise and fall of a number of such Syrian groups and Syrian Democratic Coalitions has contributed to a pessimistic view regarding the potential of expatriate groups to serve as generators of political change.

We have a different picture of the penetration and perception of other alternative media, led by satellite technology. Satellite dishes have grown in popularity and appear to be present "on every roof." Although subjected to censorship, which applies mainly to a limited number of political opposition channels, the pan-Arabic channels have penetrated a very significant number of households, bringing an array of views and opinions including those of some expatriate leaders and opposition figures. Survey data suggests that the leading Arabic networks, Al Jazeera and Al Arabiya dominate 50–70% of the Arabic TV market in the Middle East. These dynamic satellite channels, which vigorously compete for ratings and popularity, seek to bring a variety of angles (including those of the liberal opposition) and appear to make positive contributions to a more open and inclusive discourse in the region. The concept of the "other side" (also the name of one of the most popular Al Jazeera programs) has penetrated the discourse and contributed to the understanding that an "other side" exists. The contribution of the satellite channels appears significant despite the fact that these channels are colored by specific interests and party lines, often giving more credibility to non-liberal voices. The popularity of satellite dishes in both Syria and Iran (as well as in other countries of the Middle East) is such that they are described as being present in every house, consistent with David Lomax's description that the Arabs may be hungrier for television than they are for food.[6]

---

5 Mehrdad Khonsari, Political Editor and Managing Editor of *Payame Azadi TV* ("Message of Freedom").

6 Lomax, 2005.

4.4 Do Expatriate Opposition Efforts and Use of ICT Apply to the Framework of Civil Society?

Chapter II discussed at some length the issue of civil society and its dynamics in the Middle East. The term "civil society" in a democratic context has been defined as an "uncoerced collective action around shared interests, purposes and values, that is distinct from and uncontrolled by the institutional forms of the state, family and market;" or as a "society organized outside the state."[1] I have argued that ICT might help expand the civil society framework since it allows for the creation of discourse and social action that originates outside the physical borders of a given state (providing a literal interpretation of the definition "society organized outside the state").

I conclude that the civil society rationale can be applied to the work of expatriate groups based on two distinct factors: first, their own interpretation of "civil society" work and second, the aggregate effects of their efforts. Expat activists do see the majority of their work as intrinsically connected to the realities of their countries of origin. A large part of their communication is aimed at their home country with a clear intent to influence the discourse, criticize the existing government and offer a conceptual (if not a political) alternative. Attempts to establish political coalitions and governments in exile, the establishment of TV stations that broadcast to Syrians and Iranians on a daily basis as well as the publication and dissemination of political news and commentary, all indicate a clear intent to participate actively in the domestic political discourse. Likewise, the attempt to publish in other languages, targeting Western audiences and other political constituencies aims to create additional pressure on existing governments and further establish the position that the opposition-in-exile is a relevant political player. I conclude that the nature of this work, along with the changing nature of the Middle Eastern civil and political dynamic, allows for the expansion of the traditional definition of "civil society" to include such efforts even though they are physically located "beyond a border." This defined framework is particularly acute for autocratic societies that often do not allow the existence (or the free existence) of civil society.

---

1 Lomax, 2005; Bamyeh, 2006.

As I have shown while discussing Syria and Iran, in such cases the work of expatriate groups becomes more significant since it often serves as one of the very few means of expressing an alternative discourse that would otherwise (in a free society) find its place within the network of civil institutions. I would argue that this work should be analyzed within the framework of civil society as a form of cross-border activity.

4.5 The Influence of Expatriate Groups on Democratization in the Middle East

I have already discussed the difficulties in assessing the influence of media discourse, which has served as a justification for my choice of methodology and my initial engagement with this research. The overall influence of expatriate groups on democratization might be considered the most important question of this study, which attempts to measure (or at least estimate) the phenomenon of discourse in two societies that are neither open nor accessible. The acknowledged limitations of this research, which include the lack of survey or other reliable research data, lack of access to the countries under discussion, and the attempt to limit all forms of communication from them, has forced a "bypass" method which was used in an attempt to evaluate the dynamics in Syria and Iran based upon the aggregate impressions of policy players, country experts, journalists and opposition leaders. The juxtaposition of these impressions together with a review of past and current research enabled the deduction of a few conclusions about the overall influence of expatriate groups on democratization in the Middle East.

1. A limited but growing reach

As mentioned, the expatriate media relies heavily on the Internet, an instrument that arrived relatively late to Syria and Iran. Limited infrastructure, the price of computers and other means of technology, and effective censorship efforts have limited the reach of many of these outlets as direct channels of alternative discourse. At the same time, the growing reach of the Internet and the growing sophistication of Internet users has enabled, via software and proxy servers, ways of bypassing some of these censorship efforts and increased the interaction of in-country citizens with this alternative discourse. The difficulties associated with the use of software, proxy tools and the need to develop some technical skills in order to overcome new forms of censorship and tracking, naturally limits the reach of a more "free" Internet to a more savvy population. In Iran, where there was a very high Internet penetration rate (43%) prior to 2010, state-funded, individual and expatriate-led efforts have been successful in developing counter-censorship tools, along with a highly developed blog culture. In Syria, where infrastructure and education levels are less developed (and where internet penetration has reached 17% in 2010), expatriate media appears to reach a more limited circle, mainly elite and student activists.

2. *Expatriate media and media dominance, broadening the debate*

In the debate between Mills and Habermas, where the former argues that media is likely to strengthen the power of the dominant elite since it has more access to it, and the latter argues that critical media contributes to the process of democratization, I conclude that the expat media do positively contribute to the creation of a more vibrant public sphere while limiting the once-powerful media dominance of the ruling elite. I have discussed the role of the pan-Arab media as well as the state-sponsored stations (BBC, VOA, Radio Free Europe and others) that have significantly penetrated both Arabic and Farsi media markets. These stations that have successfully tackled at least some of the censorship efforts, have also brought about a culture of debate, discussion and expression of ideas that until recently could not have reached a significant public sphere. As one of the respondents stated, the media "gives the effect of a mass movement."[2] The growing circle of bloggers and innovative movements such as Kifaya, April 6th, Ma Hastim and Neda in Iran, are a direct result of these new media channels. The role of curiosity, and the attempt to reach beyond the circle of censorship, serves as a reoccurring theme throughout my interviews. The people crave alternative media and are able to consume it in a growing number of ways: via satellite, Internet, email and cell phones. Expatriate media, despite its acknowledged shortcomings, plays an increasing role in broadening the discourse and creating a public discourse with some democratic characteristics.

2 Marcella Akal, Journalist, Radio Monte Carlo.

3. Limitations: limited reach and low quality

Despite its important role in creating a more open discourse, the overall impression of expatriate media is that of a vehicle yet to fulfill its potential. A number of explanations for the relative weakness of such media were reviewed in Chapter 3. The key related points are:

- An extreme politicization which is often juxtaposed with low professional standards, creating the impression of an amateurish effort led by detached individuals who are not connected to realities on the ground
- A lack of funding which has caused the cessation of broadcasts, frequent closing of stations or a failure to update web sites and campaigns
- Fragmentation that often creates a dynamic of backstabbing among various opposition groups and negates the impression of a cohesive alternative force that is available and ready to support change

On the other hand, a number of documented cases show that despite these setbacks some expatriate efforts have been able to trigger government responses, an indication that they do carry at least some political weight. Some examples like that of Hussein Derakshan (the first developer of a Farsi blog interface), Ma Hastim or Middle East Transparent demonstrate the power and potential influence of these efforts even if executed by single individuals.

Overall, it appears that the limitations of expatriate media make their efforts weaker and less influential when compared to the broader alternative media effects described above.

Chapter 5: Media, Virtual Media and Real Revolutions

5.1 Media and Political Change

A quick review of Arab Spring writings will reveal a large number of headlines associating the virtual world of the Internet with the real world of street protests, political mobilization and Jihadi recruitment.

"Will the revolution be tweeted?" asks one article and another responded that it already is.[1] The pictures from the protest squares do still include fiery speeches where people with megaphones horn "down with the dictator." But they also include another group of scruffy young men and women staring down at their Twitter and Facebook applications, beaming the revolution away. "The main catalyst for the January 25 revolution was the Internet, so it may be accurate to describe this as an Internet-based revolution" writes Rasha Abdullah from the American University in Cairo.[2] However, while the role of the Internet and social media as a trigger to this latest wave of events is significant, its overall effect and outcome is still contested and debated, especially in relation to the role this media played at the service of the liberal and pro-democratic camp. As noted by Jeffery Swindle:

> Evidence shows that...social media played a role in bringing down dictatorships in the Middle East and North Africa. But other evidence shows that technology actually often reinforces social inequalities in other instances, giving more voice to the powerful, further drowning out the meek cries of the politically weak.[3]

The following chapter will offer an analysis on the role new media has played in the recent wave of uprisings, and will place this analysis in the context of the broader role that media has played in influencing political discourse and movements for social change. It will further attempt to explain the unique role of new media (in relation to other mediums and means of communication) and assess its contribution to triggering events

1 See Francesca Giuseppe, 2012.
2 See Abdullah, 2011, p. 42.
3 Swindle, 2011.

on the ground, particularly in relation to the moderate, pro-democracy camp in the Middle East.

5.2 What's New about New Media?

The term "new media" was added to our lexicon at the end of the last century. It describes the combination of traditional media (such as film, images, music, and the spoken and written word) with the interactive power of Information and Communication Technologies (ICT's) computer-enabled devices, and the Internet. In the aggregate, these various forms of media enable society to collectively challenge the ability of states to control the flow of information, images, and opinion. While the larger "new media outlets" of the region—mainly the satellite networks of Al Jazeera and Al Arabia—are still controlled and sponsored by states (namely Saudi Arabia and Qatar), the burgeoning Internet and social media scene has already established itself as a primary tool for sparking political debates and advancing political discourse. Among the recent examples of social media usage in politics are the wave of post-election protests in Iran in 2009 and US President Barak Obama's election campaign, which relied heavily on social network marketing.[4]

New media quickly became indigenous to the region that experienced a significant growth in Internet penetration. The number of Internet users in sub-Saharan Africa quadrupled between 2005 and 2009, an annual growth rate of 45% with a total number of 69 million users.[5] Between 2001 and 2011, Internet usage grew throughout the Middle East by 1,987%. In real numbers, Internet users in the region grew from 3,284,000 in the year 2000 to 90,000,000 in 2012. Not surprisingly, social media penetration continued to grow as events unfolded in the Middle East. Tunisia, where the first wave of protests began in December 2010, started with a relatively high (21.1%) Facebook penetration rate or about 2.20 million out of 10.4 million people in the country. The number of Facebook users in Tunisia grew in the thousands during the later months of 2011, growing by more than one hundred thousand per month once the revolution was under way.

4 Talbot, 2008.
5 Nisbet, 2012.

Egypt added more than 455,000 new users to reach 5.65 million or about 6.8% of the total population in February 2011, just a month following the beginning of the revolution there.[6] At the height of the Arab world's most recent revolutions, Facebook noticed that Arabic surpassed English and French as the predominant user language in the Middle East and North Africa (MENA) region.

5.3 From Virtual Fire to Real Flames – The Beginning of the Arab Spring

Mohamed Bouazizi, a young Tunisian university graduate who immolated himself in protest after being denied a permit to sell vegetables at a market, could not have sparked the recent wave of protests in Tunisia on his own. His compelling story— that of an educated young man supporting eight people, who could not make a living even as vendor in the market—was the story of many in Tunisia. Pictures of the incident were quickly transmitted via an existing network of bloggers, as well as Facebook, YouTube, and Twitter activists who fueled the organizational efforts of the protests that started at Sidi Bouzid. The harsh police violence, use of tear gas and eventually firearms further escalated this wave of protests. Although Tunisian media showed limited coverage of the events, the news quickly spread via the Internet and social media sites, becoming viral throughout the region and world. Despite that Tunisia was rated 164th in the World Press Freedom Index and among the leading repressors of free media, Tunisians were exposed to the Internet even before the beginning of the Arab Spring. At the end of 2011, InternetWorldStats estimated Tunisia's Internet penetration rate at 34% where 18% of Tunisians reported maintaining a Facebook profile.[7] An active network of bloggers and Internet activists was already developed and mobilized in a campaign that was focused against the government of President Ben Ali. In the weeks preceding the protests, these networks were used to distribute reports from Wikileaks, including one describing a lavish dinner held by Sakher el-Materi, the son-in-law of President Ben Ali, who

6 See <www.insidefacebook.com> March 17th, 2011. <http://www.insidefacebook.com/2011/03/17/facebooks-new-growth-in-the-middle-east-do-more-users-mean-more-protests/> accessed September 1st, 2013.

7 www.Internetworldstats.com/af/tn.htm, January 15th, 2012.

lives in an opulent villa that he shares with a pet tiger named Pasha. These reports, censored by the official Tunisian media, which had also blocked the Wikileaks web site, were quickly spread on Internet forums and sparked the creation of new alternative web sites such as Tunileaks.[8] All of this enraged the crowds, and people began to pour into the streets after Bouazizi's story became known. At this point, Facebook and Twitter were mainly used as internal communication tools (providing information about the various street protests) and as media catalysts, allowing followers all around the world to get current information on unfolding events.

A war between the government (led by ATI, the Tunisian Internet Agency) and the growing community of Internet users had been waged for some time. As Internet use grew throughout Tunisia—from 1% of the population in 2000 to 37% as of November 2010—the blacklist of banned sites swelled to more than 2,000. In 2009, when the government attempted to block proxy sites (that enabled users to bypass government censorship), the number of banned sites rose to tens of thousands, many of which were political sites.[9] Aside from blocking news and video-sharing sites such as YouTube, Dailymotion, Al Jazeera, and Al Arabiya, ATI attempted to shut down Tunisian blogs and even successfully obtained thousands of usernames and passwords for Facebook and Gmail accounts. Many journalists, bloggers, and reporters were arrested for disagreeing with the government. These include blogger Azyz Amamy; Soufiane Chourabi, a reporter working for the opposition weekly *al-Tariq al-Jadid*; Ammar Amroussia, who covered events in Sidi Bouzid for the banned newspaper *al-Badil*; Mouldi Zouabi, a journalist for the online magazine *Kalima*; and rapper El Général (Hamada Ben Aoun) for his song, Tunis ya Biladne (Tunis our Homeland). "My personal account on Facebook, including around 4,200 friends, was exposed to a failed hacking attempt last Friday, but I quickly recovered it after an unidentified person had taken control of it," Chourabi told Al Jazeera just a few days before his arrest. Lina Ben Mhenni, another Tunisian blogger, reported that at that time, Facebook users were unable to change their passwords.[10]

---

8 <https://tunileaks.appspot.com/>
9 Elkin, 2011.
10 Ryan, 2010.

Slim Amamou, a 33-year-old Tunisian blogger, programmer, and activist was another one of those arrested for his alleged involvement in the successful efforts to take a few governmental web sites offline. He was released on January 14, 2011, the date that President Ben Ali fled the country. As a testament to the blogger's role in the Tunisian uprising, four days after being freed he was appointed Minister for Youth and Sports in the interim government.

The government's harsh initial responses further clarified the importance of these voices and the degree of their perceived threat. But while censorship efforts were successful, they were not effective in halting Internet traffic altogether. The Tunisian Internet community has learned to bypass some of the government's restrictions and has developed a number of alternative distribution networks. These Internet-based efforts were not limited to Tunisia alone. Groups like "Anonymous," an international Internet activist group, used the help of "hacktivists" (hacker-activists) to take Tunisian government sites offline and assist in countering Tunisian censorship efforts. With the help of local Tunisian hackers, the group was able to bring seven government web sites down, including those of the Ministry of Industry and the Tunisian Stock Exchange.[11]

5.4 On the Way to Tahrir

Utilizing the growth of technological penetration by the general public, a similar activist network had been in existence in Egypt for some time prior to the beginning of events in January 2011. At the turn of the century there were fewer than one million mobile phone subscribers in Egypt. A decade later and shortly before the beginning of the uprising, there were already over 60 million subscribers in Egypt, a penetration rate of almost 75%.[12] In April of 2012, the Egyptian Ministry of Communications and Information Technology reported 92 million mobile phone subscribers and 31 million Internet subscribers.[13] Considering that over 25 million Egyptians are under

---

11 Ibid.

12 Egypt crossed the 60 million mobile phone users mark," *Dataxis News*, September 17, 2010, <www.dataxisnews.com/?p=22352>.

13 "90 million cell phone subscriptions in Egypt, ministry says," in Egypt Independent, August 1st, 2012, <http://www.egyptindependent.com/news/90-million-cell-phone-subscriptions-egypt-ministry-says> accessed, Sep 9th, 2013.

the age of fourteen, it appears that over 95% of Egyptian adults had access to a mobile phone as the events in Egypt unfolded. Internet access was not far behind with a 21.2% penetration rate and 4,077,520 Facebook users at the beginning of the Egyptian uprising.[14] Internet access in Egypt is more expensive than mobile phone use, but is still available to the majority of Egyptians. With that said, however, most Internet users in Egypt log on at public terminals, schools, and Internet cafes, not at home.[15]

Among a rich milieu of blogs, online forums, Facebook pages, and youth groups, a few became more prominent and played a pivotal role in the recent wave of protests. One of such groups was the April 6th Movement, founded in the spring of 2008 by young activists Ahmed Maher and Ahmed Salah, in order to mobilize support for the striking industrial workers of al-Mahalla al-Kubra. That strike, which involved textile factories employing some 30,000 people, rapidly became a citywide revolt and the workers' demands were combined with the expression of clear political opposition to the regime. Maher and his friends sought to organize demonstrations and a solidarity strike on April 6th, a symbolic date commemorating the 1952 Battle of Ismailia, when British troops surrounded the police station and killed forty Egyptian officers. Esraa Abdel Fattah, a 27-year-old student activist, opened the first Facebook page entitled "April 6" in March 2008. Within two weeks, her Facebook group had more than 70,000 Egyptian members—an astonishing number, given that only approximately 790,000 Egyptians were Facebook users at that time. [16]

The April 6th group quickly gained momentum, and was joined by many other online groups such as the "We Are All Khaled Said" group, named for a young man allegedly tortured and slain in June 2010 by the Egyptian police in Alexandria. Membership in these groups quickly reached over 800,000. Other groups and campaigns, such as "Wear Black Clothes on May 4" (Mubarak's birthday) soon surfaced, led by a growing number of activists. These campaigns did not go unnoticed by the state, which quickly responded with a counter campaign to de-legitimize Facebook and other Internet sites. Esraa Abdel Fattah was arrested in a coffee shop

---

14 See Nancey, 2011.
15 Price, 2010.
16 Faris, 2008.

close to her place of work in April 2008. She was held for two weeks on charges of helping to organize the April 6th protest and was released after a personal plea to Mubarak from her mother. Ahmed Maher and Ahmed Salah were arrested shortly thereafter. It appears that some of the intimidation worked, since Esraa emerged from prison telling reporters she would not be getting involved in any more online organizing.[17] The campaign against Facebook, however, proved less successful. Fahmy Howaidy, a prominent columnist for the Egyptian newspapers *al-Dustur* and *al-Ahram*, called the Facebook organizers the "hope for the future in Egypt."[18] A few months later, after a strike in the Tunisian city of Hawd el-Mongamy, a group of young online organizers followed the same model, setting up what later became the "Progressive Youth of Tunisia." The organizers in both countries began exchanges over Facebook, sharing experiences about strikes and blogging.[19]

These Internet dynamics further intensified during the second uprising against President Morsi in 2013. At its peak, 22 million signatures were reportedly collected mainly via the Internet and under the banner of the *Tamaroud* (revolt) Movement.[20] This number is significant both in the context of the number of votes President Morsi received (13.2 million) and because these impressive numbers helped lead to the army's eventual removal of President Mohamed Morsi. At the peak of the protest, some 30 million Egyptians were present on the streets of Cairo, Alexandria and on the streets of other major cities to support the second revolution.[21]

As previously noted, the Egyptian *Tamaroud* 2013 campaign inspired similar campaigns elsewhere, in places like Tunisia, Bahrain, Libya, Syria, Morocco, and Palestine. In Tunisia, activist have launched their own version

---

17 Ibid.

18 See Faris, 2010, p. 119.

19 Kirpatrick and Sanger, 2011.

20 "Tamarod petition has 22 million signatures," Al-Masry Al-Youm, Saturday, 29/06/2013. Also, Mahmoud Badr, a Tamarod leader, reported a total number of 22,134,460 signatures.

21 "CAPMAS estimates 35 million participated in 26 July demonstrations," Egypt Independent, July 27th, 2013 <http://www.egyptindependent.com/news/capmas-estimates-35-million-participated-26-july-demonstrations> accessed, September 7th, 2013.

of the *Tunisian Tamarud* aiming to overturn a Constituent Assembly that was charged with preparing the ground for a religious state[22]. The Tunisian campaign collected 1.6 million signatures since June 2013 with the *Free Tunisia* Facebook page along with the an unofficial *Tamarud Tunisia* Facebook pages used as main mobilization tools. [23]

5.5 Not Just Media

While traditional and social media have been in the forefront of this wave of protests, it is clear that media cannot be looked upon as the sole trigger of these events. As mentioned earlier, the frustration and unrest were percolating for some time, fed by the work of dissidents and political activists who gradually became better known, if not by name then by message. The issues of unemployment, political corruption, and unequal distribution of wealth became much more visible due to the work of dissidents and bloggers speaking to a generation that appeared ready to listen.

Tunisia is certainly a case in point. The country is considered to have a high level of social development and has an educational system that is also considered the most liberal and open in the Arab world.[24] UNESCO's data for 2006 indicates that the net enrollment in primary schools was 96% for males and 97% for females, while the rates for secondary education were 81% and 89% for males and females respectively. In 2010, The World Bank reported 100% enrollment.[25] By 2010, 36% of Tunisian youth aged 19–24 are enrolled in the country's thirteen universities and close

---

22 Amara, Tarek, "New Tunisian protest movement takes cue from Egypt" in Reuters, Kuly 3rd, 2013.

23 Hartman, Alexandra, "Tamaroud Tunisia Presence Large but Disjointed", in Tunisia Live, Jul 5 2013 (http://www.tunisia-live.net/2013/07/05/tunisian-tamarod-movement-spreads-online-but-lacks-focus/, accessed August 18th 2013).

24 For more on Tunisia's social development see <http://hdr.undp.org/en/statis tics/>; For more on its education system see Arnon Groiss, pp. 2–3.

25 Ibid and World Bank "Gross enrollment ratio, secondary, both sexes (%)" (in http://data.worldbank.org/indicator/SE.SEC.ENRR) and "Net enrollment rate, primary, both sexes (%)" (in http://data.worldbank.org/indicator/SE.PRM.NENR).

to 200 institutions of higher education.[26] On the other hand, unemployment among those educated Tunisians has increased significantly in the years leading up to the 2010 uprising. According to World Bank statistics, the number of young unemployed graduates has more than doubled in ten years—336,000 in 2006–7 compared to 121,800 in 1996–97. A 2005 survey found that eighteen months following graduation, 46% of young graduates did not have a job and that nearly 50% of those who earned an MA degree or an advanced technical diploma, remain unemployed.[27] This young generation, comprising almost 70% of the Tunisian population, grew up hating the government while understanding the available alternatives. The juxtaposition of an educated, informed, and frustrated young generation with the knowledge of potential alternatives played a crucial role in initiating this wave of protests.[28]

Egypt faced similar issues. World Bank data states that nearly 40% of Egyptians in Upper Egypt live at or below the poverty line.[29] The US estimated that 13.7 million Egyptians, 17% of the population, suffered from food insecurity in 2011.[30] Like Tunisia, Egypt also witnessed significant improvement in its educational system along with growing rates of unemployment among its graduates. In secondary education, some 78% of the population within a similar age group was enrolled in 1997, compared with only 28.4% in 1970. The improvement in the gross rates of enrollment in higher education was no less dramatic, going up from 6.9% in 1970 to 20.2% in 1996. Across all levels of education, the gender gap with respect to enrollment practically vanished over the period from 1970–97. However, data from 1998 reveals that unemployment is concentrated among the more educated class, reaching 55% of those who had received intermediate education. This trend appears to have continued: compared to 1998, in

26 Ibid.

27 "For a better integration into the labor market in Tunisia," *World Bank Report*, <http:// go.worldbank.org/3WXOHEUOG0> accessed August 28th, 2013.

28 <www.worldbank.org/progress/egypt.html>

29 See Galal, 2002.

30 See UN World Food Programme (WFP) Report and the Egyptian Central Agency for Public Mobilization and Statistics (CAPMAS), United Nations News Center, May 13th, 2013 <http://www.un.org/apps/news/story.asp?NewsID=44961#.Ui-Qt2j_Q5CI>, accessed September 2nd, 2013.

2006 the situation of Egyptian university graduates has worsened and unemployment (compared with decreased unemployment of other groups in the population) has risen.[31] Protest over basic economic needs was also a new phenomenon in Egypt. In 1977, what came to be known as the "Egyptian Bread Riots" broke out after President Sadat cancelled the subsidies on basic food staples. Hundreds of thousands of poor Egyptians took to the streets; scores were killed and hundreds injured.

Thirty years later, in 2007 and 2008, as food prices soared throughout Africa and the world, food riots again erupted in Egypt. During one of the food demonstrations in the city of al-Mahalla al-Kubra, riot police used live ammunition and rubber bullets to suppress the protests. A 15-year-old bystander was killed, apparently by police, and more than a hundred people were wounded, including some who lost eyes after being shot with rubber-coated bullets. Police also detained several journalists trying to cover the protest.[32] The response to this event, coupled with Egyptian responses to earlier events such as the Second Intifada, the invasion of Iraq, the constitutional referendum, and Presidential election campaigns demonstrated that an active civil society had developed—one that is capable of organizing. The emergence of *Kefaya* ("enough"), a movement that became a central force in the protest of 2011, appealed to reform-minded individuals and parties from diverse social backgrounds and political persuasions. This showed another indication of a certain maturity of Egypt's civil society. *Kefaya* excelled, and in many ways pioneered the utilization of information technology for civil organizations. It used electronic messages, including text messages between cell phone users, to publicize its rallies among members and the general public. *Kefaya* also pursued a multifaceted Internet strategy to disseminate its message. It used online advertisements, propagated banners, and political cartoons using its own web page as well as those of sympathetic bloggers.[33] Using available media platforms, it documented

---

31 The Egyptian Economy, Current Challenges and Future Prospects (Cairo, 2008), pp. 133–178.

32 "Egypt: Investigate Police Use of Force at Protests," Human Rights Watch, April 11th, 2008 <http://www.hrw.org/news/2008/04/10/egypt-investigate-police-use-force-protests> accessed Sep 2nd, 2013.

33 Grant Audra (2008).

abuses perpetrated by state security officers.[34] In many ways, these campaigns helped break the population's aversion to direct confrontation with the regime and opened the door for other, more confrontational voices of opposition and social movement in Egypt.

5.6 The Dark Side of the Internet

Naturally, Internet and social media platforms became available not only to liberal camps. Terrorist groups discovered the uses of the Internet and social media quite quickly, also through insights from people like Ayman al-Zawahiri who have stated that, "The media represents two-thirds of the battle."[35] Al-Qaeda developed a powerful media presence with the establishment of the Global Islamic Media Front. Likewise, the Al-Qaeda inspired Islamic State of Iraq and Syria has been expanding its presence on social media in order to implement sophisticated techniques of recruiting fighters, spreading its propaganda, and collecting financial support.

One such Internet tool is a Twitter application called "*Fajr al-Bashaer*," or "Dawn of Good Tidings."[36] This application, later flagged by Twitter as "potentially harmful," requests user data and personal information. After downloading the app, the user is sent news and updates on ISIS fighting in Syria and Iraq. The recruitment app first went into widespread use in April 2014. ISIS's posting activity has ramped up since the group's offensive, reaching an all-time high of almost 40,000 tweets in one day as ISIS marched into the northern Iraqi city of Mosul.[37]

ISIS further developed the Al Hayat Media Center, a sophisticated media platform specifically aimed at non-Arabic speakers, particularly younger audiences. Its quality appears closer to mainstream broadcast standards than anything else Islamic extremism has yet produced. In addition, the jihadist group has also launched an online magazine to recruit more fighters.

---

34 Ibid, p. IX.

35 ITAC, "Al Qaeda: Propaganda and Media Strategy," in Trends of Terrorism Series, Vol 2, 2007.

36 @Fajr991.

37 Berger, 2014.

The 10-page magazine named "The Islamic State Report," explains how life within their envisioned Islamic state would look like.[38]

These efforts appear to be working. A UN report from October 2014 found that 15,000 people have traveled to Syria and Iraq to fight alongside the Islamic State (ISIS) and similar extremist groups. They come from more than 80 countries, the report states, "including a tail of countries that have not previously faced challenges relating to al-Qaida."[39] The report was produced by a Security Council committee that monitors Al-Qaeda. It states that, "Numbers since 2010 are now many times the size of the cumulative numbers of foreign terrorist fighters between 1990 and 2010 – and are growing."[40]

5.7 Social Media, a Theoretical Framework

The relationship between media and social change was framed in a number of classic works, such as *Four Theories of the Press*, *The Power Elite*, and others in which strong and positive relationships were identified between mass media and the strength of the elite that controls it.[41] Interestingly, some of these old models that referred to old media appear still relevant to the new media realities and hence, it is important to spend some time understanding them.

Mills warned against media manipulation, a phenomenon that is likely to strengthen the power of the dominant elite. It does so by favoring a small group of elites who control or have access to the mass media over others who may think differently.[42] Further, since (until recently) mass media did not allow feedback, it thus obliterates another feature of a democratic public sphere.[43] Jürgen Habermas supported Mills's warning, but offered a remedy by arguing for the role of critical media that can revitalize the public sphere and contribute to the process of democratization. Habermas sought

---

38 Ajbali, 2014.
39 Ackerman, 2014.
40 Ibid.
41 Siebert, 1963; Mills, 1951.
42 Mills, 1951.
43 Ibid, p. 298.

to revitalize the public sphere by "setting in motion a critical process of public communication through the very organizations that mediatize it."[44]

Eliahu Katz and Paul F. Lazarsfeld (1955) developed the concept of opinion leaders and formulated the two-step flow of communication theory that frames the relationship between media and public opinion. Their study demonstrated that opinion leaders—also called leaders of "primary groups"—serve as intermediaries between messages and public opinion.[45] Primary group leaders are also the main players in the media environment, and their opinions will hence be evaluated based first on their "primary group" credential, only later on the merit of their message. This point has been corroborated in a number of studies, most notably in the work by S.C. Kalichman and T.L Hunter.[46] Data was gathered in Chicago before and after Earvin "Magic" Johnson's televised press conference on November 7, 1991, in which he announced his retirement from professional basketball because he was diagnosed with the HIV virus. The researchers found a marked increase in AIDS awareness and greater interest in AIDS-related information. They also found that all of the men interviewed in the study had heard or read about Magic Johnson's HIV infection. Most (86%) had also engaged in frequent discussion about AIDS with their friends during the three days following his news conference. Johnson, an opinion leader, was able to use his popularity to attract attention and convey a message on this issue. Inferring these conclusions to the realm of new media, one might argue that a relatively small (but popular) group of activists or citizen journalists can help form an alternative information environment that could successfully challenge the narrative presented by state-sanctioned media.

Likewise, Yochai Benkler contends that Internet technologies are transforming key social infrastructures, including those supporting the "public sphere," which he defines as "a particular set of social practices that members of a society use to communicate about matters they understand to be of public concern and that potentially require collective action or recognition."[47] For Benkler, the new media model created by

---

44 Habermas, 1989, p. 232.
45 Katz and Lazarsfeld,1955, pp. 32, 43.
46 Kalichman and Hunter, 1992, pp. 1374–1376.
47 Yochai, 2006, p. 177.

ICT is inherently more democratic, inclusive, and interactive than the old methods of mass media production and control. His assertion that Internet technologies—even under conditions of censorship—can undermine the control that was once in the hands of oppressive regimes and hence function as a catalyst for democracy has been substantiated by recent events.[48] Arguing from a slightly different standpoint, Malcolm Gladwell predicted that technology is just another form of social networking that operates like older networks when it comes to leading a change. Gladwell contended that a process of change could not be led by virtual connections since those are likely to be large in number, but low in intensity. In his "Why the revolution will not be tweeted," he argues that despite the large number of individuals involved with social networking activities around political causes, the actual number of real activists this activity generates is much smaller and is still based on ties of friendship and acquaintance.[49] Gladwell maintains that what is important is not the number of virtual members in a given group, but rather the number of real people willing to be mobilized because of their affiliation.

However, the influence of this new technology is not necessarily net-positive. Yevgeny Morozov, a "cyber-skeptic," further articulated this point in his 2010 book, *The Net Delusion*. Morozov choose to stress the limitation of social media and its negative effects such as how it may boost government's attempts at surveillance, propaganda, censorship, and even the trivialization of public discourse. Social media, he argues, can help the autocrats trace these activists and silence them, as was the case in Tunisia and Egypt. Since governments are often skilled in Internet repression, social media runs the risk of exposing the activists and curtailing their efforts.[50] In other words, while social media constitutes another tool used by activists in their struggle against governments, it also serves as a tool in the hands of governments (or other radical players) against the very same activists.

---

48 Ibid, p. 278.
49 Gladwell, 2010.
50 Ibid, pp. 212–213.

5.8 In Sum—the Virtual Difference and the Meaning of New Media

I conclude, in accordance with the most recent theorists, that new media has played a unique role in relation to the wave of uprisings in the Middle East. It has served as an alternative means of communication, enabling activists to bypass the state-controlled media mechanisms and by doing so, enabled the creation of a new "public sphere." On the other hand, and in accordance with the traditional model, the increasing popularity of the Internet, including the growing community of users and consumers it accumulates, can also be explained by the new mediating role it has begun to play. The Internet has enabled the development and creation of a new group of mediators and opinion leaders who have exerted their influence among the ranks of a new generation that is finding itself increasingly frustrated and aggravated by old and corrupt state structures. Consequently, new media played a number of specific roles in the wave of revolutions sweeping the Middle East. It served as a source of information; an internal organizational tool; a platform for dissent and for the formation of opposition groups; and an outlet to the outside world as well as to the mainstream media.

An additional few words should be written about the changing balance of power in the region, and the role of new media in relation to these new power centers. Conventional wisdom and much of the literature views the Middle East via a two-axis prism: the "autocratic" and the "theocratic." The autocrats, representing dictators that were often friendly to the West, were loyal allies who in return were allowed to crack down on opponents and ignore human rights while receiving substantial assistance. It was believed that only these types of autocrats were able to prevent a slide into extremism and fundamentalism, therefore the West believed it was best to keep these leaders in power. Others, such as "democrats" were usually ignored due to their perceived lack of power or due to the will of the autocrats who had a vested interest in keeping them silent. That system has worked for some time and for good reason—the autocrats, with their control on most policy and security structures, were able to maintain a balance, keeping the theocrats at a safe distance while making sure that the democrats remained weak and largely invisible. Historically, theocrats were also the only ones able to challenge the authority of a dictatorial state, which led many to believe that only autocrats could save the world from another Iranian Islamist revolution or a Hizbullah-style takeover in Lebanon.

That paradigm, however, has been seriously challenged in light of the recent uprisings in the Middle East. The mass wave of people who followed the steady streams of Twitter and Facebook messages demonstrated the appearance of another camp, a democratic one, which up until this moment was perceived as a non-actor due to its fragmentation and lack of institutional structures. Herein rests the greatest contribution of new media to this recent wave of events. The Internet was able to help connect isolated dissenting voices, which gradually formed groups and organizations of alternative agendas and leadership. The Internet became a catalyst for the creation of an alternative collective—a virtual public square that was able to mobilize masses for some real movement. And as the role of the virtual space increases, so grows the opening for the Expat community to play a growing role. This virtual dynamic became a new public sphere that introduced the potential to compete with the traditional structures of power. Through the Internet, it became clear that millions in the region care about some very simple and basic issues affecting their daily lives. When Mohamed Bouazizi decided to self-immolate, many of these systems were already online and a certain cadre of leadership was already in place that was able to initiate mobilization. In that sense, new media did more than just fuel a wave of protest. It helped change the dynamics of power in the region and pushed to the fore a new camp of democrats that gradually began to offer an alternative to the now debunked autocratic system. Although it is true that the Internet is not solely co-opted by the democrats, and while other studies show that Islamists groups, including the most radical ones, are able to champion its usage, it is also clear that without these new means of media, it would have been almost impossible for the democratic camp to formalize.[51]

Although the democratic hope of the Arab spring has lost steam in the past two years with the onset of a clear "Islamic winter" rather than an "Arab Spring" with the exception of Tunisia, these aforementioned dynamics should not be dismissed, irrespective of the current political landscape.

---

51 See, for example Yury 2012 and Gabriel, 2010.

One conclusion that can be drawn from these eventful years is that the wave of uprisings has not yet ended and that the region continues to struggle, change and surprise. While it is not yet clear which one of the camps will lead the Middle East in the years to come – and while the Internet continues to be an arena of struggle between moderate and radical agendas – it is now also clear that new media has triggered a new dynamic in the region, enabling a generation to leave its mark.

5.9 Epilogue

Unlike the prophesies of technological gurus (such as Gates, Glider and Clay Shirky) or futurists (such as Fukuyama) about a new world which will be transformed for the better by media and technology, the reality has conveyed a more traditional picture that leaves at least some of the old world order still intact. On the one hand, new media has engulfed the region, creating numerous new outlets accessible by satellite, Internet and mobile devices. These new media outlets have broken many of the older monopolies and forced the ruling elites to adapt to a new reality that demands more accountability and enables a freer and more diverse discourse. The media culture has changed in terms of both its consumption and production. The old state media model lost its seniority to more dynamic outlets that offer an array of opinions that were unavailable before. In order to adapt even the old state-funded media had to change and modernize. The notion of alternative opinion has penetrated the discourse and become part and parcel of a widely available new media. The old monopoly was effectively broken, allowing dissenting opinions to enter the discourse via participation in newly established mainstream outlets like Al Jazeera or Al Arabiya in the Arab world. Expat groups, activists and bloggers have grown in number and increased their participation in a discourse that, via technology, is now able to overcome borders and distances. This concept, which has been framed herein as a cross-border civil society, has created a new media arena that is more vibrant, more dynamic and more diverse than ever before. This diversity, however, has not always led the media in a way that encourages more openness and tolerance of a democratic discourse.

On the other hand, the new media, and certainly the liberal media that has been the subject of this work, is far from winning the battle of ideas.

Newly created media structures, led by the satellite networks, have gained popularity due to their quality and reliability in spite of their other agendas, which remain associated with the old guard and governments of the region. The scene in November of 2010, when Mubarak went to Qatar in order to discuss the editorial line of Al Jazeera as it prepared to cover the Egyptian parliamentary elections, was not a rare one in the formation of a new regional media market. Facing the parliamentary elections, Mubarak defaulted to familiar "old school" methods of closing down media outlets, including shutting down the internet in Egypt, arresting journalists and activists and enforcing limitations on text messaging, since these were actively being used for political campaigns against his ruling party. His trip to Qatar was meant to secure an agreement that the major Arab network would not discredit his efforts. This example points to how the ruling elites have adapted to new media realities, and how they are successfully using a number of strategies aimed at securing a friendly and less-critical media discourse. These elites demonstrated a degree of success in retaining some control over the new media, using a number of strategies including: ownership, political alliances, the development of new "alternative" state media outlets and censorship. In addition, and as noted earlier, the Iranian and Syrian regimes have been somewhat successful in using intimidation tactics and discrediting opposition-related outlets. On the other hand, the recent wave of uprisings in the region has shown the most radical departure of the Pan Arab networks from supporting the existing ruling elite of the region.

This mixed picture is intimately connected to the broader debate about the way technology interacts with our world. The so-called "cyber-optimists" have argued that the new tools of social media are reinventing social activism. For them, Facebook, Twitter and other ICT applications are expected to change the traditional relationship between political authorities and the populace, making it easier for the powerless to collaborate, coordinate, and give a voice to their concerns. In his book *Here Comes Everybody*, Shirky analyses a number of examples of how the Internet age enables individuals and groups to make a difference, create communities and engage others in personal and public issues. However, as Gladwell points out, the ability to become active does not always translate into the willingness do so, a fact that might even be truer when measuring Internet activism. In 2010, the Facebook page of the Save Darfur Coalition had an impressive number of members, 1,282,339. However, the average financial contribution of each member to this cause is nine cents apiece.[52]

The expat opposition often sees itself as a trigger for social change and a catalyst for civil action stemming from its work from across the border. While this claim can be substantiated, as the documented cases have shown, the effect of their virtual work often remains "cyber" in nature, gaining sympathy and support but not causing any real change on the ground. This conclusion corresponds with the observations made by Gladwell that internet-based social mobilization results mainly in engaging the circles of passive participation rather than triggering large-scale political action. This "social media noise effect" (the notion that the new media generates more attention and noise than actual change) can help explain why the majority of my interviewees concluded that the media by itself is not the strongest driver for influencing political change in the Middle East.

Nevertheless, the examples I have brought from Syria and Iran (as well as other countries such as Tunisia, Egypt and Morocco) provide some indication that this remote expat work can assist and even trigger political activism efforts, which are perceived as significant as they continue to force governments to respond and take action against them. The growing ability of expat (and in-country) groups to make their voices heard, and trigger activities both on the ground as well as in the international arena, is substantive enough to conclude that their work has made a positive contribution to the public and political discourse on democratization in the Middle East.

My analysis also supports the more nuanced picture that emerged from interview question number 11 (What are the other possible drivers of political change in the Middle East?): ICT, led by the new media, is perceived as a platform and a catalyst for change. However, its ability to trigger change is highly dependent on other drivers such as the social and economic climate, education and leadership. The move beyond "virtual work" requires in-country dissidents who could benefit from the work of the expat groups. The opposite scenario, meaningful and significant expat work that is solely based on remote efforts without local support, is unlikely to move the needle on the ground.

---

52 See Gladwell, 2012, p. 2.

I began this work as a cyber-optimist. My interaction with expat activists and with those who create expat media triggered the initial assumption that I would be able to prove the effectiveness of their work and the changes they would be able to trigger from afar. While I was able to show the unique contribution of expat groups that work to advance democracy in Syria and Iran, I have somewhat tempered my initial enthusiasm about the power of ICT and the "new media" revolution.

A number of variables stifle the work of the expat opposition. These include:

1. A lack of resources and a lack of professional level efforts
2. The internal rivalries among their ranks
3. Their perception as "outsiders" who often represent foreign interests
4. The successful censorship and intimidation efforts of regimes operating against them
5. The limitations of the Internet and satellites as virtual tools that are dependent on additional support in order to trigger a change

In addition, it appears that without an "on the ground" support base, the effects of these efforts are limited.

Nevertheless, and despite these obstacles, expat efforts are continually increasing and gradually gaining visibility while generating success stories. Agreeing with Benkler, I conclude that this expat "cross-border" civil activity, even under the conditions described above, can undermine the control that was once in the hands of oppressive regimes, enhance the democratic discourse, and contribute its share as a catalyst for the process of greater openness and democratization in the region. While it is true that this process of openness and democratic discourse will not necessarily result in a more democratic political system (at least not in the short term) the influence of these dynamics should not be dismissed facing a new generation that is gradually coming of age in the Middle East. These more educated, able and savvy youth—many who have already marched to Tahrir or Manama to demand freedom and democracy—have not yet had their last word.

Appendix I – Methodology and Delphi Interviewees

The research scope along with the objective difficulties of data collection in countries such as Syria and Ira - has led me to adopt a multidisciplinary research model with a Delphi component at its core. The Delphi technique may be characterized as a method for structuring a group communication process by allowing a group of individuals, as a whole, to deal with a complex problem for which precise information may be unavailable, and to elicit group judgments on values for which information is a matter of opinion. It is questioner based methodology that seeks to find consensus amongst interviewees on key issues and this work used modified Delphi technique based on a Delphi model of Linstone and Murray[1] The research was conducted in three phases:

1) **The "pre-Delphi" phase,** or an initial consultation aimed at the structuring of the Delphi process itself. This began with my own advisors and continued with an initial list of experts, with the aim of further defining the research process, identifying key questions and establishing the criteria for the selection of interviewees.
2) **The construction of the Delphi questionnaire.** This phase, which progressed along with the pre-Delphi process, was intended to develop the actual questionnaire which would accompany the research itself. Ongoing feedback from the "pre-Delphi" group should help ensure that adequate questions are selected, that important questions are not left out and that the structure of the questionnaire should enable further analysis once data is collected.
3) **The Delphi Process-** The process of locating, reaching and interviewing a group of 50 relevant experts worldwide with a priority on conducting in-person rather than telephone interviews. The interviews were recorded and in many cases, the notes of the interview were sent to the interviewee for confirmation (and, sometimes, for clarification).

---

1 See Linstone and Murray, 1975.

For the purpose of this work and in light of the complexity of the question at hand, I decided to utilize a "pre-Delphi" pilot process which was focused on constructing the Delphi process itself: (a) defining the research process, (b) identifying key questions, (c) identifying criteria for the selection of interviewees, and (d) identifying an initial list of potential interviewees.

The Delphi Questionnaire and list of Interviewees

Following the pre-Delphi process, a main Delphi line-up was established for scholars and experts who deal with media, democratization and the Middle East. A secondary line-up for opposition activists, and for those involved in media production on behalf of *Expat*riate communities, was also established with the aim of generating more questions for those interviewees who play a more prominent role in the opposition, and who agreed to respond to a longer set of questions.

The Delphi interview sample

The Delphi interviews were conducted between 2005- 2010 in a variety of locations including Cairo, Jerusalem, Los Angeles, Paris, London and Washington D.C. A strong preference was given to in-person interviews since those were found to be more effective and comprehensive. A small number of telephone interviews were held in cases where time and resources did not allow another journey.

Based on the pre-Delphi process, it became evident that a large variety of interviewees would be needed in order to cover the various dimensions associated with my research question. To that end, the Delphi sample focused on seven different categories of interviewees totaling 51 interviews[2]:

1. **Scholars who work on Iran, with a focus on Iranian media and the work of the Iranian opposition (n=6)**

- **Dr. Dariush Homayoun**, Author, opposition leader, former minister.

2 I should note that some of the interviews may fit more than one category (i.e. scholars who are also journalists, policy experts who are also activists etc.). For the purpose of this list only the primary category is noted.

- **Mariam Memarsadeghi,** Senior Program Manager on Iran, Freedom House.
- **Pro. Uzi Rabi,** Senior Lecturer at The Department for Middle Eastern History, Tel Aviv University and a senior researcher at the Center for Iranian Studies.
- **Dr. Mina Nima,** Professor of Languages and Cultures of the Near and Middle East at SOAS and a fellow of the George C. Marshall Center for Security Studies.
- **Dr. Eldad Pardo,** Head of the "Iran in Global Perspectives" group at the Truman Institute.
- **Prof. David Menashri,** Head of the Center for Iranian Studies, Tel Aviv University.

2. **Scholars who work on Syria, with a focus on the Syrian media and the work of the Syrian opposition (N=6)**

- **Tony Badran,** Research fellow, The Foundation for the Defense of Democracies, author *Syria Monitor.*
- **Andrew Exum,** Fellow, Washington Institute for Near East Policy.
- **Dr. Joshua M. Landis,** Professor of Middle Eastern Studies in the School of International and Area Studies, editor, *Syria Comment.*
- **Seth Wikas,** Fellow, Washington Institute for Near East Policy
- **Professor Eyal Zisser,** head of the Department of Middle East and African Studies at Tel Aviv University.
- **David Schenker**- Washington Institute Senior Fellow, Former US Secretary of Defense Country director for the Levant.

3. **Scholars and policy experts who work on issues of democratization and media in the Middle East (N=10)**

- **Ali El Ahmed,** Director, Saudi Institute/Gulf Institute.
- **Nadia al-Alami,** Regional Director for the Middle East and North Africa, Internews.
- **Michael Allan,** Fellow, National Endowment for Democracy.
- **Abdulwahab Alkebsi,** Senior Program Officer for the Middle. East and North Africa, National Endowment for Democracy
- **Nick Grace,** Founder, ClandestineRadio.com.

- **Ambassador Dr. William Rugh,** US Ambassador to Yemen and UAE, DCO in Damascus.
- **Dr. Walid A. Phares,** Associate professor of Middle East Studies, fellow, Foundation for the Defense of Democracies.
- **Dr. Shibley Talhami,** Chairman, The Anwar Sadat Center for Peace and Development, University of Maryland.
- **Yotam Feldner,** Director, Memri TV project.
- **Scott Carpenter-** Former Undersecretary of State, responsible for democracy programs, US State Department.

4. **Journalists and writes who write from and/or about the region** (N=9)

- **Pierre Akal,** Editor, Middle East Transparent.
- **Anna Mahjar Barducci,** Tunisian journalist.
- **Bahram Bathaee,** Iranian journalist.
- **David Keyes,** Founder and Director, CyberDissidents.org
- **Mehrdad Khonsari,** Political Editor and Managing Editor of *Payame Azadi TV* ("Message of Freedom").
- **Dr. Shaker al-Nabulsi,** Scholar, author and writer, Elaph and MetTransparent, al-Aharam, al-Watani and other Arab newspapers.
- **Roee Nachmias,** Correspondent for Arab Affairs, YNET.
- **Rima Mustafa,** Israeli correspondent for Israeli and Palestinian affairs, al-Arabiya.
- **Dr. Reza Bayagan,** Iranian journalist, Paris-based scholar and writer.

5. **Journalists and professionals who work/ed in state-funded agencies** (i.e. **VOA, BBC Arabic/Farsi, Kol Israel**) (N=6)

- **Marcella Akal,** Journalist, Radio Monte Carlo.
- **Menashe Amir,** Director, Voice of Israel Persian-language service.
- **Abdelilah Bouasria,** Researcher, former Radio Sawa Correspondent.
- **Dr. Arnon Groiss,** Deputy Director of Israel Broadcasting Authority, Arabic Services.
- **Dr. William Royce,** Former head of Voice of America's Farsi Division.
- **Mehdi Khalaji,** Author, senior fellow at the Washington Institute, Former BBC and VOA broadcaster.

6. **Activists in the *Expat* pro-democracy camp in Iran** (n=6)

- **Shayan Arya,** Director of the Foreign Relations Committee, Constitutional Party of Iran.
- **Potkin Azarmehr,** Blogger, Iranian activist.
- **Dr. Daniel Dana (Jamshid Hassani),** Iranian legal scholar
- **Farzad Farhani,** Broadcaster, Channel One TV.
- **Ghazal Omid,** Iranian author and activist.
- **Roozbeh Farahanipour,** Student activist, political prisoner and co-founder of the Marze Por Gohar Party.

7. **Activists in the *Expat* pro-democracy camp in Syria** (n=8)

- **Ammar Abdulhamid-** Dissident, human rights activist and a US representative of Syrian NSF.
- **Bassam Bitar,** Former Syrian Embassy official and US representative of the National Salvation Front.
- **Bashar Elsbihi,** Vice-Chairman of Alenfetah Party of Syria and chief for the Washington, DC office of Zenobia Satellite Channel
- **Farid Ghadry,** Founder and President, Syrian Reform Party.
- Ahed al-Hendi- Young Syrian blogger, founder of the online forum www.akhnwia.com.
- **Ausama Monajed,** Director of International Relations, Movement for Justice & Development in Syria.
- **Tariq al-Mzawi-** Political Activist, former broadcaster and station manager for Arabic News Network.
- **Dr. Radwan Ziadeh,** Founder and director of the Damascus Center for Human Rights Studies; a principal figure and activist in the "Damascus Spring" and initiator of the Damascus Declaration.

Appendix 2 – Delphi Questionnaire

1. Please describe your position/responsibility in relation to Middle East democratization and or/the media in the Middle East
2. What, do you think, is the potential influence of the media on the process of openness/democratization/liberalization?
3. Can you give specific examples?
4. Can you describe the changes in the Middle East "media market"? Who controls the media in the Middle East today? Do you see a change in that control in the last few years; and if so-in what way?
5. Can you give examples regarding media influence in the Middle East?
6. What is the role and influence of media generated from outside the region, particularly opposition radio and satellite programs, VOA and Radio Free Europe?
7. Can expatriate groups, using forms of media, influence the discourse in a given country? If so, can you give examples?
8. What do you think is the penetration of alternative forms of media into the Middle East? How can it be measured?
9. What is the official media response to these efforts? Does the official- and usually government-controlled media- respond to these alternative forms of media?
10. What is the government's response to these efforts? Does it acknowledge the existence of such media and/or the opposition they represent? If so, how? Can you provide any examples?
11. What are the other drivers that may influence a political change in the Middle East?

Bibliography

Abramson, J. B, Atherton, C. and Orren, G. R. (1988) *The Electronic Commonwealth: The Impact of New Media Technologies on Democratic Politics,* New York: Basic Books.

Abdulla Rasha A. (2011) "The Revolution Will Be Tweeted" in *The Cairo Review of Global Affairs,* Vol 3, pp. 40–49.

AbuKhalil, As'ad. (1997) "Change and Democratization in the Arab World: the Role of Political Parties," in *Third World Quarterly,* Vol. 18 (1), pp. 149–163.

Ad-Dajani, Ahmad Sudqi. (1984) "The Development of the Concepts of Democracy in the Modern Arab Thought." Beirut, Arab Unity Studies Centre.

Addison, Tony and Heshmati Almas. (2003) "The New Global Determinants of FDI Flows to Developing Countries: The Importance of ICT and Democratization," in *World Institute for Development Economics Research,* Discussion Paper No. 2003/45, United Nations University.

Addison, Tony, and Rahman A. (2005) "Capacities to Globalize: Why Are Some Countries More Globalized than Others?," in G. W. Kolodko (ed.), *Globalization and Social Stress. Hauppauge,* NY: Nova Science Publishers, Inc.

Adler, M. and Ziglio, E. (1996) "Gazing into the oracle." Jessica Kingsley Publishers: Bristol, PA.

Aghion, Philippe & Howitt, Peter. (1992) "A Model of Growth through Creative Destruction," in *Econometrica*, Econometric Society, vol. 60 (2), pp. 323–351.

Al-Ali, Nadje. (2004) "The Relationship between Migration within and from the Middle East and North-Africa and Pro-Poor Policies," in *A Report by the Institute of Arab & Islamic Studies, University of Exeter for the Department for International Development,* Institute of Arab & Islamic Studies, University of Exeter, pp. 1–48.

Al-Azm, Sadik, J. (2014) "Syria in Revolt – Understanding the Unthikable War" in *Boston Review*, August 18, 2014.

Albright, Madeleine K. and Weber, Vin. (2005) in *Support Of Arab Democracy: Why and How: Report of an Independent Task Force*, Council on Foreign Relations Press.

Alimardani, Masha. *(2014)* "Iran's Internet Users Outsmart Government in Cat-and-Mouse Censorship Game" in *Global Voices Online*, August 12, 2014 <http://globalvoicesonline.org/2014/08/12/irans-internet-users-outsmart-government-in-cat-and-mouse-censorship-game/>.

Alimardani, Masha. (2014) "Iranian Minister Says Government 'Never Promised' to End Web Censorship" *in Golbal Voices Online*, August 22, 2014 <http://globalvoicesonline.org/2014/08/22/iranian-minister-says-government-never-promised-to-end-web-censorship/>.

Allan, Michael. (2008) "Demanding Arab Democracy," in *Democracy Digest*, October 22, 2008 <http://www.demdigest.net/blog/2008/10/demanding-arab-democracy/, accessed August 31, 2011>.

Allsopp Harriet. (2014) *The Kurds of Syria: Political Parties and Identity in the Middle East*, London, I.B Tauris.

Altman, Israel. (2009) "Strategies of the Muslim Brotherhood Movement 1928–2007," in *Research Monographs on the Muslim World*, Series No 2, Paper No 2, January, 2009, Hudson Institute, Washington, DC, pp. 1–43.

Altschull, Herbert, J. (1995) "Agents of Power: The Media And Public Policy," White Plains, NY: Longman Pub.

Appadurai, Arjun. (1996) *Modernity at Large: Cultural Dimensions of Globalization*, Minneapolis: University of Minnesota Press.

Aristotle. (1932) *Politics*, tr. H. Rackham, Cambridge: Harvard University Press.

Assad, Ragui. (2008) "Unemployment and Youth Insertion in the Labor Market in Egypt," in *The Egyptian Economy, Current Challenges and Future Prospects*, Cairo, pp. 133–178.

At-Tunisi, Khairuddin. (1972) "Aqwam Al-Masalik Fi Taqwim Al-Mamalik" Tunis, in Azzam, *Democracy in Islamic Political Thought*, paper based on a lecture given at the Belfast Mosque in October 1997.

Ayubi, Nazih. (1995) *Overstating the Arab State: Politics and Society in the Middle East,* London: I. B. Tauris, pp. 81–95.

Babet, Dean V. (1964) "Elective Governments- A Force for Peace," in *The Wisconsin Sociologist*, Vol. 3, pp. 9–14.

Badran, Tony. (2006) "Divided They Stand: The Syrian Opposition," in *Mideast Monitor*, Vol. 1(3).

Bamyeh, Mohammed A. (2003) "Global Order and the Historical Structures of Dar al-Islam," in *Rethinking Globalism,* ed. Manfred Steger, Lanham: Rowan & Littlefield.

Bamyeh, Mohammed A. (2005) "Civil Society and the Islamic Experience," in *ISIM Review*, Vol. 15, pp, 40–42.

Barber, Benjamin. (2000) "A Place for Us," in E. J. Dionne, ed., *Community Works: The Revival of Civil Society in America,* Washington, DC: The Brookings Institution, p. 3.

Basch, Linda G., Nina Glick Schilier, and Cristina Blanc-Szanton. (1994) *Nations Unbound: Transnational Projects, Post-colonial Predicaments, and De-territorialized Nation-States*, Langhorne, PA: Gordon and Breach.

Baylouny, Anne Marie. (2005) "Alhurra, the Free One: Assessing U.S. Satellite Television in the Middle East," in *Strategic Insights*, Volume IV, Issue 11.

Beissinger, Mark; Jamal, Amaney & Mazur Kevin (2012) "Who Participates in Democratic Revolutions? A Comparison of the Egyptian and Tunisian Revolutions" in *Prinston University Press,* ASPA conference paper.

Benarie, Michel. (1988) "Delphi and Delphilike approaches with special regard to environmental standard setting," in *Technological Forecasting and Social Change*, Vol. 33 (2), pp. 149–158.

Benkler, Yochai. (2006) *The Wealth of Networks: How Social Production Transforms Markets and Freedom,* New Haven: Yale University Press.

Bennett, W. Lance. (1998) "The Media and Democratic Development: The Social Basis of Political Communication." In P. H. O'Neil, ed., *Communicating Democracy: The Media and Political Transitions*, London: Lynne Rienner.

Berman, Sheri. (2003) "Islamism, Revolution, and Civil Society," in *Political Science and Politics*, Vol.1 (2), pp. 257–272.

Bernal, Victoria. (2006) "Diaspora, Cyberspace and Political Imagination: the Eritrean Diaspora Online," in *Global Networks: A Journal of Transnational Affairs,* Vol. 6 (2), pp. 161–179.

Blackstone, William. (1979) *Commentaries on the Laws of England: A Facsimile of the First Edition of 1765–1769*, Chicago: The University of Chicago Press.

Briggs, Asa and Burke, Peter. (2002) *A Social History of the Media: From Gutenberg to the internet*, Oxford: Oxford University Press, pp 20–21.

Brockhoff, Klaus. (1975) "The performance of forecasting groups in computer dialogue and face to face discussions," in Linstone and Turoff (ibid.), pp. 291–321.

Brown, Brendan F. (1960) *The Natural Law Reader*, New York: Oceana Publications.

Bryant, Christopher. (1995) "Civic Nation, Civil Society, Civil Religion," in J. Hall, ed., *Civil Society: Theory, History, Comparison*, Cambridge, MA: Polity Press, pp. 136–157.

Buchanan, James M. (1984) "Politics without romance: a sketch of positive public choice theory and its normative implications", in James M. Buchanan and Robert Tollison, eds., *The Theory of Public Choice*, Ann Arbor: University of Michigan Press.

Bulliet, Richard W. (1999) "Twenty Years of Islamic Politics," in *Middle East Journal*, Spring 1999, pp. 189–200.

Carapico, Sheila. (1998) *Civil Society in Yemen*, Cambridge: Cambridge University.

Carothers, Thomas. (2012) *Democracy Promotion Under Obama, Revitalization or Retreat,* Washington, DC: Carnegie Endowment for International Peace.

Carothers, Thomas. (1997) "Think again: democracy," in *Foreign Policy*, Vol. 17.

Carothers, Thomas. (1999) *Aiding Democracy Abroad: The Learning Curve*, Washington, DC: Carnegie Endowment for International Peace.

Carothers, Thomas and Marina Ottaway. (2005) *Uncharted Journey: Promoting Democracy in the Middle East*, Washington, DC: Carnegie Endowment for International Peace.

Carothers, Thomas. (2007) *U.S. Democracy Promotion During and After Bush,* Washington, DC: Carnegie Endowment for International Peace.

Cavalli-Sforza, Luigi, and Cavalli-Sforza, Francesco. (1996) *The Great Human Diasporas*, New York, Addison-Wesley.

Center for Civil Society (CCS). (2004) "What is civil society?," London School of Economics (LSE), March 1, 2004.

Chadwick, Andrew and Howard, Philip N., eds. (2008) *Handbook of Internet Politics*. London: Routledge.

Chailand, Gerard, and Rageau, Jean-Marc. (1995) *The Penguin Atlas of Diaspora*, New York: Viking.

Chander, Anupam. (2001) "Diaspora Bonds," *New York University Law Review*, Vol. 76, pp. 1005–1099.

Cleveland, Harlan. (1987) "The twilight of hierarchy: speculations on the global information society," in *International Journal of Technology Management*, Vol. 2 No. 1, pp. 45–66.

Cohen, Jean L. and Arato, Andrew. (1992) *Civil Society and Political Theory*, Cambridge: MIT Press, pp.18–19.

Cohen, Ronen. (2013) "The Hojjatiyeh Society in Iran: idology and Practice from the 1950 to the Presence," Palgrave Macmillen <http://www.timesofisrael.com/saudi-general-tells-israeli-tv-of-peace-hopes/?fb_comment_id=1155724527786750_1157086520983884>.

Colecchia, A., Anton-Zabalza, E., Devlin, A., Montagnier, P. (2002) *Measuring the information economy 2002, Global statistics on use and economic impact of information technologies*, OECD Publishing, Annex 1.

Comunello, Francesca & Giuseppe Anzera. (2012) "Will the revolution be tweeted? A conceptual framework for understanding the social media and the Arab Spring," in *Islam and Christian–Muslim Relations,* Vol 23:4.

Cornelius, Wayne A. (1992) "Controlling illegal immigration: lessons from Japan and Spain." Working paper, Center for U.S.-Mexico Studies, University of California, San Diego.

Cornelius, Wayne A. (1994) "Japan: The Illusion of Immigration Control," in *Controlling Immigrationi: A Global Perspective*, P.L. Martin, W. A.Cornelius, and J.F. Hollifield, eds., Stanford, CA: Stanford University Press., pp. 375–410.

Coronel, Sheila S. (2008) "The Media as Watchdog," in *The Role of the News Media in the Governance Reform Agenda*, Harvard-World Bank Workshop.

Crafts, Nicholas. (2001) "The Solow Productivity Paradox in Historical Perspective," London School of Economics Seminar Series, <http://

www.j-bradford-delong.net/articles_of_the_month/pdf/Newsolow.pdf, accessed August 31, 2011>.

Crawley, Richard. tr. (1952) *Thucydides: The History of the Peloponnesian War*. Chicago: The University of Chicago Press, pp. 104–106.

Dabahhi, Hamid. (2013) "What happened to the Green Movement in Iran?" in *Al-Jazeera online*, June 13, 2013.

Dahan, Michael. (2003) *Computer Mediated Communication, Civil Society and Global Civil Society*, PhD. Dissertation, Hebrew University of Jerusalem (in English).

Dahl, Robert A. (1971) *Polyarchy: Participation and Opposition*, New Haven: Yale University Press.

Dahl, Robert A. (1975) "Governments and Political Oppositions," in Fred I. Greenstein and Nelson W. Polsby, eds., *Handbook of Political Science*, Vol. 3, Massachusetts: Addison-Wesley.

Dahl, Robert A. (1989) *Democracy and its Critics*, New Haven: Yale University Press.

Dajani, Mohammad Dauodi. (2009) *Wasatia – the Sprit of Islam*, Jerusalem: Wasatia Publishing.

Dalacoura, Katerina. (2005) "US democracy promotion in the Arab Middle East since 11 September 2001: a critique" in *International Affairs*, Vol. 81, No. 5, pp. 963–979.

Davis, David R., and Will H. Moore. (1998) "Transnational Ethnic Ties and Foreign Policy." In *The International Spread of Ethnic Conflict: Fear, Diffusion, and Escalation*, eds. D. A. Lake and D. S. Rothchild, Princeton, NJ: Princeton University Press.

Deibert, Ronald J., Palfrey, John G., Rohozinski Rafal, Jonathan, eds. (2008) *Access Denied: The Practice and Policy of Global internet Filtering*, Cambridge: The MIT Press.

Denison, Edward F. (1962) *The Sources of Economic Growth in the US and the Alternatives before us*, New York: Committee For Economic Development.

Dews, Fred. (2014) "Syria's Refugee Crisis Threatens Regional Stability," in *Brookins Instiute*, 21st, February, 2014.

Doherty, T. (2003) '*Cold War, Cool Medium: Television, McCarthyism, and American Culture*' New York.

Denison, Edward F. (1968) *Why Growth Rates Differ: Postwar Experiences in Nine Western Countries,* Washington, DC: Brookings Institution.

Dholakia, N., Dholakia R. and Kshetri N. (2003) "Global Diffusion of the internet," in *The internet Encyclopedia*, Hossein Bidgoli, Ed., New York: Wiley, Vol. 2, pp. 38–51.

Diamond, Larry. (1992) "Rethinking Civil Society: Toward Democratic Consolidation," in *Journal of Democracy*, Vol. 5, pp. 4–17.

Diamond, Larry. (1996) "Democracy in Latin America," in Tom Farer, ed., *Beyond Sovereignty: Collectively Defending Democracy in a World of Sovereign States*, Baltimore: Johns Hopkins University Press.

Diamond, Larry. (2000) "A Report Card on Democracy," in *Hoover Digest*, Vol. 3 pp. 1–15.

Diamond, Larry. (2003) "Can the Whole World Become Democratic? Democracy, Development, and International Policies," Center for the Study of Democracy. Paper 03–05, <http://repositories.cdlib.org/csd/03–05, accessed August 31, 2011>.

Diamond, Larry. (2009) "Democracy in the Arab world, and the role of the USA," Lecture at Ambassador Hotel, Jerusalem, April 7, 2009.

Dijk, Jan van. (2006) "The network society: social aspects of new media," SAGE, Social Science.

Doherty, Thomas. (2003) *Cold War, Cool Medium: Television, McCarthyism, and American Culture*, New York: Columbia University Press.

Eckstein, Harry and Apter, David E., eds. (1963) *Comparative Politics-A Reader*, Glencoe: Free Press.

Emery, Walter B. (1971) *Broadcasting and Government: Responsibilities and Regulations*, Michigan State University Press.

Encarnación, Omar G. (2003) "Beyond civil society: promoting democracy after September 11," in *ORBIS*, Vol. 47 (4), pp.115–128.

Entezarkheir, Mahdiyeh. (2005) *Why is Iran Experiencing Migration and Brain Drain to Canada?*, PhD. abstract, University of Waterloo.

Entman, Robert M. (1989) *Democracy Without Citizens: Media and the Decay of American Politics,* Oxford University Press US.

Escobar, A. (1999) "Gender, place and networks: a political ecology of cyberculture", in W. Harcourt (ed.) *Women@internet: Creating New Cultures in Cyberculture*, Zed: London: pp. 31–54.

Esman, Milton J., and Rabinovich, Itamar, eds. (1988) *Ethnicity, Pluralism and the State in the Middle East*, Ithaca: Cornell University Press.

Esposito, John L., and Voll, John O. (2001) "Islam and democracy," in *Humanities*, November/December 2001, Vol. 22 (6) <http://www.neh.gov/news/humanities/2001-11/islam.html> accessed August 31, 2011).

Etzioni, Amitai, ed. (1988) *The Essential Communitarian Reader*, Lanham, Md.: Rowman and Littlefield Press.

Euro-Mediterranean Partnership. (2009) *Euro-Mediterranean Partnership/ Barcelona Process*, EU Official Website <http://europa.eu.int/comm/external_relations/euromed/index.htm> accessed June 13, 2009.

Faris, David. (2008) "Revolutions without revolutionaries? Network theory, Facebook, and the Egyptian blogosphere," *Arab Media and Society*, Vol. 6, <www.arabmediasociety.com/?article=694> accessed July 13, 2011.

Fix, Michael and Jeffrey S. Passel. (1991) "The Door Remains Open: recent immigration to the United States and a preliminary analysis of the Immigration Act of 1990" in Working Paper, The Urban Institute and the RAND Corporation.

Fishman, Joel. (2005) "Hidden in Plain Sight: Alexis de Tocqueville's recognition of the Jewish origin of the idea of equality," in *Jewish Political Studies Review*, vol.17 (2).

Fong, Timothy P. (1994) *The First Suburban Chinatown: The Remaking of Monterey Park, California*, Philadelphia: Temple University Press.

Freedom House. (2001) *Freedom in the world: 2000–2001* <www.freedomhouse.org> Washington, DC: Freedom House.

Freedom House. (2004) *Democracy Survey*,<www.freedomhouse.org> Washington, DC: Freedom House.

Freedom House. (2005) *Freedom in the world: 2004–2005* <www.freedomhouse.org> Washington, DC: Freedom House.

Freedom House. (2011) *Freedom in the world: 2010–2011* <www.freedomhouse.org> Washington, DC: Freedom House.

Freedom House. (2013) *Freedom in the Press: 2013* <www.freedomhouse.org> Washington, DC: Freedom House.

Fukuyama, Francis. (1992) *The End of History and the Last Man*, London: Penguin Press.

Fukuyama, Francis. (1999) *The Great Disruption: Human Nature and the Reconstitution of Social Order*, New York: The Free Press.

Galal, Ahmed. (2002) "The paradox of education and unemployment in Egypt," Working Paper No. 67, The Egyptian Center for Economic Studies.

Gambil, Gary C. (2004) "Kurdish reawakening in Syria." In *Middle East Intelligence Bulletin*. Vol. 6 (4). pp. 1–8, <http://www.meib.org/articles/0404_s1.htm> accessed April 3, 2010).

Gambil, Gerry C. (2006) "Dossier: Abdul Halim Khaddam," in MidEast Monitor Vol. 1 (1).

Gans, Herbert. (1992) "Second-generation decline: scenarios for the economic and ethnic futures of the post-1965 American immigrants," in *Ethnic and Racial Studies*, 15, pp. 173–192.

Geremek, Bronisilaw. (1994) "Civil society then and now," in *Journal of Democracy*, Vol. 3 (2), pp. 3–12.

Gellner, Ernst. (1994) *Conditions of Liberty: Civil Society and Its Rivals*, London: Hamish Hamilton.

Gieseler, Steven G. (2004) "Debate on the 'democratic peace," in *American Diplomacy*, Vol. 2 <http://www.unc.edu/depts/diplomat/, accessed May 4, 2010>.

Glazer, Nathan, Daniel P. Moynihan, and Corinne Saposs Schelling, eds. (1975) *Ethnicity: Theory and Experience,* Cambridge: Harvard University Press.

Glick-Schiller, Nina, Linda Basch, and Cristina Szanton-Blanc. (1992) "Transnationalism: a new analytic framework for understanding migration", in *Towards a Transnational Perspective on Migration: Race, Class, Ethnicity and Nationalism Reconsidered*, New York: New York Academy of Sciences.

Goldstein, Joshua. (2007) "The role of digital networked technologies in the Ukrainian Orange Revolution," in *Berkman Center Research Publication* No. 2007–14.

Goldstein, Eric, Megally, Hanny, PoKempner, Dinah, McClintock, Michael. (1999) "The internet in the Mideast and North Africa: free expression and censorship," Human Rights Watch.

Govrin, David. (2014), "The Journey to the Arab Spring: the Ideological Roots of the Middle East Upheaval in Arab Liberal Thought," Valentine Mitchell.

Graddol, David. (1997) *The Futire of English*, The British Council, English Language publications.

Granick. Jackie. (2005), "Nixing the News: Iranian internet censorship," in *Harvard International Review*, Vol. 27 (2), pp. 11–17.

Grant, Audra. (2008) "The *Kefaya* Movement: A Case Study of a Grassroots Reform Initiative," Santa Monica: RAND Corporation, 2008, pp. 1–81, <www.rand.org/pubs/monographs/2008/RAND_MG778.pdf> accessed July 28, 2011.

Groiss, Arnon (2009) "Peace and the 'other' in Tunisian schoolbooks," in *The Institute for Monitoring Peace and Cultural Tolerance in School Education* (IMPACT-SE), November, 2009, pp. 1–42.

Grossman, Lawrence K. (1995) *The Electronic Republic: Reshaping Democracy in the Information Age,* New York: Viking.

Grzegortz, Ekiert and Jan Kubik. (1999) *Rebellious Civil Society: Popular Protest and Democratic Consolidation in Poland, 1989–1993*, Ann Arbor: University of Michigan Press.

Gupta, Uma, Clarke, Robert. (1996) "Theory and applications of the Delphi Technique: a bibliography (1975–1994)," in *Technological Forecasting and Social Change*, Vol. 53 (2), pp. 185–211.

Habermas, Jurgen. (1989) *Structural Transformation of the Public Sphere*, Cambridge, Mass.: MIT Press, Pp. 232–235.

Hakimzadeh, Shirin and Dixon, David. (2006) "Spotlight on the Iranian Foreign Born," in *Migration Information Source,* Migration Policy Institute, July, 2006.

Hakimzadeh, Shirin, (2006) "Iran: A Vast Diaspora Abroad and Millions of Refugees at Home," in *Migration Information Source,* Migration Policy Institute, September, 2006.

Hamdy, Naila. (2006) "Alternate Arab Voices: A depiction of the Usage of Blogs in Cyberspace," Paper prepared for presentation at the International Association for Mass Communication Research, The American University in Cairo, Egypt, July, 23–29 2006, <http://www1.aucegypt.edu/conferences/iamcr/uploaded/CD_Naila%20Hamdy.pdf> accessed November 10, 2010.

Hansen, Gary. (1996) *Constituencies for Reform: Strategic Approaches for Donor-Supprorted Civic Advocacy Programs*, Washington, DC, USAID.

Harik, Iilya. (2004) "Pluralism in the Arab World," in *Journal of Democracy*, Vol. 5 (3), pp. 3–17.

Hassan, Hassan. (2013) "How the Muslim Brotherhood Hijacked Syria's Revolution" in *Forigen Policy Magazine*, The Council on Forigen Realations, March 13, 2013.

Hasson, F., Keeney S and McKenna H. (2000) "Research guidelines for the Delphi survey technique," in *Journal of Advanced Nursing,* Vol. 32, (4), pp. 1008–1015.

Helmer, O. (1977) "Problems in futures research: Delphi and causal cross-impact analysis" in *Futures*, February 1977, pp. 17–31.

Hockenos, Paul. (2003) *Homeland Calling: Exile Patriotism and the Balkan Wars,* Ithaca: NY, Cornell University Press.

Horrocks, Ivan and Pratchett, Lawrence. (2000) "Electronic democracy: central themes and issues," in Hoff, Jens, Horrocks, Ivan and Tops, Pieter eds. (2000): *Democratic Governance and New Technology: Technologically Mediated Innovations in Political Practice in Western Europe.* Routledge/ECPR Studies in European Political Science 9, London: Routledge, pp. 1218–1225.

Hourani, Albert. (1983) *Arabic Thought in the Liberal Age, 1798–1939*, Cambridge: Cambridge University Press.

Hudson, Michael C. (1977) *Arab Politics: The Quest for Legitimacy*, New Haven: Yale University Press.

Hunter Price, J. (2010) "The new media revolution in Egypt: understanding the failures of the past and looking towards the possibilities of the future," in *Democracy and Society*, VII:2.

Huntington, Samuel P. (1991) *Democratization in the Late Twentieth Century,* Norman: University of Oklahoma Press.

Huntington, Samuel P. (1991) *The Third Wave*, Norman: University of Oklahoma Press.

Huntington, Samuel P. (1993) "The clash of civilizations?," in *Foreign Affairs*, Vol. 72 (3).

Huntington, Samuel P. (1997) "The erosion of American national interests," in *Foreign Affairs,* Vol. 76 (5).

Inglehart, Ronald. 1997. *Modernization and Postmodernization: Cultural, Economic and Political Change in 43 Societies*. Princeton: Princeton University Press.

Inglehart, Ronald and Paul Abramson. (1999) "Measuring postmaterialism," *American Political Science Review* (September), pp. 665–677.

Inglehart, Ronald. (2003) "How solid is mass support for democracy—and how can we measure it?," in *Political Science and Politics*, Vol. 36 (1), pp. 51–57.

Inglehart, Ronald. (2007) "Values Change the World– World Value Survey" (Brochure) World Value Survey, <http://margaux.grandvinum.se/SebTest/wvs/SebTest/wvs/articles/folder_published/article_base_110/files/WVSbrochure4.pdf>.

Javid, Jahanshah. (1995)" Interests conflict over control of internet access," in *Iran Business Monitor,* Vol. 4 (9).

Jenkins, Henry. (2006) *Convergence culture: where old and new media collide*, New York: New York University Press, pp. 6–10.

Johari, Abbas. (2002) "internet use in Iran: access, social, and educational issues," in *Educational Technology Research and Development,* Vol. 50 (1), pp. 81–84.

Jones, Sydney J. (2009) "Syrian Americans," in *Multicultural America,* <http://www.everyculture.com/multi/Sr-Z/Syrian-Americans.html> accessed in February, 2009.

Kalichman, S. C., & Hunter, T. L. (1992) "The disclosure of celebrity HIV infection: its affects on public attitudes," in *American Journal of Public Health*, Vol. 82, pp. 1374–1376.

Kant, Immanuel. (1981) "Eternal Peace", in *Eternal Peace and Other International Essays* Boston: World Peace Foundation.

Kaplan, Lawrence F. and Kristol William. (2003) *The War over Iraq: Saddam's Tyranny and America's Mission*, New York: Encounter Books.

Katz, E., & Lazarsfeld, P. F. (1955) *Personal Influence: The Part Played By People in the Flow of Mass Communication,* Glencoe, IL: Free Press.

Katzenstein, Peter J. ed. (1978) *Between Power and Plenty: Foreign Economic Policies of Advanced Industrial States*, Madison, Wisconsin: University of Wisconsin Press.

Kawakibi, Salam. (2010) "internet or Enter Not: the Syrian experience" in *Knowledge Programme, Civil Society in West Asia,* Working paper #10, pp. 1–13. <http://www.hivos.net/Hivos-Knowledge-Programme/Themes/Civil-Society-in-West-Asia/News/internet-or-Enter-Not-the-Syrian-Experience> accessed August 31st, 2011.

Kayal, Philip M. (1973) "Religion and assimilation: Catholic Syrians in America," in *International Migration Review*, Vol. 7 (4), pp. 409–425.

Keane, John. (2003) *Global Civic Society?*, Cambridge: Cambridge University Press.

Kearney, Michael. (1995) "The local and the global: the anthropology of globalization and transnationalism," in *Annual Review of Anthropology*, Vol. 24, pp. 257–65.

Kedourie, Elie. (1994) *Democracy and Arab Political Culture.* Portland: Frank Cass.

Kelass, Games, J. (1991) *The Politics of Nationalism and Ethnicity*, New York: St. Martins.

Kellner, Douglas. (2000) "Habermas, the public sphere, and democracy: a critical intervention," in *Perspectives on Habermas*, ed. Lewis Edwin Hann, pp. 259–288.

Kelly, John.& Etling, Bruce. (2008) "Mapping Iran's online public: politics and culture in the Persian blogosphere," in *Berkman Center for internet and Society at Harvard University,* <http://cyber.law.harvard.edu/sites/cyber.law.harvard.edu/files/Kelly&Etling_Mapping_Irans_Online_Public_2008.pdf> accessed October 31, 2010.

Kelsay, John. (2002) "Civil society and government in Islam," in *Islamic Political Ethics: Civil Society, Pluralism, and Conflict*, ed. Sohail Hashmi.

Khosravi, Shahram. (2006) "Religion and nation: Iranian local and transnational networks in Britain – a review," in *International Migration Review*, Vol. 40 (1), pp. 253–254.

Kleinrock, L. (2003) "An internet vision: the invisible global infrastructure," in *Ad Hoc Networks*, Vol. 1. p. 5.

Klenow, Peter J. and Andres Rodriguez-Clare. (1997) "The neo-classical revival in growth economics: has it gone too far?," In *NBER Macroeconomics Annual*, eds. Ben S. Bernanke and Julio J. Rotemberg. Cambridge, MA: MIT Press.

Kolsto, Pal, and Andrei Edemsky. (1995) *Russians in the Former Soviet Republics*, Bloomington: Indiana University Press.

Kuneralp, Sinan. (2009) "L'émigration syro-libanaise en Amérique latine et la diplomatie ottoman," in *Syrian Studies Association Newsletter,* Vol. 15 (1), pp. 4–19.

Kymlicka, Will. (1996) "Social unity in a liberal state," in *Social Philosophy and Policy*, Vol. 13, pp.105–136.

Lagon, Marp P. (2011) "Promoting Democrcy: The Why and How for the United States and the international Community" in The Council on Forigen Relations, a Market and Democrcay Brief, February 2011.

Lal, Vinay. (1999) "A political history of Asian Indians in the United States", in Leela PrAssad, ed., *Live Like the Banyan Tree: Images of the Indian American Experience*, Philadelphia: Balch Institute for Ethnic Studies.

Landis, Joshua. (2009a) "Muslim brotherhood breaks with Khaddam and NSF," in *Syria Comment*, Monday, April 6, 2009, <http://joshualandis.com/blog/?p=2627, accessed April 16, 2010>.

Landis, Joshua. (2009b) "Bashar Elsbihi Clarifies," in *Syria Comment*, Sunday, August 9, 2009, <http://joshualandis.com/blog/?p=3853, accessed August 31, 2011>.

Landis, Joshua. (2011) "National Initiative for Change" Program of Syrian Opposition: the liberal wing", in *Syria Comments*, posted on April 29, 2011.

Lefèvre, Raphaël. (2014) "*A Revolution in Syria's Muslim Brotherhood"* in Carnagie Endowmnment for Middle East Peace, January 23, 2014.

Leiken, Robert S. (2005) "Europe's angry Muslims," in *Foreign Affairs*, July/August, pp. 120–135.

Leiner, Barry M, Cerf, Vinton G., David, Clark D., Kahn, Robert E., Kleinrock, Leonard, Lynch, Daniel C., Postel, Jon, Roberts, Lawrence G. and Wolff, Stephen. (2003) *A Brief History of the Internet,* <http://www.isoc.org/internet/history/brief.shtml> accessed August 31, 2011.

Lewis, Bernard. (2002) *What Went Wrong? Western Impact and Middle Eastern Response,* Oxford: Oxford University Press.

Lichtenberg, Judith. (1990) *Democracy and the Mass Media: A Collection of Essays,* Cambridge: Cambridge University Press.

Linstone, Harold A., Turoff, Murray. (1975) *The Delphi Method: Techniques and Applications*, Reading, MA: Addison-Wesley.

Linz, Juan J., and Alfred Stepan. (1996) *Problems of Democratic Transitions and Consolidation: Southern Europe, South America, and Post-Communist Europe*, Baltimore: John Hopkins University Press.

Locke, John. (1680) *Two Treatises on Government*, Book II, Chapter IV, "On Slavery," <http://www.ecn.bris.ac.uk/het/locke/government.pdf> accessed August 30, 2011.

Lowe, Robert. (2006) "The Syrian Kurds: a people discovered," in *Chatham House briefing paper series*, MEP BP 06/01, pp. 1–8.

Lucas, Robert E. (2005) "International migration and economic development: lessons from low-income countries," Expert Group on Development Issues, Ministry of Foreign Affairs, Sweden <http://www.egdi.gov.se/migraiton.htm> accessed May 16, 2009.

Lyons, Terrence. (2004) "Engaging diasporas to promote conflict resolution: transforming hawks into doves," in *Institute for Conflict Analysis and Resolution* (working paper), George Mason University.

Mardin, Serif. (1995) "Civil Society and Islam" in J Hall (ed), *Civil Society: Theory, History and Comparison*, Cambridge, Polity, pp. 278–9.

McChesney, Robert W. (1997) "The mythology of commercial broadcasting and the contemporary crisis of public broadcasting," the 1997 Spry Memorial Lecture, Montreal, 2 December 1997.

McColm, Robert. (1992) "The comparative survey of freedom 1991–1992: Between two worlds," in *Freedom in the World: Political Rights and Civil Liberties 1991–1992*, New York: Freedom House.

McDougall, Walter A. (1997) "Back to bedrock," in *Foreign Affairs*, Vol. 72 (3).

McFaul, Michael. (2004) "Democracy promotion as a world value," in *The Washington Quarterly,* Volume 28, Number 1, Winter 2004–05, pp. 147–163.

McLeod, Jack M., and Blumler, Jay G. (1989) "The macrosocial level of communication science," in *Handbook of Communication Science*, eds. Charles R. Berger and Steven H. Chaffee, California: SAGE Publications, pp. 271–322.

March, James G. and Johan P. Olsen. (1989) *Rediscovering Institutions: The Organizational Basis of Politics*, New York: The Free Press.

Martin, Philip and Martin, Susan. (2006) "GCIM: a new global migration facility," in *International Migration,* Vol. 44 (1).

Meijl, H van. (1995) "Endogenous technological change: the case of information technology. Theoretical considerations and empirical results," *MERIT*, University of Limburg, Maastricht, p. 289.

Meernik James. (1996) "United States military intervention and the promotion of democracy," in *Journal of Peace Research*, Vol. 33 (4).

Mills, C. Wright. (1951) *The Power Elite*. Boston: Beacon Press.

Moniquet and Dombart. (2010) "Does the syrian opposition have the resources to match its ambitions?," *European Strategic Intelligence and Security Center*, Analysis, February 28, 2010.

Mottahedeh, Roy. (2001) *Loyalty and Leadership in an Early Islamic Society*, London: I. B. Tauris.

Moubayed, Sami. (2005) "The history of political and militant Islam in Syria," in *Terrorism Monitor*, Vol. 3 (16), pp. 1–7.

Moussalli, Ahmad S. (2001) *The Islamic Quest for Democracy, Pluralism, and Human Rights*, Gainesville: University of Florida Press.

Münz, Rainer and Rolf Ulrich. (1995) "Changing patterns of migration, the case of Germany, 1945–1994." Paper presented at the German-American Migration and Refugee Policy Group, American Academy of Arts and Sciences, Cambridge, Mass. March 23–26.

Negroponte, Nicholas. (1995) *Being Digital*, New York: Alfred A. Knopf.

Neumann, Peter (2014). "Foreign fighter total in Syria/Iraq now exceeds 20,000; surpasses Afghanistan conflict in the 1980s" in *The International Centre for the Study of Radicalisation and Political Violence.*

Nevo, Joseph. (1998) "The Jordanian, Palestinian and Jordanian-Palestinian identities," paper presented at the Fourth Nordic Conference on Middle Eastern Studies: *The Middle East in a Globalizing World,* Oslo, 13–16 August 1998.

Noveck, B.S. (2000) Paradoxical partners: electronic communication and electronic democracy," in *Democratization*, Vol. 1, pp. 18–35.

O'Bagy, Elizabbeth. (2012) "Jihad in Syria," in *Middle East Security Report*, Vol. 6. pp, 1–43.

O'Donell, Guillermo and Schmitter, Philippe C. (1986) *Transitions from Authoritarian Rule: Tentative Conclusions about Uncertain Democracies,* Baltimore: John Hopkins University Press.

OECD. (2003) *ICT and economic growth, evidence from OECD countries, industries and firms*, OSCD, <http://www1.oecd.org/publications/e-book/9203031E.PDF> accessed August 14, 2009.

OECD. (2003) *Seizing the benefits of ICT in a digital economy*, Meeting of the OECD Council in Ministerial Level, OECD, <http://www.oecd.org/dataoecd/43/42/2507572.pdf> accessed August 14, 2009).

Ogundimu, Folu F. (2002) "Media and democracy in Twenty-First Century Africa." in *Media and Democracy in Africa*, edited by G. Hyden, M. Leslie and F. F. Ogundimu. New Brunswick: Transaction Publishers. Quote from Page 234.

Ohliner, S. D. and Sichel, D. E. (2000) "The resurgence of growth in the late 1990s: is information technology the story?," *Journal of Economic Perspectives*, vol. 14, pp. 3–22.

Ohliner, S. D. and Sichel, D. E. (2001) "Response from Stephen E. Ohliner and Daniel E. Sichel", *Journal of Economic Perspectives*, vol. 15, pp. 259–273.

O'Neil, Patrick H. (1998) "Democratization and mass communication: what is the link?," in *Communicating Democracy: The Media and Political Transitions*, ed. P.H. O'Neil, London: Lynne Rienner.

Pal, Leslie A. (1997) "Virtual policy networks: the internet as a model of contemporary governance?," Paper presented to the Seventh Annual Conference of the internet Society, INET '97, Pp 4–5. <http://www.isoc.org/inet97/proceedings/G7/G7_1.HTM> p. 3.

Palmer, Robert, R. (1959), *The Age of the Democratic Revolution. A Political History of Europe and America, 1760–1800,* Princeton: Princeton University Press.

Pasek, Josh. (2006) "Fueling or following democracy? Analyzing the role of media liberalization in democratic transition," Paper prepared for delivery at the Political Communication section of the 2006 Annual Meeting of the American Political Science Association, Philadelphia, August 30–September 3, 2006. pp 11, 23.

Pee, Robert. (2014) "The Cold War and the Origins of US Democracy Promotion," in *USSO*, May, 2014 <http://usstudiesonline.com/cold-war-democracy-promotion/>.

Peck, Connie. (1998) *Sustainable Peace: The Role of the UN and Regional Organizations in Preventing Conflict*, Lanham, NY: Rowman & Littlefield.

Pedersen, Anders. (2009) "ICTs for democracy information and communication technologies for the enhancement of democracy, with a focus on empowerment," in *Association for Progressive Communications, APC*, SIDA52470en.

Percy, Allum A. and Amyot, Grant. (1970) "Regionalism in Italy: old wine in a new bottle?," in *Parliamentary Affairs*, Vol. 24, pp. 53–78.

Plato. *The Republic* (Translated by Benjamin Jowett), The Internet Classics Archive, <http://classics.mit.edu/Plato/republic.9.viii.html, accessed August 31, 2011>.

Pollock, David. (2012) "Syria's Kurds Unite against Assad, but Not with Opposition," in *Washington Institute for Near East Policy*, Policy Watch 1967, July 31st, 2012.

Portes, Alejandro and Kincaid, Douglas A. (1990) "The crisis of authoritarianism: state and civil society in Argentina, Chile and Uruguay," in R.G. Braungart & M.M. Braungart, ed., *The Political Sociology of the State*, Greenwich, London: JAI Press Inc., pp. 151–179.

Portes, Alejandro and Guarnizo, Luis E. (1990) "Tropical capitalists: U.S.-bound immigration and small enterprise development in the Dominican Republic," in S. Diaz-Briquets and S. Weintraub, ed., *Migration, Remittances and Business Development: Mexico and Caribbean Basin Countries*, Boulder, Colo.: Westview Press, pp. 101–131.

Portes, Alejandro. (1995) "Economic sociology and the sociology of immigration: a conceptual overview," in Alejandro Portes, ed., *The Economic Sociology of Immigration: Essays on Networks, Ethnicity, and Entrepreneurship*, New York: Russell Sage Foundation.

Portes, Alejandro. (1997) "Globalization from below: the rise of transnational communities," Transnational Communities Programme working paper series, Princeton University, WPTC-98–01.

Przeworski, Adam. (1991) *Democracy and the Market*, Cambridge: Cambridge University Press.

Przeworski, Adam, Neto, Limongi, Papaterra, Fernando, Alvarez, Michael M. (1996) "What makes democracies endure?" in *Journal of Democracy*, Vol. 7, No. 1 1996, pp. 39–55.

Przeworski, Adam. (2002) "Democracy as an equilibrium," in *Public Choice*, Vol. 123, pp. 253–273.

Putnam, Robert D. (1993) *Making Democracy Work- Civic Traditions in Modern Italy*, Princeton: Princeton University Press, pp. 8–9.

Putnam, Robert. (2000) *Bowling Alone: The Collapse and Revival of American Community*, New York: Simon and Schuster.

Raa, Ten, T. and Wolff, E.N. (1999) *Engines of Growth in the US Economy*, ECIS/SCED Conference on Economic Growth, Trade and Technology, 3–4 October, Eindhoven.

Rahimi, Babak. (2003) "CyberDissent: The internet in revolutionary Iran," in *Middle East Review of International Affairs*, Vol. 7 (3), pp. 101–115.

Richardson, M. E. J. (2000) *Hammurabi's Laws*, Sheffield: Academic Press.

Rieff, David. (1994) "The false dawn of civil society," in *Nation*, Vol. 2, p. 22.

Roberts, Ha, Zuckerman, Ethan, & Palfrey, John G. (2009) "2007 Circumvention landscape report: methods, uses, and tools," in *The Berkman Center for internet & Society,* <http://cyber.law.harvard.edu/sites/cyber.law.harvard.edu/files/2007_Circumvention_Landscape.pdf>accessed November 12 2010).

Rousseau, Jean-Jacques. (1792) *The Social Contract, or Principles of Political Right*, tr. G. D. H. Cole, <http://www.constitution.org/jjr/socon.htm, accessed August 31st, 2011>.

Rudolph, J. (1997) *Power Kills: Democracy as a Method of Nonviolence*, New Brunswick, N.J.: Transaction Books.

Rumbaut, Rubén G. (1994) "Origins and destinies: Immigration to the United States since World War II," in *Sociological Forum* 9(4), pp. 583–621.

Rummel, R. J. (1991) "Political systems, violence, and war," in W. Scott Thompson and Kenneth M. Jensen, eds., *Approaches to Peace: An Intellectual Map*. Washington, DC: United States Institute of Peace, pp. 347–370.

Rummel, R. J. (1998) "The politics of cold blood," in *Society*, Vol. 27, pp. 32–40.

Sahal, Devendra, Yee, King. (1975) "Delphi: An investigation from a Bayesian viewpoint," in *Technological Forecasting and Social Change*, Vol. 7 (2), pp. 165–178.

Sajoo, Amyn B. (2004) "Civil society in the Muslim world: contemporary perspectives," London: I.B.Tauris, Institute of Ismaili Studies.

Sakr, Naomi, ed. (2007) *Arab Media and Political Renewal: Community, Legitimacy and Public Life*, London: I.B.Tauris.

Salzman, Philip Carl. (2008) "The Middle East's tribal DNA," in *Middle East Quarterly,* Winter 2008, pp. 23–33.

Sassen, Saskia. (1988) *The Mobility of Labor and Capital: A Study in International Investment and Labor Flow*. New York: Cambridge University Press.

Sassen, Saskia. (1989) "New York City's informal economy," pp. 60–77 in A. Portes, M. Castells, and L.A. Benton, eds., *The Informal Economy: Studies in Advanced and Less Developed Countries*, Baltimore, MD: Johns Hopkins University Press.

Sassen, Saskia and Portes, Alejandro. (1993) "Miami: a new global city?," in *Contemporary Sociology* 22, pp. 471–477.

Satloff, Robert & Schenker, David (2013). "Political Stability in Jordan" in Contingency Planning Memorandum Vol 19, the Council on Forigen Relations.

Savage, Timothy M. (2004) "Europe and Islam: crescent waxing, cultures clashing," in *The Washington Quarterly*, Vol. 27 (3), pp. 25–50.

Schraeder, Peter. (2002) *Exporting Democracy: Rhetoric vs. Reality*, Boulder, CO: Lynne Rienner.

Schumpeter, Joseph. (1947) *Capitalism, Socialism and Democracy*, New York: Harper & Brothers.

Schwedler, Jillian. (2002) "Yemen's aborted opening," in *Journal of Democracy* Vol. 13 (4), pp. 48–55.

Schwedler, Jillian. (2006) *Faith in moderation: Islamist parties in Jordan and Yemen,* Cambridge: Cambridge University Press.

Schweizer, Peter. (2003) *Reagan's War: The Epic Story of His Forty-Year Struggle and Final Triumph over Communism*, New York: Doubleday.

Selian, Audrey N. (2002) "ICTs in support of human rights, democracy and good governance," background paper in preparation for the World Summit on the Information Society.

Sen, Amartya Kumar. (1999) "Democracy as a universal value," in *Journal of Democracy*, Vol. 1 (3), pp. 3–17.

Shahab, Cameron J. and Mousoli, Reza. (2010) "Traffic analysis, anonymity, freedom and digital "cat and mouse" in cyberspace: a case study," paper submitted to the Cybercrime Forensic and Education Conference in the UK <http://payvand.com/news/10/sep/Traffic-Analysis--C.Shahab--R.Mousoli.pdf> accessed November 7, 2010.

Shain, Yossi. (2000) "American Jews and the construction of Israel's Jewish identity," in *Diasporas*, Vol. 9, pp. 163–201.

Shain, Yossi. (2002) "The role of diasporas in conflict perpetuation or resolution," in *SAIS Review of International Affairs*, Vol. 22 (2).

Shain, Yossi. (2004) "Ethnic Diasporas and U.S. Foreign Policy in *Political Science Quarterly* Vol. 109, No. 5, pp. 811–841.

Sharabi, Hisham. (1988) *Neopatriarchy: A Theory of Distorted Change in Arab Society*, New York: Oxford University Press.

Sheffer, Gabriel, ed. (1986) *Modern Diasporas in International Politics*, London and Sydney: Croom Helm.

Sheffer, Gabriel. (1997) "Middle Eastern diasporas: introduction and readings" in *Middle East Review of International Affairs*, Vol. 1 Issue 2.

Sheffer, Gabriel. (2002) "Middle Eastern diasporas: an overview," in: G. Sheffer and M. Maoz, eds., *Middle Eastern Minorities and Diasporas*, Brighton: Sussex Academic Press, pp. 195–218.

Sidky, Baker. (2014). "The Kurds and the Syrian Revolution – Statehood & Participation,"in Heinrich-Böll-Stiftung, Middile East, March 3, 2014.

Shirky, Clay. (2008) *Here Comes Everybody. The Power of Organization Without Organizations*, London: Penguin Books.

Shuval, Judith T. (2000) "Diaspora migration: definitional ambiguities and a theoretical paradigm," in *International Migration,* Vol. 38, pp. 41–56.

Siebert, Frederick S., Peterson, Theodore, and Schramm, Wilbur. (1956) *Four Theories of the Press*, Urbana: University of Illinois Press.

Sigarchi, Arash. (2008) "Jail for Iranian journalists," in *Middle East Quarterly,* Vol. 15 (4), pp. 49–52.

Small, Melvin and Singer, David J. (1976) "The war proneness of democratic regimes, 1816–1965," in *The Jerusalem Journal of International Relations*, Vol. 1, pp. 50–69.

Smith, Anthony D. (1981) *The Ethnic Revival in the Modern World*, Cambridge: Cambridge University Press.

Smith, Anthony D. (1992) "Ethnic identity and territorial nationalism in comparative perspective," in Motyl, A., ed., *Thinking Theoretically about Soviet Nationalism*, New York: Columbia University Press.

Smith, Christopher and Min Zhou. (1995) "Flushing: capital and community in a transnational neighborhood" (manuscript), New York: Russell Sage Foundation.

Smith, Elizabeth. (2005) "Development of the American democracy transnational social movement," in *Strategic Insights*, Vol. 5, Issue 5, pp. 1–11.

Sohamanesh, Sassan Sam. (2009) "On the Iranian diaspora," in *Global Brief*, <http://globalbrief.ca/blog/author/sasanshoamanesh/> accessed August 31, 2011.

Solow, Robert M. (1957) "Technical change and the aggregate production function," in *Review of Economics and Statistics*, Vol. 39, pp. 214–231.

Sorenson, George. (1993) *Democracy and Democratization: Process and Prospects in a Changing World*, Boulder: Westview Press.

Stack, James F. (1997) "The ethnic challenge to international relations theory," in D. Carment and P. James, eds., *Wars in the Midst of Peace: The International Politics of Ethnic Conflict*, Pittsburgh: University of Pittsburgh Press.

Taylor, Richard and Judd, Larry. (1994) "Delphi forecasting," in Stephan F. Witt and Luiz Moutinho, eds., *Tourism, Marketing and Management Handbook,* London: Prentice Hall.

Tessler, Mark. (2002a) "Do Islamic orientations influence attitudes toward democracy in the Arab world: evidence for the world values survey in Egypt, Jordan, Morocco, and Algeria," in *International Journal of Comparative Sociology*, Vol. 43, pp. 229–249.

Tessler, Mark. (2002b) "Islam and democracy in the Middle East: The impact of religious orientations on attitudes toward democracy in four Arab countries," in *Comparative Politics*, 34, pp. 337–254.

Tessler, Mark. (2003) "Arab and Muslim political attitudes: stereotypes and evidence from survey research," in *International Studies Perspectives,* Vol. 4:2 pp. 175–181.

Tessler, Mark and Amaneny, Amal. (2008) "Has the United States poisoned democracy?," In *Arab Reform Bulletin*, Carnegie Endowment for International Peace, Washington DC, October, 2008.

Tibi, Basam. (1999) "From pan-Arabism to the community of sovereign Arab states: redefining the Arab and Arabism in the aftermath of the Second Gulf War," in Michael Hudson, ed., *The Politics and Economics of Arab Integration*, New York: Columbia University Press, p. 101.

Tilly, Charles. (1998) "Regimes and contention," in *Columbia International Affairs Online*, <http://www.ciaonet.org/wps/tic09/index.html> accessed March 3, 2009.

Tocqueville, Alexis de. (1840) *Democracy in America*, Vol. 2, Chapter 1, <http://xroads.virginia.edu/~HYPER/DETOC/ch2_01.htm> accessed August 31, 2011.

Tomlinson, John. (1991) *Cultural Imperialism*, Baltimore: John Hopkins University Press.

Triplett, J, J. (1999) "The Solow productivity paradox: what do computers do to productivity?," *Canadian Journal of Economics*, vol. 32, pp. 309–334.

Trucano, M (2005) "What do we know about the effective uses of information and communication technologies in education in developing countries?," Infodev "Knowledge Maps" series, The International Bank for Reconstruction and Development, The World Bank.

Turoff, Murray. (1970) "The design of a policy Delphi," in *Technological Forecasting and Social Change*, Vol. 22 (2).

Ulrich, Marybeth Peterson. (1999) *Democratizing Communist Militaries – the Cases of the Czech and the Russian Armed Forces*, Ann Arbor: the University of Michigan Press.

UNDP. (2002) "The role of civil society in local governance and poverty alleviation: concepts, realities and experiences," discussion paper for the Regional Workshop on Promoting Effective Participation of Civil Society in Local Governance and Poverty Alleviation in the ECIS region – Challenges and Good Practices, UNDP, Tirana, 5–9 May 2002.

UNDP. (2002) *Deepening Democracy in a Fragmented World*, New York: Oxford University Press.

UNDP. (2011) "International human development indicators," <http://hdr.undp.org/en/statistics/> accessed July 28, 2011.

Ungar, Stanford J. (1990) "The role of a free press in strengthening democracy," in.

Democracy and the Mass Media, edited by J. Lichtenberg. New York: Cambridge.

USIP, Peace Briefing. (2006) "Syria's role in Lebanon," <http://www.usip.org/files/resources/syria_lebanon.pdf> accessed July 12, 2009.

Van Rooy, Alison and Robinson, Frank. (1998) "Out of the Ivory Tower: civil society assistance and the aid system," in Alison Van Rooy, ed., *Civil Society and the Aid Industry*, London: Earthscan.

Venturelli, Shalini. (1998) *Liberalizing the European Media*, Oxford: Clarendon Press.

Verspagen, B. (2001) "Economic Technological Change: An Evolutionary Interpretation," OECD Science, Technology and Industry Working Papers, 2001/1, OECD Publishing.

Vertovec, Steven and Cohen, Robin. (1999) "Global Diasporas, an Introduction," in Steven Vertovec and Robin Cohen, eds., *Migration and Transnationalism*. Aldershot: Edward Elgar, pp. xiii–xxviii.

Vertovec, Steven. (2005) "The political importance of diasporas," in *Migration Information Source*, Migration Policy Institute, (http://www.migrationinformation.org/Feature/display.cfm?ID=313,accessed July 17th 2011).

Wald, Kenneth D. and Williams, Bryan. (2005) "Diaspora political consciousness: Variation in the transnational ethnic alliance of American Jews," Paper presented at the Annual Meeting of the American Political Science Association, September 1–4, 2005.

Walker, Thomas C. (2000),"The Forgotten Prophet: Tom Paine's cosmopolitanism and international relations," in *International Studies Quarterly*, XLIV:1, pp. 521–557.

Waltz, Kenneth. (1979) *Theory of International Politics*, Reading, MA: Addison-Wesley.

Waltz, Kenneth. (1996) "International politics is not foreign policy," *Security Studies* Vol. 6, pp. 51–57.

Wapner, Paul. (1995) "Politics beyond the state: environmental activism and world civic politics," *World Politics*, Vol. 47, pp. 311–340.

Waterbury, John. (1994) "Democracy without democrats? The potential for political liberalization in the Middle East," in Ghassan Salame, ed., *Democracy without Democrats*, London: I.B Tauris, pp. 23–48.

Weber, George. (1997) "Top languages: the world's 10 most influential languages," in *Language Monthly*, Vol. 3, pp. 12–18.

Webler, Thomas, Levine, Debra, Rakel, Horst, Renn, Ortwin. (1991) "A novel approach to reducing uncertainty: The group Delphi," in *Technological Forecasting and Social Change*, Vol. 39 (3), pp. 253–263.

Weimann, Gabriel. (2004) "www.terror.net: How modern terrorism uses the internet," United States Institute of Peace, Special Report #116. p. 4, 6.

Weiss, Michael and Stuart, Hannah. (2011) "The Syrian opposition: political analysis with original testimony from key figures," Hennery Jackson Society, London.

Wheeler, M. (1998). "Democracy and the information superhighway," in *Democratization*, Vol. 5 (2), pp. 217–248.

Wissema, J.G. (1982) "Trends in technology forecasting," in *R & D Management*, Vol. 12(1), pp. 27–36.

Woudenberg, Fred. (1991) "An evaluation of Delphi," in *Technological Forecasting and Social Change*, Vol. 40 (2), pp. 131–150.

Yerkes, Sarah E & Wittes, Tamara Cofman. (2006) "What Price Freedom? Assessing the Bush Administration Freedom Agenda" in Saban Center Middle East Policy, Brookings Institutions, Analysis Paper series.

Zakaria, Fareed. (1997) "The rise of illiberal democracy," in *Foreign Affairs* Vol. 76 (6), pp. 22–43.

Zarwan, Elija. (2005) *False Freedom: Online Censorship in the Middle East and North Africa*, Human Rights Watch, (http://hrw.org/reports/2005/mena1105/, accessed August 31st, 2011).

Ziada, Radwan. (2009) "The Kurds in Syria, fueling separatist movements in the region?," in *United States Institute of Peace Special Report*, pp. 1–11.

Zimmt, Raz, "Telegram: The Most Popular Social Network in Iran" in *BeeHive,* Volume 4, Issue 1, January 2016.

Zohry, A. and Harrell-Bond, B. (2003) "Contemporary Egyptian migration: an overview of voluntary and forced migration," Country Background Papers (WP-C3), Development Research Center on Migration, Globalization, and Poverty, University of Sussex.

Zunz, Olivier and Kahan, Alan S. (2002) "Introduction", in Olivier Zunz and Alan S. Kahan, eds., *The Tocqueville Reader*, Oxford: Blackwell Library.

עברית

טרדמן, משה (2011) "מחאות סביבתיות במצרים הפוסט-מהפכנית: המקרה של אגם קארון", *זווית אחרת*, 10 לאוגוסט, 2011 (http://www.zavita.co.il/index.php/archives/2948#3, נבדק ב 11 לאוגוסט 2011).

כדורי, אלי (1993) *דמוקרטיה והתרבות הפוליטית הערבית*, ירושלים: כרמל.

פורר, ענת (2003), *אוטוריטריזם בנסיגה: הסיבות לליברליזציה פוליטית במזרח התיכון – מבט השוואתי*, חיבור לשם קבלת תואר "דוקטור לפילוסופיה", אוניברסיטת חיפה.

שיין, יוסי (2004) *גבולות הנאמנות–גולים פוליטיים בעידן מדינת הלאום*, רמות, אוניברסיטת תל אביב.

Speeches and Official Statements

Baghdadi, Abu Baker, Isis Leader and Caliph of the Islamis State, Translation of audio mesagae from Januery 19, 2014 <http://pietervanostaeyen.wordpress.com/>.

Bush, George, President of the United Sates, Speech at the National Endowment for Democracy, Nov 6, 2003.

Bush, George, President of the United Sates, Second Inaugural Address, Jan 20, 2005.

Eisenhower, Dwight, special message to Congress on the policy of the United States in the Middle East countries, Jan 14, 1957.

Carter, Jimmy, President of the United Sates. Inaugural Address, January 20, 1977.

Obama, Barak, President of the United Sates, Inaugural Address, January 20, 2009.

Obama, Barak, President of the United Sates, Remarks by the President on a Beginning, Cairo University, Cairo, Egypt June 4، 2009.

Obama, Barak, President of the United Sates, Remarks by the President to the United Nations General Assembly, United Nations Headquarters, New York, September 23 2009.

Obama, Barak, President of the United Sates, Remarks by the President on the Middle East and North Africa, Remarks by the President on the Middle East and North Africa on D.C, May 19, 2011.

Ahmadinejad, Mahmoud, President of Iran. Address to the representatives of Hamas and Islamic Jihad, members of the Society for the Defense of the Palestinian Nation, and members of the Islamic Students Union in Teheran. The Middle East Media Research Institute, Special Dispatch Series-No. 1013, October 28, 2005.

Bulliet, Richard W. "Twenty years of Islamic politics," address at the Middle East Institute Annual Conference, Washington, DC, October 16, 1999.

Dobriansky, Paula J.(2005) "Remarks given to the Hudson Institute on June 20th 2005," Press Release, U.S. Department of State, Washington, DC.

Fried, Daniel. Assistant Secretary for European and Eurasian Affairs, Department of State. Address to the Baltimore Council of Foreign Relations, January 19, 2006.

Haas, Richard N. Director, Office of the Policy Planning Staff, U.S. Department of State, Remarks to the World Affairs Council of Northern California, San Francisco, CA November 16, 2001.

Laden, Osama Bin, al-Qaeda terrorist network, text of a speech broadcast by al-Jazeera, October 7, 2001.

Laden, Osama Bin, al-Qaeda terrorist network, Text of speech broadcast by al-Jazeera, December 26, 2001.

Laden, Osama Bin. "The Solution"- A Video Speech from Osama bin Laden Addressing the American People on the Occasion of the Sixth Anniversary of 9/11 – 9/2007, SITE Intelligence Group, <http://counterterrorismblog.org/site-resources/images/SITE-OBL-transcript.pdf> accessed August 31, 2011.

Posner, Michael H. Assistant Secretary, Bureau of Democracy, Human Rights, and Labor, Statement Before the House Foreign Affairs Committee, Subcommittee on the Middle East and South Asia, Washington, DC, July 27, 2011.

Reagan, Ronald, President of the United States, Address to the British Parliament, June 8 1982.

Shelby, David. "Middle East Forum for the Future produces solid initiatives," an official report by the State Department posted on December 11, 2004 at <http://www.america.gov/st/washfile-english/2004/December/20041211152049ndyblehs0.1221735.html> accessed August 31, 2011.

Truman, Harry. President of the United States, address before a joint session of Congress, March 12 1947.

Newspaper and Magazine Articles

Agence France-Presse (AFP) (2006) "Iran cracks down on satellite dishes," August 14, 2006.

Agence France-Presse (AFP) (2011) "In Iran, internet surfers battle cyber police," Feb 3, 2011.

Alavi, N. (2004) "Freedom in Farsi blogs," *The Guardian*, December 20, 2004.

al-Awsat, Ashark. (2006) " تنسحب من جبهة الخلاص الوطني السورية المعارضة جماعة الإخوان المسلمين?," Sunday, April 5th 2009.

Associated Press (2012) "Syria Civil War Spills Violance Scross Boarder into Jorden, Lenanon," 22, October 2010.

Associated Press, (2004) "Bashar Orders Partial Amnesty to Mark Four Years in Power,"18, July 2004.

Bogert, Carrol. "Chat rooms and chadors," *Newsweek*, August 21, 1995, p. 36.

Boms, Nir and Arya Shayan. "Ayatollahs desert Iran's besieged regime," *The Australian,* January 14, 2010.

Cohler-Esses, Larry. (2009) "An inside look at New Jersey's Syrian-Jewish enclave," *Haaretz,* August 8, 2009.

Dataxis News (2010) "Egypt crossed the 60 million mobile phone users mark," *Dataxis News*, September 17, 2010, <www.dataxisnews.com/?p=22352> accessed July 28, 2011.

Elkin, Mike. (2011) Interview with Kamel Saadaoui, director of the Tunisian internet Agency, *Wired Magazine*, January 28, 2011, <www.wired.com/dangerroom/2011/01/as-egypttightens- its-internet-grip-tunisia-seeks-to-open-up/> accessed August 31, 2011.

Erdbrink, Thomas (2010), "Iran bans the country's two remaining official opposition parties" in Washington Post, April 20th 2010, <http: http://www.washingtonpost.com/wp-dyn/content/article/2010/04/19/AR2010041903636.html> accessed August 31, 2011.

Fathi, Nazila. (2009) "Protesters defy Iranian efforts to cloak unrest," *New York Times,* June 18, 2009, p. A1.

Flock, Elizabeth. (2011) "Syria internet services shut down as protesters fill streets," *Washington Post*, June 3, 2011, <http://www.washingtonpost.com/blogs/blogpost/post/syria-internet-services-shut-down-as-protesters-fill-streets/2011/06/03/AGtLwxHH_blog.html> accessed August 18, 2011).

Gilder, George. (1994) "Life after television, updated," *Forbes*, February 23, 1994.

Gladwell Malcolm. (2010), "Small change: Why the revolution will not be tweeted," *The New Yorker*, October 4, 2010.

Ghazal, Mohammad, (2015), "Jordan launches 2015 Syrian refugee response plan" in *Al-Shofra*, Januery 27, 2015.

Hammersley, Ben. (2002) "Iran nets another revolt: The Iranian government may be draconian, but the internet remains uncensored," *The Guardian*, February 21, 2002.

Homles, Oliver & Siddiq azih. (2013), "Bombs kill 42 outside mosques in Lebanon's Tripoli," *Reuters,* 23, August 2013.

Khalili, Laleh. (1998) "Mixing memory and desire: Iranians in the United States," *The Iranian*, May 13, 1998, www.Iranian.com/Features/May98/Iranams/index.html, accessed September 16, 2010.

Khouri, Rami. (2010) "Aid the jailer or the prisoner, not both," *The Daily Star*, July 21, 2010.

Lebanon News. (2015) "Lebanon minister appeals for winter aid for winter aid for Syrian refugees," *Daily Star*, Januery 7, 2015.

Lomax, David. (2005) "Iraq's television revolution," *BBC*, 25 February, 2005, <http://news.bbc.co.uk/1/hi/programmes/newsnight/4298455.stm> accessed November 10, 2010.

Maclucas, Neil (2014) "Refugee Numbers in Iraq Rise By 300,000 Amid Fighting" in *Wall Steet Journal*, June 13, 2014.

Mendels, Pamela. (1996) "Worldwide, internet restrictions are growing," *New York Times*, September 10, 1996.

Morozov, Evgeny. (2009) "Moldova's Twitter revolution," *Foreign Policy*, April 7, 2009, <http://neteffect.foreignpolicy.com/posts/2009/04/07/moldovas_twitter_revolution> accessed August 18, 2011.

Najibullah, Farangis. (2007) "Iran: internet cafes shut down over un-Islamic behavior," *Radio Free Europe*, Wednesday, December 19, 2007, <http://www.rferl.org/content/article/1079274.html> accessed November 10, 2010.

Ormanchi, Metin. "Scores of Syrian refugees in Turkey struggle in cold without shelter," in *Today Zeman,* Istanbul, November 28, 2014.

Parsa, Telmah. (2009) "Mir-Sayafi: Iranian blogger's writings bring him to life," *Huffington Post,* 20 March, 2009, <http://www.huffingtonpost.com/2009/03/20/mir-sayafi-iranian-blogge_n_177553.html> accessed November 10, 2010*)*.

Ryan, Yasmine. (2011) "Tunisia's bitter cyberwar," *al-Jazeera*, January 6, 2011 <http://english. aljazeera.net/indepth/features/2011/01/20111614145839362.html> accessed July 12, 2011.

Saletan, William. (2011) "Is the internet driving the revolutions of the *Arab Spring?" Future Tense: a collaboration among Arizona State University, the New America Foundation, and Slate,* July 18, 2011, (http://www.slate.com/id/2299214/, accessed August 1st, 2011).

Salhani, Claude. (2005) "Khaddam, the Syrian tsunami," UPI, Dec. 31, 2005.

SANA (1999), "Syria: STE central server said to control internet traffic," SANA news agency, Damascus, March 29, 1999.

Sharabi, Hisham. (2003) *al-Hayat* (London), July 18, 2003.

Sherlock, Ruth, "One of Syria's richest men to help fund a rebel army," The Telegraph, September 12, 2012.

Sinha, Shereeya & Beachy, Susan Campbell (2015), "Timeline on Iran's Nuclear Program," *New York Times*, April 2, 2015.

Singh, Shubha. (2008) "Like India, Syria has a large diaspora," *Thailand News,* June 18, 2008.

Soone, Paul and Stecklow, Steve. (2011) "U.S. Restricts U.A.E. Firm for Web Filter Sale to Syria," Washington Post, December 16, 2011.

Stecklow, Steve. (2011) "Web's openness is tested in Tunisia: Post-uprising freedoms are under pressure, journey from internet activist to official- and back again," *Wall Street Journal,* July 7, 2011.

Taylor, Guy. (2007) "After the Damascus spring: Syrians search for freedom online," *Reason Online*, February 2007 <http://www.reason.com/news/show/118380.html> accessed March 15, 2009.

Veerasamy, N & Grobler, M. (2011) "Terrorist use of the Internet: exploitation and support through ICT infrastructure" in *6th International Conference on Information Warfare and Security,* George Washington University, Washington, DC, 17–18 March 2011.

Worth, Robert. (2010) "Web tastes freedom inside Syria, and it's bitter," *New York Times*, September 29, 2010.

Yacoub, Khaled Oweis. (2009) "U.S. pledges to keep taking in Iraqi refugees," *Reuters,* Nov 18, 2009.

Statements, Reports and other official Documents

ASDA'A Burson-Marsteller Arab Youth Survey. (2015), 7th Annual Survey, <http://www.arabyouthsurvey.com>.

Carnagie, Middle East. (2012) Syria Resources, The Muslim Brotherhood in Syria, February 1, 2012.

Committee to Protect Journalists. (CPJ) (2009) "10 worst countries to be a blogger," April 30, 2009, <http://www.cpj.org/reports/2009/04/10-worst-countries-to-be-a-blogger.php> accessed August 18, 2010.

Emarketer. (2014) "In theMiddle East and Africa, Nearly All Web Users Are Mobile," January 6, 2014, <http://www.emarketer.com/Article/Middle-East-Africa-Nearly-All-Web-Users-Mobile/1010507#sthash.0xCcFiy9.dpuf>.

GAO. (2005) "Middle East partnership initiative offers tools for supporting reform, but project monitoring needs improvement," Report to Congressional Requesters, United States Government Accountability Office.

Human Rights Watch. (2008) "Egypt: investigate police use of force at protests," Human Rights Watch special report, April 10, 2008 <www.hrw.org/en/news/2008/04/10/egypt-investigate-police-use> accessed July 28, 2011.

Internet World Stats <http://www.internetworldstats.com/, accessed at various times 2007–2012>.

International Monetary Fund (IMF). (2008) Article IV Consultation with the Syrian Arab Republic, Public Information Notice (PIN) No. 09/07, January 26, 2009.

Kandel, William A. (2011) The *U.S. Foreign-Born Population*: Trends and Selected Characteristics. William A. *Kandel*. Analyst in Immigration Policy. Congressional Research Service, January 18, 2011 <http://www.fas.org/sgp/crs/misc/R41592.pdf> accessed January 16, 2012).

Media Sustainability Index (MSI). (2009) "Development of sustainable independent media in Africa," in IREX/USAID, pp. 392–405.

Museum Victoria. (2010) "History of immigration from Syria," (http://museumvictoria.com.au/origins/history.aspx?pid=61, accessed March 17, 2010).

OpenArabNet. (2010) "Online Syria, Offline Syrians" in *One Social Network With a Reballious Message* <http://old.openarab.net/en/node/162>.

The OpenNet Initiative. (ONI) (2005) *internet Filtering in Iran in 2004–2005: A Country Study*, (http://www.opennetinitiative.net/studies/iran/, accessed November 12, 2010).

The OpenNet Initiative. (ONI) (2009) *internet Filtering in Iran in 2009: A Country Study*, pp. 1–14, <http://opennet.net/sites/opennet.net/files/ONI_Iran_2009.pdf> accessed October 10, 2010.

The OpenNet Initiative (ONI). (2009) "Syria", published on August 7, 2009, <http://opennet.net/research/profiles/syria> accessed September 12, 2010).

The OpenNet Initiative (ONI). (2011) "New data added to ONI's global timeline of YouTube censorship," published on July 21st, 2011 by Matt Lavigueur <http://opennet.net/blog/2011/07/new-data-added-oni%E2%80%99s-global-timeline-youtube-censorship,> accessed July 30, 2011).

The Washington Institute for Near East Policy (WINAP). (2011) "The Syrian opposition and its key players: a working model," Published on August 4, 2011. <https://www.washingtoninstitute.org:8011/mapImages/4e3ad7ec3db31.pdf> accessed August 5, 2011.

Reporters without Borders (RSF). (2007) "2007 Annual Report," <http://www.rsf.org/IMG/pdf/rapport_en_bd-4.pdf> accessed October 17, 2010.

Reporters without Borders (RSF). (2009) "internet Enemies," March 12, 2009, internet Freedom desk.

Reporters without Borders (RSF). (2010) "internet Enemies: Web 2.0 versus Control 2.0," 18 March 2010, pp. 1–4 <http://en.rsf.org/web-2-0-versus-control-2-0-18-03-2010,36697> accessed October 31, 2010).

Reporters without Borders (RSF). (2010) "Iranian journalist Jila Bani Yaghoob wins "Freedom of Expression" award sponsored by Reporters without Borders," <http://en.rsf.org/iran-iranian-journalist-jila-bani-15-04-2010,37030.html> accessed November 8, 2010.

The Barcelona Declaration, adopted at the Euro-Mediterranean Conference by European Foreign Minstrels on November 28, 1995 <http://europa.eu.int/comm/external_relations/euromed/bd.htm, accessed January 6, 2008>.

The MEDA II Regulation, European Council Regulation, (EC) No 2698/2000 of 27 November, 2000, <http://europa.eu.int/comm/external_relations/euromed/meda2_reg.htm> accessed January 6, 2008.

The Moscow Meeting Document of the Conference on the Human Dimension of the CSCE, Moscow, October 1, 1991 <http://www.legislationline.org/legislation.php?tid=168&lid=5366> accessed January 6, 2008.

World Bank Report. (2011) "For a better integration into the labor market in Tunisia," *The World Bank Group* <http://bit.ly/g3IemR> accessed July 28, 2011.

World Bank Report (2011) "Egypt: improving measurements", *The World Bank Group* <www.worldbank.org/progress/egypt.htm> accessed July 28, 2011.

World Bank Report (2012) "The transformational use of information and communication technologies in Africa."

Statute of the Council of Europe, founding document for the Council of Europe, London, May 28, 1949, <http://conventions.coe.int/Treaty/EN/Treaties/HTML/001.htm> accessed, August 31, 2011.

Stanford, Mapping Militant Organistaion Research Project, 2011–2015, <http://web.stanford.edu/group/mappingmilitants>

Total Registered Refugees per Country and Area (30/06/2008), UNRWA: the United Nations Relief and Works Agency for Palestine Refugees in the Near East, <http://www.unrwa.org/userfiles/rr_countryandarea.pdf> accessed July 28, 2010.

United Nations, "World population at the turn of the century," New York, United Nations, 1989.

United Nations (26/06/1945) "Charter of the United Nations," <http://www.un.org/en/documents/charter/index.shtml> accessed August 31, 2011.

United Nations Children's Fund (UNICEF). (2010) "Child poverty and disparities in Egypt: building the social infrastructure for Egypt's future," in *Global Study on Child Poverty and Disparities*, United Nations Children's Fund (UNICEF), Egypt, February, 2010.

United Nations Refugee Agency. (2002) "Iran: Status and treatment of pro-monarchists," in *Immigration and Refugee Board of Canada*, IRN40084.E, 15 October 2002, <http://www.unhcr.org/refworld/publisher,IRBC,,IRN,3f7d4dae15,0.html> accessed September 1, 2011.

United Nations Refugee Agency. (2014), "World Refugee Day: Global forced displacement tops 50 million for first time in post-World War II era"June 20, 2014 <http://www.unhcr.org/53a155bc6.html>.

United Nations Refugee Agency. (2014), "Syria Regional Refugee Response," Inter Agency Informtaion Sharing Portal, December 2014 <http://data.unhcr.org/syrianrefugees/regional.php>.

United State Department of State (2010) background notes <http://www.state.gov/r/pa/ei/bgn/index.htm> accessed August 31, 2011.

U.S. Census Bureau (2000), Census 2000 special tabulations.

U.S. Census Bureau (2006) American Community Survey, People Reporting Ancestry.

Public Opnion Polls

Emmerson College Polling Sociery. (2015), "2015 National Public Opinion Survey of Iranian Americans," Iranian American Majority.

PAIAA. (2015), "National Public Opnion Survey 2015, Iranian Americans and the American Public," Zogby Research Services.

NATIONAL PUBLIC OPINION SURVEY 2015 IRANIAN AMERICANS & AMERICAN PUBLIC.

Pechter Polls. (2011) "Tripoli and Benghazi media-use data, October-November 2009," <http://www.pechterpolls.com/> accessed July 13, 2011.

Pew Global Attitudes Project. (June 2006) "The Great Divide: how westerners and Muslims view each other," <http://pewglobal.org/reports/> accessed February 6, 2010).

Pew Research Center. (Januery 2011), "The Future of Global Muslim Population, prediction 2010–2030."

Pew Research Center (March 2014), "Emerging Nations Embrace Internet Mobile Tecnology."

Manuals and Technical References

Platinum, Inc (2010) Manual for Thundercache, a Wall of Trust, <http://www.thundercache.com/index.php?m=3> Accessed October 17, 2010).

Democracy, Human Rights, Integration, Radicalisation and Security

Edited by the / Herausgegeben von der
European Foundation for Democracy

Vol./Bd. 1 Wahied Wahdat-Hagh: Der islamistische Totalitarismus. Über Antisemitismus, Anti-Bahaismus, Christenverfolgung und geschlechtsspezifische Apartheid in der „Islamischen Republik Iran“. 2012.

Vol./Bd. 2 Nir T. Boms: Expat-ing Democracy. Dissidents, Technology, and Democratic Discourse in the Middle East. 2016.

www.peterlang.com

www.ingramcontent.com/pod-product-compliance
Ingram Content Group UK Ltd.
Pitfield, Milton Keynes, MK11 3LW, UK
UKHW041825031026
15587UKWH00002B/563

9 783631 654699